PRODUCT DEVELOPMENT AND WASTE RECYCLING

ENV BOOKS SERIES

PRODUCT DEVELOPMENT AND WASTE RECYCLING

Editor

Dr. Pawan Kumar 'Bharti'

Society for Environment, Health
Awareness of Nutrition & Toxicology (SEHAT)
B-225/5D, Top Floor, Subhash Gali, Road No. 7, Block B
Ashok Nagar, Shahdara
Delhi-110093
(India)

DPH

DISCOVERY PUBLISHING HOUSE PVT. LTD.
INDIA

Published by:

Namit Wasan

DISCOVERY PUBLISHING HOUSE PVT. LTD.

4383/4B, Ansari Road, Darya Ganj

New Delhi-110 002 (India)

Phone : +91-11-23279245; 23253475; 43596065

E-mail : discoverybooksindia@gmail.com
discoverypublishinghouse@gmail.com
namitwasan9@gmail.com

web : www.discoverypublishinggroup.com

***First Edition:* 2019**

ISBN: 978-93-86841-94-0

Product Development and Waste Recycling

Printed at:

Infinity Imaging Systems

Delhi

PREFACE

The creation of products with new or different characteristics that offer new or additional benefits to the customer. Product development may involve modification of an existing product or its presentation, or formulation of an entirely new product that satisfies a newly defined customer want or market niche.

Product development typically refers to all of the stages involved in bringing a product from concept or idea, through market release and beyond. In other words, product development incorporates a product's entire journey, including: Identifying a market need; Conceptualizing and designing the product; Building the product roadmap; Developing a minimum viable product (MVP); Releasing the MVP to users; Iterating based on user feedback.

When you understand product development this way, you can see that it is not synonymous with product management, although many people mistakenly use the terms interchangeably. Indeed, product development does not refer to a single role at all.

As the consumption of the society grows, more and more waste are produced both from consumers as for manufacturing industries. A large amount of waste is produced in the mining, paper, steel and food industries. Metals, chemicals, plastics and other usable materials are still today considered to be waste and in fact only slightly more than 10% of all industrial waste is recycled. Apart from the industries, significant volume of waste material is produced from household, commercial hubs and agriculture fields. These wastes must be recycled and converted into value added products for the use of mankind.

The present book updates the subject content of waste recycling, composting, cellulose from plant biomass, degradable packaging film from plant cellulose, mosquito repellent from wild grass, biogas, activated charcoal, soilless media for plants from tannery waste, car perfume gel from carrageenan, and many other value added products from waste materials.

Thanks are due to publisher and contributors from various institutions and universities.

The book will be helpful for the researchers, academia working in the field of waste recycling, composting, cellulose from plant biomass, degradable packaging film from plant cellulose, mosquito repellent from wild grass, biogas, activated charcoal, soilless media for plants from tannery waste, car perfume gel from carrageenan and many other value added products from waste materials.

Editors
(envbooks@gmail.com)

CONTENTS

Product Development and Waste Recycling **Pages 1-13**
Edited by: Pawan Kumar 'Bharti'
ISBN: 978-93-86841-94-0
Edition: 2019
Published by: Discovery Publishing House Pvt. Ltd., New Delhi (India)

1

Integrated Strategy to Combat against Tannery Solid Waste and Its Utilization in Multiple Applications

[1]Pawan Kumar 'Bharti'

ABSTRACT

Due to industrialization, quantity of solid waste generated from industrial operations is increasing day by day causing pollution to the environment. Leather processing industries are not exception to this. Tanneries generate considerable amount of solid wastes comprising a portion of hazardous materials which is a threat to modern society. The industrial tanning of leather produces considerable amounts of solid wastes and liquid effluents and raises many concerns regarding the environmental effects and escalating landfill costs. These disposal problems are increasingly becoming a hindrance to this industrial activity, suggesting the need for alternative methods of residue disposal and their effective utilization. In the present study, an integrated strategy is framed up for turning tannery wastes into several valuable resources. Energy is produced from tannery waste in the form of biogas and compost from degradable fraction of the waste. Activated carbon is manufactured from solid tannery waste for use as adsorption media. Besides these, a soilless media for growing plants as well as hollow bricks for pavements are developed from the tannery waste.

Keywords: Tannery waste, waste utilization, compost, biogas, activated carbon, soilless media for plants

Introduction

The leather tanning industry is one of the oldest and fastest growing industries in South and South East Asia. There are more than 3000 tanneries located in India with a total processing capacity of 700,000 tons of hides and skins per year. Tannery clusters in India are mainly located in four states, namely, Tamilnadu, West Bengal, Uttar Pradesh and Punjab (Gupta et al., 2014).

The global tanning industry generates 4 million tonnes of solid waste per year. As the economic and environmental costs of tannery waste disposal and the cost associated with the use of fossil fuels to generate energy from

[1] R&D Division, Shriram Institute for Industrial Research, 19 University Road, Delhi-110007, India

these wastes continue to be spiral and the search for viable alternative waste solutions becomes increasingly critical. The present proposal deals with the disposal of solid waste generated from leather processing industries including the discarded reverse osmosis (RO) rejects by means of utilizing its various valuable constituents. Our approach will be an integrated system of disposal of tannery wastes comprising utilization of various valuable ingredients of the disposables generating certain value added products. Our efforts are multidimensional as we are interested to utilize maximum possible quantity of the waste to generate multiple products to be utilized in various sectors including power, agriculture, horticulture, construction, and water purification. We have proposed here to work on the disposition of common tannery wastes including RO rejects along with utilization of its valuable ingredients to the tune of a pilot plant operation. Once the operation is stabilized by means of optimization of operating parameters in order to maximum utilization of valuable constituent materials of the tannery disposables, the same methodology can be scaled up to the commercial capacity.

Table 1.1: States having Major Leather Clusters in India

S.N.	State	Places	Cluster
1	Tamil Nadu	Ambur, Dindigul, Melpudupet, Melvisharam, Pallavaram, Pernambut, TALCO Ranipet, SIDCO Phase-I, Ranipet, Erode, Madhavaram, SIDCO Phase-II, Ranipet, Trichy, Vaniyambadi,	15
2	Uttar Pradesh	Jajmau, Unnao, Banther, Agra	13
3	West Bengal	Kolkata	7
4	Punjab	Jalandhar, Phillaur	15

Table 1.2: States having Minor Leather Clusters in India

S.N.	State	Cluster
1	Haryana	9 clusters
2	Maharashtra	13 clusters
3	Bihar	12 clusters
4	Andhra Pradesh,	7 clusters
5	Rajasthan	11 clusters
6	Gujarat	2 clusters
7	Karnataka	1 cluster at Bangalore
8	Odisha	4 Clusters
9	Delhi	2 clusters
10	Himachal Pradesh	1 cluster
11	Uttarakhand	1 cluster
12	Goa	scattered units

Table 1.3: Solid Waste Management Practices in Tannery Intensive States and Utilization of Wastes (Gupta et al, 2014)

<table>
<tr><th>Solid Wastes</th><th>Tamil Nadu</th><th>Uttar Pradesh</th><th>West Bengal</th><th>Punjab</th></tr>
<tr><td>Trimmings</td><td>Major percentage taken away by the raw hide suppliers Sold to Glue manufacturers</td><td colspan="3" rowspan="5">Same as Tamil Nadu</td></tr>
<tr><td>Salt</td><td>Partly reused for curing Rest Sold to raw hide merchants</td></tr>
<tr><td>Hair</td><td>Disposed off as solid waste</td></tr>
<tr><td>Fleshings & Pelt</td><td>Sold to glue manufacturer</td></tr>
<tr><td>Trimmings</td><td>Sold to chicken feed manufacturer</td></tr>
<tr><td>Lime Sludge</td><td>Sold on truck load basis for construction activities. Used for filling up low lying areas</td><td>Same as Tamil Nadu + Used by Labors for construction of huts</td><td>Sold on truck load basis for construction activities</td><td>Same as Uttar Pradesh</td></tr>
<tr><td>Organic waste from Vegetable Tanning</td><td>Used in boilers after drying
Sold to be used as fuel in brick kilns</td><td colspan="3">Same as Tamil Nadu +</td></tr>
<tr><td>Vegetable Tanned</td><td>Used for making leather boards</td><td colspan="3" rowspan="2">Same as Tamil Nadu</td></tr>
<tr><td>Trimmings</td><td>Larger cuttings used for Footwear Manufacturing & repair</td></tr>
<tr><td>Chrome Shavings</td><td>Used for making leather boards Biometha-nation of Chrome free shavings</td><td>Used for making leather Boards Sold as fertilizer</td><td rowspan="2">Same as Uttar Pradesh</td><td>Same as Uttar Pradesh</td></tr>
<tr><td>Chrome Trimmings</td><td>Used for making Leather Boards</td><td>Used for making Leather Goods Sold to Fertilizer manufacturers</td><td>Used for making leather boards</td></tr>
<tr><td>Buffing dust</td><td>Disposed off as MSW</td><td>Same as Tamil Nadu + As Fuel for Boilers</td><td>Used for filling low lying areas Partly used as fuel in boilers in few tanneries</td><td>As Fuel for Boilers</td></tr>
<tr><td>Pre-Treatment Sludge</td><td>Disposed off in SLF</td><td>Partly stored within premises Dumped near tannery cluster</td><td>Stored within premises and sent off to SFL</td><td>Same as Uttar Pradesh</td></tr>
</table>

Table 1.4: Major Components of Tannery Waste (Kangaraj, et al., 2006)

S.N.	Component	Quantity (%)
1	Fleshing waste	50-60
2	Shaving, Chrome split & Buffing waste	23-40
3	Skin trimming	5-7
4	Hairs	2-5

Research Work So Far

Various research works have been carried out in different countries on various aspects of waste utilization of tannery waste. Hughes (1988) described the disposal of leather tanning wastes by land treatment in a review. Imai and Okamura (1991) made some studies on incineration of chrome leather waste. Alves *et al.* (1991) emphasized on utilization of leather waste especially animal feedstuff from chrome shavings. Taylor *et al.* (1991) find out the efficiency of enzymic solubility of chrome shaving as influence by choice of alkalinity-inducing agent. Heidemann (1991) explained the disposal and recycling techniques of chrome tanned materials. Veeger (1993) pointed out some ecological procedure to solve the tannery waste problems. Simeonova and Dalev (1996) emphasized on the utilization of a leather industry waste in different ways. Brown *et al.* (1996) find out the production and potential uses of co-product from solid tannery waste. Taylor *et al.* (1997) made a study on extraction of value added by products from the treatment of chromium containing collagenous leather industry waste. Cabeza *et al.* (1998) explained the processing of leather waste and carried out pilot scale studies on chrome shavings-isolation of potentially valuable protein products and chromium.

Bajza and Vrèek (2001) worked on thermal and enzymatic recovering of proteins from untanned leather waste. Kowaslki and Walawska (2001) described the utilization of tannery wastes for the production of sodium chromate. Mu *et al.* (2003) presented a strategy towards zero discharge of chromium-containing leather waste through improved alkali hydrolysis. Li *et al.* (2006) highlighted the phosphate removal from aqueous solutions using raw and activated red mud and fly ash. Luiz *et al.* (2006) used solid waste from leather industry as adsorbent of organic dyes in aqueous-medium. Yilmaz *et al.* (2007) emphasized on conversion of leather wastes to useful products. Ozgunay *et al.* (2007) worked on characterization of leather industry wastes. Oliveira *et al.* (2007) utilized the solid waste from leather industry as adsorbent of organic dyes in aqueous-medium. Oliveira *et al.* (2008) performed the preparation of activated carbon from leather waste, which was a new material containing small particle of chromium oxide. Tahiri and de la Guardia (2009) made a review on treatment and valorization of leather industry solid wastes. Wang *et al.* (2009) explained a novel way of transformation of tannery waste to environmentally friendly formaldehyde scavenger. Gil *et al.* (2009) explained the valorization of solid wastes from the leather industry and emphasized on preparation of activated carbon by thermochemical processes. This study has been conducted to establish conditions for the pyrolysis of leather wastes (LW) in order to recover gas and condensable fractions. The pyrolized sample was later activated by means of alkaline hydroxides in order to develop its porous structure. The activated carbons prepared are microporous with specific surface area values up to 2700 m^2/g. Mohamed and Kassem (2010) pointed out the utilization of waste leather shavings as filler in paper making. Famielec and Krystyna (2011) explained the nature and conditions of waste materials from leather industry and highlighted the associated threat to the environment. Jing *et al.* (2011) explained ecological methods of utilization of leather tannery waste with circular economy model. Paul *et al.* (2013) indicated towards zero solid waste and focused on utilizing tannery waste as a protein source for poultry feed. Hasnat *et al.* (2013) made a study for the assessment of environmental impact for tannery industries in Bangladesh.

Many Indian researchers are also engaged in the utilization of leather tannery waste in different applications. Reddy *et al.* (1977) proposed conceptual modeling of non-point source pollution from land areas receiving animal wastes with special reference to nitrogen transformations. Nair *et al.* (1985) highlighted the bacterial accumulation of chromium in tannery waste. Prasad *et al.* (1987) presented a critical review on prospects for chromium management in tanneries. Ramasami and Prasad (1991) highlighted the environmental aspects of leather processing. Warrier *et al.* (1995) explained the safe utilisation of chrome containing sludges in brick making.

Ramasami (1996) pointed out the greening of chrome tanning in Indian leather industry. Sekaran *et al.* (1998) emphasized on characterization and utilisation of buffing dust generated by the leather industry. Dasgupta (1998) focused on minimising the environmental impact of chrome tanning with special reference to the thrublu process. Chakraborty and Sarkar (1998) explained the enzyme hydrolysis of solid tannery wastes and stated solid state enzyme production. Rao *et al.* (1999) focused on some strategies towards mitigation of pollution from tanneries in a review. Chakraborty *et al.* (1999) find out the effect of detanning agents on the utilisation of tannery wastes. Muralidharan *et al.* (2001) explained a new approach for chrome management which was based on two stage tanning. Suresh *et al.* (2001) focused on an improved product-process for cleaner chrome tanning in leather processing. Rao *et al.* (2002) highlighted the green route for the utilization of chrome shavings (chromium-containing solid waste) in tanning industry. Sandeep *et al.* (2003) studied on the performance of waste activated carbon as a low-cost adsorbent for the removal of anionic surfactant from aquatic environment. Rao *et al.* (2004) performed some tanning studies with basic chromium sulfate prepared using chrome shavings as a reductant. It was a model for 'wealth from waste' approach to the tanning industry. Saha *et al.* (2005) gave the status of waste leather in India and proposed an integrated business with value creation opportunities. Fathima *et al.* (2005) studied on adsorption of chromium (VI) by iron complexed protein waste, in which solid waste removes toxic liquid waste. Kanagraj *et al.* 2006) explained the solid waste generation in the leather industry and its utilization for cleaner environment. Vasudevan and Ravindran (2007) invented a biotechnological process for the treatment of fleshing from tannery industries for methane generation. Fathima *et al.* (2009) emphasized on utilization of organically stabilized proteinous solid waste for the treatment of coloured waste-water.

Saravanan *et al.* (2010) explained a cleaner leather manufacturing process using enzymes. Fathima *et al.* (2011) used stabilized protein waste as a source for removal of color from wastewaters. Nishad *et al.* (2012) gave a new holistic paradigm for tannery solid waste to treat toxic liquid wastes. This work presents an overview of the solid wastes emanating from tanneries and the various disposal methods practiced with special emphasis on the utilization of these wastes to treat toxic liquid pollutants. Puri *et al.* (2013) emphasized on the utilization of recycled wastes as ingredients in concrete mix. Pati and Chaudhary (2013) made some studies on the generation of biogas from collagen hydrolysate obtained from chrome shavings by alkaline hydrolysis and gave a greener disposal method. In this work, proteinous matter recovered from chrome shaving through chemical process was feed to the anaerobic digester to generate biogas. Two different modes of alkaline chromed shaving dust hydrolysis i.e. using lime and KOH followed by neutralization with HCl and H_3PO_4 subsequently. The Full scale investigations conducted to evaluate the performance of anaerobic digestion of collagen hydrolysate.

Recently, few research groups have worked on various aspects of solid waste management, handling and utilization and suggest various value added products from solid waste. Bharti (2007); Sharma et al., (2011); Bharti (2012); Bharti and Gajananda (2013); Bharti and Haldar (2014); Bharti (2015); Bharti et al., (2015a); Bharti et al., (2015b) have also carried out various studies and filed some patents.

UTILIZATION OF TANNERY WASTE IN THE PRESENT CONTEXT

Hypothesis

The objective of the present study is to frame up strategies for turning tannery wastes into worthy resources like production of biogas, compost, activated carbon, hollow bricks and soilless growing media in horticulture and to develop a technology for 100 % utilization of tannery solid waste.

Methodology

However, many standard methodologies are recommended for the solid waste management and handling studies, but we are following our self developed and patented methodology. The strategy of our work includes the specific work elements as described in the standard protocol given by Bharti and Haldar (2014). The tannery solid waste was segregated and utilized as per their characteristics. Wheter this is degradable and able to produce biogas, it will be utilize in that purpose. Otherwise, most inert and less degradable portion is to be utilized accordingly.

Process

The entire process of utilizing tannery solid waste is given in the following points:

1. Tannery waste including shaving, trimming and buffing from various sources will be mixed and homogenized in order to results a uniform solid waste.
2. The homogenized waste on storage will evolve a mixture of energy rich gases, e.g. methane, ammonia and hydrogen sulfide, which can be collected and used as fuel like biogas.
3. The mixed waste will be pyrolysed at a temperature of 800 °C in an inert and closed atmosphere. As a result of pyrolysis of mixed solid waste, flue gases (CO_2 and CO) are liberated living a carbonaceous residue (char) behind. Energy of flue gases can be recovered and utilized
4. The carbonaceous Char as generated above will be impregnated with certain activating agents like $ZnCl_2$, H_3PO_4, KOH, NaOH, etc. followed by heating at 750°C to yield activated carbon, a valuable agent for water purification.
5. A portion of the homogenized tannery waste mixed with RO reject will be utilized to make following important products after removal of chromium salts:
   - Compost; mixing with biodegradable domestic wastes to use as fertilizer in agriculture
   - Hollow bricks; mixing with concrete to use in construction
   - Soil less media for plants; treating with tropical peat to use in horticulture

Flow chart 1: Showing the All Steps Involved in the Proposed Hypothesis of Integrated Strategy

Schematic representation of the method/design is as follow:

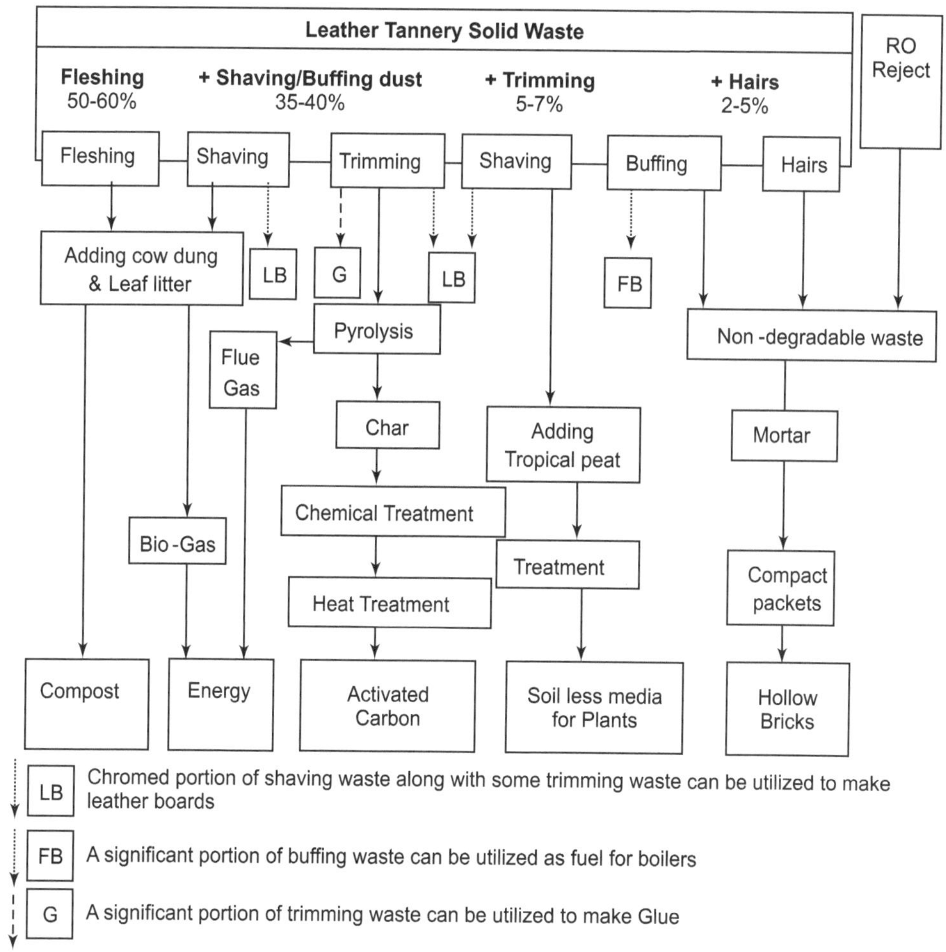

Utilization of Waste

Tannery waste is dangerous to environment and is not being utilized in effective way in the country. It is a matter of great importance to utilize this tannery in some useful applications. Tannery waste as raw material for the proposed work is available in many states of India in plenty. It can be achieved at very low cost and can be utilized for the welfare of environment also. The outcomes of proposed study will give benefits to human society as well as will conserve the environment.

Raw material used for the production of biogas, compost, development of activated carbon, preparation of soilless media for plants will be waste materials originating from leather tanneries, which is available in plenty. Therefore the developed material would be cheaper. As the developed products will be eco-friendly, its end use will reduce the environmental burden because it will get degraded after utilization. As the proposed integrated utilization scheme is not adopted in the country and development of an integrated process for multiple uses of tannery waste is an original idea and patented (Bharti and Haldar, 2014).

Outcomes

We proposed and claim the following process/techniques/product development:

1. Multiple useful products (More than five) from tannery solid waste as given below:
   (*a*) Compost (manure) for agriculture use, which is prepared using fleshing and shaving (degradable portion of tannery solid waste), when mixed with cow dung and leaf litter in appropriate ratio.
   (*b*) Energy in the form of biogas, which is evolved from the decomposition of biodegradable portion of tannery solid waste.
   (*c*) Activated charcoal is achieved through pyrolysis process and chemical treatment by an activating agent and followed by heat treatment at high temperature. Trimming portion of tannery solid waste will be pyrolysed at a temperature of 800-850°C in an inert and closed atmosphere. As a result of pyrolysis of mixed solid waste, flue gases (CO_2 and CO) are liberated living a carbonaceous residue (char) behind. Energy of flue gases can be recovered and utilized. The carbonaceous Char as generated above will be impregnated with certain activating agents like $ZnCl_2$, H_3PO_4, KOH, NaOH, etc. followed by heating at 750ºC to yield activated carbon, a valuable adsorbing agent for water purification.
   (*d*) Soilless media for plants is prepared from buffing dust and adding tropical peat into it.
   (*e*) Hollow bricks/blocks are prepared by adding most inert/useless portion of tannery solid waste inside the concrete blocks.
   (*f*) Beside these, Chromed portion of shaving waste along with some trimming waste can be utilized to make leather boards. A significant portion of buffing waste can be utilized as fuel for boilers and a significant portion of trimming waste can be utilized to make Glue.
2. Process for 100% utilization of tannery solid waste in making various useful products.
3. No dumping and land-filling is required for tannery waste, as the complete waste is utilized for making valuable products. Hence, this will help to conserve the environment and minimizing pollution.
4. A process in which bio-degradable as well as non-degradable portions are completely utilized and nothing is remnant.

5. An eco-friendly process of waste management, where waste can be converted into worthy resources and no solid waste remains at dumping sites.

Conclusion

In the recent developmental era, generation of solid waste is a big problem. Proper disposal of this waste is extremely required to protect the environmental components. The recycling of waste materials can also combat against pollution. It is necessary to find out the latest techniques to maximize the recycling and utilization of waste materials in various useful applications. Hence, it will be the best solution to utilize waste in multidisciplinary manner to develop some useful products from it like biogas, compost, activated carbon and soilless media for plants.

Industries working in the field of waste management can utilize the results of the proposed work. Biogas producing and compost making industries can also get benefitted with the outcome of the study. The developed technology for integrated utilization of tannery waste & production of biogas, compost, activated carbon & soilless media for plants will be scaled-up before commercialization. Initially the process for production of biogas and compost and development of activated carbon & soil less media for plants will be executed at laboratory scale. During the scale-up studies the design parameter for technology will be taken care.

REFERENCES

Alves Dos, Reis, M. and Beleza, V. (1991): Utilization of Leather Waste: Animal Feedstuff from Chrome Shavings, Part I. J. Am. Leather. Chem. As., 75: 15-19.

Bajza, Ž. and Vrèek, V. (2001): Thermal and Enzymatic Recovering of Proteins from Untanned Leather Waste. Waste Manage., 21: 79-84.

Bharti, P. K. (2015): Solid Waste Management at Indian Research Stations over East Antarctica, In: Waste Disposal and Management (Eds.- Bharti, P. K.; Tabassum, B. and Bajaj, P.), Discovery Publishing House, Delhi, pp. 1-17 (ISBN: 978-93-5056-729-6).

Bharti, P. K. and Gajananda, Kh. (2013): Environmental Health and Problems, Discovery Publishing House, Delhi, pp. 210 (ISBN: 93-5056-263-4).

Bharti, P. K.; Sharma, B.; Pal, N.; Singh, R.K. and Niyogi, U.K. (2015): Environmental Monitoring at Maitri Station, East Antarctica, In: Environment and Chemistry (Eds.- Kumar, S. and Vandana), Campus Books International, Delhi, pp. 1-17 (ISBN: 978-81-8030-432-3).

Bharti, P. K.; Tabassum, B. and Bajaj, P. (2015): Waste Disposal and Management, Discovery Publishing House, Delhi, pp. 202 (ISBN: 978-93-5056-729-6).

Bharti, P.K. (2007): Why are Indian Standards not so Strict?, Current Science, 93(9): 1202.

Bharti, P.K. and R.S. Haldar (2014): A Process to Utilize 100% Tannery Solid Waste, No.-3851/ DEL/2014.

Bharti, Pawan K. (2012): Solid Waste and River Ecology, Lambert Academic Publishing GmbH & Co. KG, Saarbrucken, Germany, pp. 65 (ISBN: 978-3-659-12852-3).

Brown, E.M., Taylor, M.M. and Marmer, W.N. (1996): Production and Potential Uses of Co-product from Solid Tannery Waste. J. Am.. Leather. Chem. As., 91: 270-276.

Cabeza, L.F., Taylor, M.M., Dimaio, G.L., Brown, E.M., Marmer, W.N., Carrió, R., Celma, P.J. and Cot, J. (1998): Processing of Leather Waste: Pilot Scale Studies on Chrome Shavings-Isolation of Potentially Valuable Protein Products and Chromium. Waste Manage, 18: 211-218.

Chakraborty S, Bhoumik H, Mondal C and Biswas K. (1999): Effect of Detanning Agents on the Utilisation of Tannery Wastes. In: Science and Technology for Leather into the Next Millennium. Tata McGraw-Hill Publishing Company, New Delhi, pp. 484-88.

Chakraborty, R. and Sarkar, S.K. (1998): Enzyme Hydrolysis of Solid Tannery Wastes: Solid State Enzyme Production. J. Soc. Leather Technol. Chem. 82: 56.

Dasgupta, S. (1998): Minimising the Environmental Impact of Chrome Tanning: The Thrublu Process. J Soc Leather Technol Chem; 82: 15-21.

Famielec S. and Krystyna W.C. (2011): Waste from Leather Industry: Threat to the Environment, Biblioteka Cyfrowa Politechniki Krakowskiej, 108(8): 43-48.

Fathima, N.N., Aravindhan, R., Rao, J.R., and Nair, B.U. (2005): Solid Waste Removes Toxic Liquid Waste: Adsorption of Chromium (VI) by Iron Complexed Protein Waste. Environ. Sci. Technol. 39: 2804.

Fathima, N.N., Aravindhan, R., Rao, J.R., and Nair, B.U. (2009): Utilization of Organically Stabilized Proteinous Solid Waste for the Treatment of Coloured waste-water. J. Chem. Technol. Biotech.., 84: 1338.

Fathima, N.N., Aravindhan, R., Rao, J.R., and Nair, B.U. (2011): Stabilized Protein Waste as a Source for Removal of Color from Wastewaters. J. Appl. Polym. Sci., 120: 1397.

Gil R.R., R.P. Girón, B. Ruiz, M.S. Lozano, M.J. Martín and E. Fuente (2009): Valorization of Solid wastes from the Leather Industry: Preparation of Activated Carbon by Thermo-chemical Processes. 1st Spanish National Conference on Advances in Materials Recycling and Eco-Energy, Madrid, 12-13 November 2009 S01-7.

Gupta Shradha, Mita Sharma and U.N Singh (2014): Tannery Clusters in India and Waste Management Practices in Tannery Intensive States – Inventory and Status. IOSR Journal of Environmental Science, Toxicology and Food Technology, 8 (4): pp. 88-96.

Hasnat Abul, Istiakur Rahman, and Mosabbir Pasha (2013): Assessment of Environmental Impact for Tannery Industries in Bangladesh, Int. J. of Environmental Science and Development, 4(2): 217-220.

Heidemann E. (1991): Disposal and Recycling of Chrome Tanned Materials. J Am Leather Chem Assoc.; 86: 331-33.

Hughes, J.C. (1988): The Disposal of Leather Tanning Wastes by Land Treatment: A Review. Soil Use Manag., 4: 107-111.

Imai, T. and Okamura, H. (1991): Studies on Incineration of Chrome Leather Waste. The Journal of the American Leather Chemists Association. 86: 281-294.

Jing Hu, Zuobing Xiao, Rujun Zhou, Weijun Deng, Mingxi Wang and Shuangshuang Ma (2011): Ecological Utilization of Leather Tannery Waste with Circular Economy Model, Journal of Cleaner Production, 19 (2–3): 221–228.

Kanagraj, J.; Velappen, K.C.; Chandra Babu, N.K. and Sadulla, S. (2006): Solid Waste Generation in the Leather Industry and Its Utilization for Cleaner Environment – A review, Journal of Scientific and Industrial Research, 65: 541-548.

Kowaslki, Z. and Walawska, B. (2001): Utilization of Tannery Wastes for the Production of Sodium Chromate. Ind. Eng. Chem. Res. 40: 826-832.

Li, Y.Z., Liu, C.J., Luan, Z.K., Peng, X.J., Zhu, C.L., Chen, Z.Y., Zhang, Z.G., Fan, J.H. and Jia, Z.P. (2006): Phosphate Removal from Aqueous Solutions using Raw and Activated Red Mud and Fly Ash. J. Hazardous Mater. 137: 374-383.

Luiz C.A. Oliveira, Maraýsa Goncalves, Diana Q.L. Oliveira, Mario C. Guerreiro, Luiz R.G. Guilherme and Rogerio M. Dallago (2006): Solid Waste from Leather Industry as Adsorbent of Organic Dyes in Aqueous-medium, J. Hazardous Mater. doi:10.1016/j.jhazmat.2006.06.111.

Mohamed, O. A. and Kassem, N. F. (2010): Utilization of Waste Leather Shavings as Filler in Paper Making. J. Appl. Polym. Sci., 118: 1713–1719. doi: 10.1002/app.32315.

Mu, C.D., Lin, W., Zhang, M.R. and Zhu, Q.S. (2003): Towards Zero Discharge of Chromium-Containing Leather Waste Through Improved Alkali Hydrolysis. Waste Manage., 23: 835-843.

Muralidharan C, Sundar VJ, Rao VSS and Ramasami T. (2001): Two Stage Tanning-A New Approach for Chrome Management. J Am Leather Chem Assoc; 96: 61-66.

Nair S, Ramasami T and Krishnamoorthy VS. (1985): Bacterial Accumulation of Chromium. Leather Sci.; 32: 88-90.

Nishad Fathima, Raghava Rao and Balachandran Unni Nair (2012): Tannery Solid Waste to Treat Toxic Liquid Wastes: A New Holistic Paradigm, Environmental Engineering Science, 29(6): 363-372.

Oliveira, L.C.A., Goncalves, M., Oliveira, D.Q.L., Guerreiro,M.C., Guilherme, L.R.G., and Dallago, R.M. (2007): Solid Waste from Leather Industry as Adsorbent of Organic Dyes in Aqueous-medium. J. Hazard. Mater. 141: 344.

Oliveira, L.C.A., Guerreiro, M.C., Goncalves, M., Oliveira, D.Q.L., and Costa, L.C.M. (2008): Preparation of Activated Carbon from Leather Waste: A New Material Containing Small Particle of Chromium Oxide. Mater. Lett., 62: 3710.

Ozgunay, H.; S. Colak; M.M. Mutlu and F. Akyuz (2007): Characterization of Leather Industry Wastes. Polish J. of Environ. Stud., 16(6): 867-873.

Pati Anupama and Chaudhary Rubina (2013): Studies on the Generation of Biogas from Collagen Hydrolysate Obtained from Chrome Shavings by Alkaline Hydrolysis: A Greener Disposal Method, Research Journal of Recent Sciences (ISSN 2277-2502), 2: 234-240.

Paul, H., Antunes, A. P. M., Covington, A. D., Evans, P. and Phillips, P. S. (2013): Towards Zero Solid Waste: Utilizing Tannery Waste as a Protein Source for Poultry Feed. Paper Presented to: 28th International Conference on Solid Waste Technology and Management, Philadelphia, PA, USA, 10-13 March 2013. Philadelphia USA: The Journal of Solid Waste Technology and Management. ISSN: 1091-8043.

Prasad BGS, Chandrasekaran B, Rao JR, Chandrababu NK, Kanthimathi M and Ramasami T. (1987): Prospects for Chromium Management in Tanneries: A Critical Review. Leather Sci; 34:132-48.

Puri Nitish, Brijesh Kumar, Himanshu Tyagi (2013): Utilization of Recycled Wastes as Ingredients in Concrete Mix. International Journal of Innovative Technology and Exploring Engineering, 2 (2): 74-78.

Ramasami T. and Prasad B.G.S. (1991): Environmental Aspects of Leather Processing. Proc. LEXPO XV, Calcutta, India.

Ramasami, T. (1996): Greening of Chrome Tanning in Indian Leather Industry. ILIFO J Cleaner Tanning; 1(2): 12-14.

Rao JR, Sreeram KJ, Nair BU, Ramasami T. (1999): Some Strategies Towards Mitigation of Pollution from Tanneries: A Review. In: Advances in Industrial Wastewater Treatment (Goel PK, editor). Technoscience Publications, Jaipur, India, pp. 135-52.

Rao JR, Thanikaivelan P, Sreeram KJ and Nair BU (2002): Green Route for the Utilization of Chrome Shavings (Chromium-containing Solid Waste) in Tanning Industry. Environ. Sci. Technol.; 36:1372-76.

Rao, J.R., Thanikaivelan, P., Sreeram, K.J., and Nair, B.U. (2004): Tanning Studies with Basic Chromium Sulfate Prepared using Chrome Shavings as a Reductant: A Call for 'Wealth from Waste' Approach to the Tanning Industry. J. Am. Leather Chem. Assoc. 99: 170.

Reddy, K.R., Khaleel, R., Overcash, M.R and Westerman, P.W. (1977): Conceptual Modeling of Non-Point Source Pollution from Land Areas Receiving Animal Wastes. I. Nitrogen Transformations. Am. Soc. Agric. Eng., 77: 4046.

Saha, Nabanita, Mukhopadhya, Satyanarayan , Siddique, Imran and Saha, Petr (2005): Waste Leather in India – An Integrated Business with Value Creation Opportunities, 7th World Congress on Recovery, Recycling and Re-integration (R'05) in Beijing, China.

Sandeep, G., Anjali, P., Pranab, K. G. et al., (2003): Performance of Waste Activated Carbon as a Low-cost Adsorbent for the Removal of Anionic Surfactant from Aquatic Environment. Journal of Environmental Science and Health - Part A. Toxic/Hazardous Substance and Environ. Engineering, 38(2): 381-397.

Saravanan, P., Ramanaiah, B., Glowthaman, M.K., Kamini, Babu, C., Amudeswari, A., Mandal, A.B. and Ramasami, T. (2010): Cleaner Leather Manufacturing Process Using Enzymes, Leather Age, pp. 67-70.

Sekaran, G., Shanmugasundaram, K.A., and Mariappan, M. (1998): Characterization and utilisation of Buffing Dust Generated by the Leather Industry. J. Hazard. Mater. 63: 53.

Sharma, B.; Bharti, P.K.; Pal, N.; Singh, R.K.; Niyogi, U.K. and Khandal, R.K. (2011): Waste Management Practices at Indian Research Station 'Maitri', East Antarctica, In: 'Proceedings of Brainstorming Session on Polar Sciences' Published by Indian Meteorological Department, MoES, Govt. of India, pp. 67-76.

Simeonova, L.S. and Dalev, P.G. (1996): Utilization of a Leather Industry Waste. Waste Management, 16:765-769.

Suresh V, Kanthimathi M, Thanikaivelan P, Rao JR and Nair BU (2001): An Improved Product-Process for Cleaner Chrome Tanning in Leather Processing. J Cleaner Prodn.; 9: 483-91.

Tahiri, S., and de la Guardia, M. (2009): Treatment and Valorization of Leather Industry Solid Wastes: a Review. J. Am. Leather Chem. Assoc. 104: 52.

Taylor, M. M.; Diefendorf, E. J.; Thompson, C. J.; Brown, E. M.; Warmer, W. N. and Cabeza, L. F. (1997): Extraction of Value Added by Products from the Treatment of Chromium Containing Collagenous Leather Industry Waste. Journal of the Society of Leather Technologies & Chemists, 81(1): 5-13.

Taylor, M.M., Diefendorf, E.J. and Marmer, W.N. (1991): Efficiency of Enzymic Solubility of Chrome Shaving as Influence by Choice of Alkalinity-inducing Agent. J. Am. Leather. Chem. As., 86: 199-208.

Vasudevan, N., and Ravindran, A.D. (2007): Biotechnological Process for the Treatment of Fleshing from Tannery Industries for Methane Generation. Curr. Sci., 93: 1492.

Veeger, L. (1993): Ecological Procedure to Solve the Tannery Waste Problems. JALCA. 88 (9): 326.

Wang, X.C., Ren, L.F., and Qiang, T.T. (2009): Novel Way of Transformation of Tannery Waste to Environmentally Friendly form Aldehyde Scavenger. Environ. Prog. Sustain. Energy, 28: 285.

Warrier, K.G.K., Nair, K.M., Vries, A.H., van der Zwan, J., Prasad, B.G.S., Nair, B.U., Venba, R., Mahadevan, T.S.K., and Ramasami, T. (1995): Safe Utilisation of Chrome Containing Sludges in Brick Making. Friedrichshafen: XXIII IULTCS Congress.

Yilmaz, O., Kantarli, I.C., Yuksel, M., Saglam, M., and Yanik, J. (2007): Conversion of Leather Wastes to Useful Products. Res. Conserv. Recycl. 49: 436.

Product Development and Waste Recycling **Pages 14-35**
Edited by: Pawan Kumar 'Bharti'
ISBN: 978-93-86841-94-0
Edition: 2019
Published by: Discovery Publishing House Pvt. Ltd., New Delhi (India)

2 Design, Physical and Biological Analysis of Novel Surfactants Derived from Thermally Abused Cooking Vegetable Oils

[1]Renu Bhutra, [2]Rashmi Sharma, [3]Arun kumar Sharma

ABSTRACT

Various edible oils used in deep fat frying in Indian market are available easily and economically. The use of treated oils as potential biocidal agents and wood preservatives and analysis of their physico-chemical studies will generate new hopes in biological and pharmacological fields.

Surface active agents derived from oils using metal ions are vital components in biological systems, form key ingredients in consumer products and play an important role in many industrial processes. Exact information about micellar feature of copper (II) surfactants play a vital role in its selection in various fields such as foaming, wetting, detergents, emulsifier, herbicides, pesticides, paints, varnishes, wood preservatives, lubricants etc.

The following points will be discussed in the chapter:

1. Synthesis of copper soaps from various untreated and treated oils.
2. Spectral studies (UV and IR) for structural aspects and to confirm the formation of copper soaps.
3. Their biological activities and applications of synthesized surfactants as antifungal agents, their toxicity against various fungi.

Introduction

Surfactants or surface active agents are materials that tend not only to accumulate at surfaces but also by their presence, change the properties of surfaces. Generally, they are active at interfaces that can be between solid/liq, liq/liq or liq/gas pairs of phases.

The surfactant molecule is typically composed of a strongly hydrophilic (water loving) groups or moiety and a strong hydrophobic (water hating) moiety. The active surfactant monomer is referred to as amphiphilic because

[1] Departmentof Chemistry, Rajesh Pilot Govt. Polytechnic College Dausa-303303, Raj. India
[2] S.P.C. Govt. College Ajmer-305001 Raj. India
[3] Govt. P.G. College Jhalawar-326001 Raj. India

of its dual nature. The hydrophobic portion of the surfactant monomer is typically a long hydrocarbon chain referred as the tail of the molecule. The hydrophilic portion of the surfactant monomer is referred to as the 'head' of the molecule and often includes anions or cations. Thus surfactant monomer is illustrated as a tadpole structure.

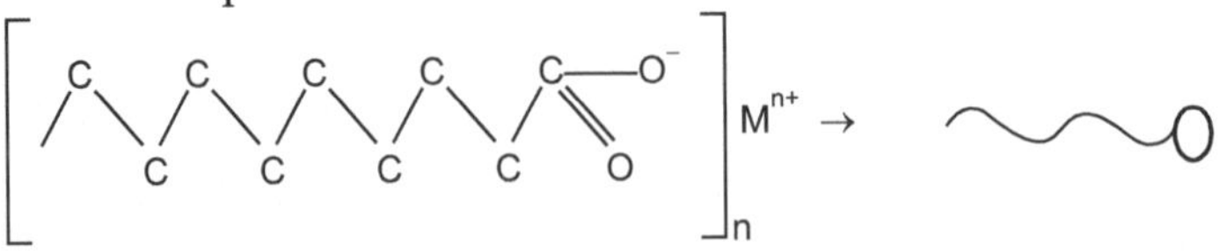

According to nature of their hydrophilic head group, surfactants are classified into three main category i.e. anionic, cationic, and non-ionic surfactants. Anionic surfactants containing Copper ion are gaining popularity on account of their utilitarian effect such as foaming, herbicide, fungicide etc. These Copper bearing surfactants play a vital role in various fields such as rubber industries, paints, varnishes, water proofing and repellency, protection of crops, stabilization of nylon threads, preservation of wood, lubrications etc. All these properties led us to study micellar features and fungicidal activities of Copper soaps derived from various edible oils, available in the market, for their possible uses and applications in agriculture and industries.

Transition Metalcopper-An Introduction

Copper (Cu) is a metal in I B group of the periodic table with atomic number 29. Its natural isotopes are ^{63}Cu (69.1%) and ^{65}Cu (30.9%). Copper is highly ductile and malleable and an excellent conductor of heat and electricity being second to silver in the latter respect.

Copper has a single s-electron outside the filled 4*d* shell but can not be classed with alkalis. Since it has little in common with the alkalis except formal stoichiometries in the +1 oxidation state because ten d-electrons are rather ineffective in shielding the outer s-electron from the coulomb field of the nucleus. Since the electrons of the d-shell are also involved in metallic binding, the heat of sublimation and the melting point of Copper are also higher than those of alkalis. These factors are responsible for the more noble character of Copper and the effect is to make the compounds more covalent and to give them higher lattice energies. The charge +2 is common in Copper. The d^9 arrangement of Cu^{+2} gives rise to square arrangements in which two ligands are attached by somewhat longer bonds above and below the plane of the other four.

Copper has a wide diversity of uses in the electrical, refrigeration and heavy industries, in powder metallurgy and in communications, much of the Copper produced is utilized in various alloys. Many Copper compounds are employed as pesticides either alone (as Cu (I) oxide and Cu (II) sulphate) or in mixtures. Some examples of the later are the pesticide cupronil which contains

35% Cu (II) carbonate hydroxide and 15% zinc N,N-dimethyldithiocarbamate, the fungicide cuprozan containing 37.5% Cu (II) chloride hydroxide and 15% Zineb (zinc ethylene-bis-dithiocarbamate, Bordeaux mixture-a fungicide prepared by reacting Cu (II) sulphate with hydrated lime, and Burgundy mixture-a fungicide similar to Bordeaux mixture but containing sodium carbonate instead of lime. Copper compounds have catalytic properties in many chemical reactions and can activate formation of chlorinated dioxins and dibenzofurans during incineration processes [Schienberg]. Reed reviewed methods of preparation of Copper soaps described by several workers.

Fats and Oils: An Overview

Oils and fats are invaluable for human dietary regimen. They are not only a concentrated source of energy but also source of essential fatty acids, which in turn act as building block of fats and oils.

The edible vegetable oils are a rich source of fatty acids which are having diverse applications in various fields of industries like textile, paints, cosmetics, food and pharmaceutical both in their natural form and as derivatives.

Natural fats are mixtures of mixed glycerides in which the three fatty acids esterifying glycerol differ from each other[11]. The available analysis of natural fats are usually based on an analysis of fatty acids rather than the actual mixed glycerides which occur in the natural product. To describe precisely the structure of fatty acid molecule, one must give the length of the carbon chain, the number of double bonds and also the exact position of double bonds. This will define the biological reactivity and even of the lipid containing the fatty acids.The simplest fatty acids are referred to as saturated fatty acids. They have no unsaturated linkage and can not be altered by hydrogenation or halogenation. When double bonds are present, fatty acids are said to be unsaturated, monounsaturated (MUFA) if only one double bond is present and polyunsaturated (PUFA) if they have two or more double bonds, generally separated by a single methylene group.

COMMON FATTY ACID COMPONENTS OF EDIBLE OILS

Saturated Fatty Acids

Commonly they have straight chains and even number of carbon atoms (4-30). They have the general formula $CH_3(CH_2)_nCOOH$. The following is a list of the most common saturated fatty acids-

Systematic name	Trivial name	Shorthand designation	Molecular weight	Melting point (°C)
Butanoic	Butyric	4:0	88.1	-7.9
Hexanoic	Caproic	6:0	116.1	-3.4
Octanoic	Caprylic	8:0	144.2	16.7

Decanoic	Capric	10:0	172.3	31.6
Dodecanoic	Lauric	12:0	200.3	44.2
Tetradecanoic	Myristic	14:0	228.4	53.9
Hexadecanoic	Palmitic	16:0	256.4	63.1
Octadecanoic	Stearic	18:0	284.4	69.6
Eicosanoic	Arachidic	20:0	412.5	75.3
Docosanoic	Behenic	22:0	340.5	79.9
Tetracosanoic	Lignoceric	24:0	368.6	84.2

Fatty acids with 4-12 carbon atoms are found mainly in milk fats but the higher members are found in seed oils.

- Lauric acid (12:0) occurs extensively in Lauraceae seeds (Laurusnobilis) where it was discovered. It is dominant in cinnamon oil (80-90%), coconut oil (40-60%) and is found in Cuphea species.
- Myristic acid (14:0) is present in major amount in seeds of the family Myristicaceae (nutmeg butter 60-70%). Coconut and Palm Kernel oils are convenient sources of C_8-C_{14} fatty acids.
- Palmitic acid (16:0) was purified first by Chevreul. Palmitic acid is present in major proportions in cottonseed oil (20%), Palm oil (35-40%) and Chinese vegetable tallow (60-70%).
- Stearic acid (18:0) is a major component acid of several familiar animal depot fats (tallows) where it occurs to the extent of 10-30%.
- Arachidic acid (20:0) occurs in appreciable quantities in groundnut oil (3%) but larger amounts are found in seeds of Sapindaceae.
- Behenic acid (22:0) was first reported as a constituent of ben oil (seeds of Moringooleifera). This fatty chain is present in nearlly all seed oils but in amounts lower than 1%.
- Lignoceric acid (24:0) is present at trace levels in plant oils except in groundnut oil and notably in a Leguminous seed oil.

Mono Unsaturated Fatty Acids-MUFA

Chevreul discovered the monoenoic fatty acids. These monounsaturated normal acids are wide spread in the living world where they occur mostly as the cis-isomer. They have the general structure-

$$CH_3(CH_2)_XCH{=}CH(CH_2)_yCOOH$$

They can have unique double bond in a number of different positions, but the commonest are n-9 series, as oleic acid from olive oil. Some important monoenoic acids are given below-

Systematic name	Trivial name	Shorthand designation	Molecular weight	Melting point (°C)
cis-9- hexadecenoic	Palmitoleic	16:1	254.4	0.5
cis-9- octadecenoic	Oleic	18:1	282.4	16.2
cis-11-eicosenoic	Gondoic	20:1	310.5	-
cis-13- docosenoic	Erucic	22:1	338.6	33.4

- Oleic acid is the most common fatty acid. Olive oil has a high content of this acid; about 60-70%, but it is also found in a large variety of nuts.
- Erucic acid with 22 carbon atoms is found in high amounts (up to 50%) in seed oils of the Cruciferae such as Nasturtium, rape, mustard and of the Tropacolaceae.

Poly Unsaturated Fatty Acids - PUFA

The common poly unsaturated fatty acids are listed below-

Systematic name	Trivial name	Shorthand designation	Molecular weight	Melting point (°C)
9,12- octade-cadienoic	Linoleic	18:2(n-6)	280.4	−5
	-linolenic	18:3(n-6)	282.4	16.2
	-linolenic	18:3(n-3)	278.4	−11
	arachidonic	20:4(n-6)	304.5	−50

- Linoleic acid (18:2) is the most common polyunsaturated fatty acid in plants. It was isolated by Sacc. Walnut, peanut, seeds of sunflower, grape, corn, sesame and soya contain large amounts of this fatty acid.
- Arachidonic acid (20:4) is a major constituent of membrane lipids (phospolipids) and is the principal precursor of hormone-like compounds known as prostaglandins (prostanoids).
- Linolenic acid (18:3) is the major fatty acid of plant leaves, stems and roots.

Four edible oils (Groundnut, Mustard, Sesame, Soyabean oil) have been chosen for the investigations possesing some of the above described fatty acids in their composition. Copper soaps are synthesised from them and studied for cmc by various physical parameters (viz. density, viscosity, ultrasonic velocity etc.).

Solubilization and Solubility

The phenomenon of solubilization was first discovered by Gad. A moderately concentrated aqueous soap solution is able to take into thermodynamically stable solution of various organic compounds, which in the absence of soaps show only a very small solubility in water. This phenomenon was termed as solubilization by McBain and co-workers. The difference between solubilization and protective action has been pointed out by Lawrence and by McBain et.al. and the similarity between hydrotropy and solubilization has been suggested by Von H Lindane and by Winsor.

Demchenko has investigated the solubilization of dichloro methane, chloroform and hydrocarbon in sodium soap and the effect of electrolytes and non-electrolytes on the solubilizing capacity of sodium and potassium soaps. Hellar and Clevans have studied the solubilization of hydrocarbon by opacity method.

The dissolving power of aqueous soap solution has been compared with that of other detergents by McBain and co-workers Solubilization pertaining to Copper, cobalt, cadmium and iron have been studied by number of workers. Solubilization action of different basic organic compounds on zinc soaps was studied by Chatterje and Palit. Relph studied physical properties of zinc and their relation to solubility parameters of the solvent. Solubilization of silver stearate by non-ionic surfactants in organic solvents was studied by Jain and Singh.

Dobry determined the solubility of Copper stearate in water and benzene at 25°C. The solubility of Copper soaps of wool wax acid in non-aqueous solvents was studied by Nobel, Scalane and Fisher. The chemical behaviour of Copper stearate and oleate in dioxane and pyridine was explained by Matuura and Nagasue.

On the basis of solubility measurements at different temperatures, it was pointed out by Nelson and Pink that Copper laurate aggregates in toluene and the association effect is reduced in iso-butyl alcohol. Wolff observed that degree of association depends on the nature of the solvent. Mehrotra and Rai et.al. and Mehta et.al. confirmed the dimeric nature of Copper soaps in chloroform and benzene by the determination of the molecular weights ebullioscopically. Number of scientists studied the micellar features of the transition metal containing soaps in different solvents.

Applications and Structural Scenario

Schulman and Riely from the X-Ray diffraction of Copper (II) soaps propounded the concept that the structure consists of closely packed uniform water sphere in oil or of oil in water. It has been pointed out by Anacker that the molecular weight obtained for soap solutions are incompatible with the assumption of spherical micelle and according to McBain and Jhonson, the spherical micelles are wholly inadequate to account for the solubilization of hydrocarbon. In conformity with X-Ray diffraction data, McBain has postulated the existence of lamellar micelles. This has been supported by Shinoda by the results obtained from the affects of alcohols on cmc. This has been suggested by Ooshika that the change in cmc by addition of alcohol is due to lamellar micelles.

Later McBain has pointed out that it is not possible to account for all the properties of the soap solutions with only one kind of micelle and he suggested the existence of both spherical ionic micelle and lamellar micelles.

McBain and coworkers have suggested that soap solutions contain different proportions of the various micelles at different concentrations. It has been pointed out by Kolthoff and Stricks that different types of micelles with different solubilizing power are formed and that with increase in soap concentration, more of the micelles with greater solubilizing power are formed. Matuura investigated the IR spectra and X-Ray diffraction patterns of Copper oleate. Barclay and Kennard studied the crystal structure of Copper formate by X-Ray technique. The infra red spectra of Copper soaps and Copper soaps with benzidine were also studied. Grant studied the nuclear magnetic resonance spectra of Copper stearate.

Bespyatov and Palstyanoi studied the rate of hydrolysis of sunflower oil at high temperature in presence of Copper soaps as catalyst. Fukuda and Tsurugi pointed out the utility of butyrates of lead, Copper, cobalt and cadmium as an activator in the reaction of mercaptobenzo thiazole. The decomposition of ethyl-diazo acetate in presence of Copper stearate in cyclohexane was studied by Dyakonov *et al.* Stouthamer and Vlugte studied the hydrogenation of unsaturated fatty acids to alcohols in presence of mixed soaps.

Surfactants form a unique class of chemical compounds. These are able to alter surface and interfacial properties and to self-associate and solubilize themselves in micelles. These properties provide the means to apply surfactants in wettability modification, detergency and the displacement of liquid phases through porous media on one hand, and to stabilize dispersions (including foams, froths and emulsions), or to destabilize dispersions (again including foams and emulsions) on the other hand. These in turn lead to a vast array of practical application areas, which are illustrated in terms of mineral and petroleum processing, biological systems, health and personal care products, foods, and crop protection.

Several workers described the uses of Copper soaps as stabilizers for nylon threads, synthetic polyamides and polyesters. The protection of fabrics, nets, cordage etc from fungi and decay by impregnating them in ammonical solution of Copper soaps was described by several workers. The effectiveness of Copper soaps as fungicides, bactericides, insecticides and herbicides were also studied.

The water repellency of Copper soaps was studied by Varkonj and Szell and it was observed that water proofing and water repellent coating were formed by treating the heavy fabrics with Copper naphthenates. It was observed by Zahradhik *et al.* that Copper soaps were more effective for protection of stored sugar beets. It was pointed out by Leyland and Stanford, Gebhardt and by

Pedersen that the oxidation of natural rubber increases rapidly by the addition of Copper stearate.

Recent development in metalic soaps preservation shows that zinc and Copper napthanates, exhibiting no specific fungal weakness, can be used to prevent attack by woodboring insects. Bartleson and Hughes used Copper soaps in lubricants which were stable to oxidative deterioration. To decrease wear of drawing dies, the lubricant containing Copper soaps is more effective. Mattiello described the use of Copper soaps as driers for the preparation of paints, varnishes and other protective coating. It was observed that the addition of Copper soaps to fuel oil reduces the smoke and fumes of burning oil. The use of Copper linoleate as heavy-duty wood preservative and many other biological activities of Copper metal containing surfactants have also been studied.

Copper naphthenate is a widely used, broad-spectrum wood preservative. It has several properties which make it a highly valued commodity, including effective control of decay fungi and excellent control or mitigation of wood destroying insects, including termites, beetles carpenter ants and other host organisms. Metal soaps of naturally occurring plant-based acids such as oleic, stearic, and tall oil acids were inferior to naphthenates when used to protect cellulosic material (Marsh, 1944). Metal soaps of synthetic acids are frequent substitutes for naphthenate soaps in paint driers and other applications because of their lower cost and higher metal content.

Formulated proprietary brands of cuprous oxide are extensively employed as fungicides and seed dressings. Another important application of cuprous oxide is in anti-fouling paints. Copper oxychloride has a number of applications, by far the most important being as an agricultural fungicide for which purpose it is extensively employed in formulated form as dusts, wettable powders and pastes. Copper stearate, Copper oleate and Copper abietate (from resins) are employed mainly for rot-proofing textiles, ropes, etc. They are also used in paints, as they are soluble in oils, white spirits, etc. The main applications of Copper sulphate are in the production of proprietary wood preservatives and agricultural fungicides as well as for the production of a number of Copper compounds.

Recent uses of lauric acid are in the manufacture of soaps, shampoos and other surface-active agents, including special lubricants. Lauric acid as monoglyceride is known to the pharmaceutical industry for its good antimicrobial properties. It may play a role in combating lipid-coated RNA and DNA viruses. It was recently shown that polyenoic fatty acids are able to reduce plasma triglycerides and VLDL in rats? Linoleic acid is the first intermediate formed and claims have been made for its therapeutic properties.

Survey of literature shows that Copper soaps play a vital role in biological activities and have sufficient pharmaceutical, industrial and analytical applications. Biocidal studies have been done of Copper soaps derived from various oils to assess their comparative toxicity on two easily available fungi *Alternaria alternata* and *Aspergillus niger*.

The synthesized Copper soaps may be biodegradable so they may play a very important role in wood preservation and in other biological activity.

EXPERIMENTAL

Four edible oils available in the market (Groundnut, Mustard, Sesame, Soyabean) were chosen for the investigation. Their compositions are recorded in Table 2.1. They were treated for 15 and 60 minutes. Copper soaps were synthesized from them.

Preparation of Treated Oils

(*a*) Preparation of Treated Oils for 15 Minutes: About 500 gm oil was taken in a iron pan. The oil was heated to the highest temperature and 5 gm potato chips were deep fried while maintaining the frying temperature between 180-200 °C. The oil was heated for 15 minutes in the open air and sunlight in iron pan at 180-200 °C. The volume of the oil was not replenished to the original volume after frying operations. The frying experiment with all the four oil samples at 180-200 °C for 15 minutes were conducted in similar manner.

(*b*) Preparation of Treated Oils for 60 Minutes: About 500 gm untreated oil was taken in a iron pan. The oil was heated to the highest temperature and potato chips in 5 gm batches were deep fried while maintaining the frying temperature between 180- 200 °C. Four batches were fried after every 5 minutes after the heating started. The oil was heated for 60 minutes in the open air and sunlight in iron pan at 180-200 °C. The volume of the oil was not replenished to the original volume after frying operations. The frying experiment with all the four oil samples at 180-200 °C for 60 minutes were conducted in similar manner.

Preparation of Copper Soaps

Copper soaps were prepared by refluxing the oils with 2N KOH solution and alcohol for about 3 h. The excess of KOH was neutralised using 1N HCl. Saturated solution of Copper sulphate was added to it. The Copper soap obtained was filtered, washed with warm water followed by alcohol, dried at 50°C and recrystallised from hot benzene. The formation of Copper soap was confirmed by using UV, IR techniques. The metal was analysed by standard procedure.

The Copper soaps synthesized are abbreviated as follows-

A. From untreated oils-

1. Copper soap of Groundnut oil CG

2. Copper soap of Mustard oil — CM
3. Copper soap of Sesame oil — CSe
4. Copper soap of Soyabean oil — CSo

B. From treated oils for 15 minutes-
1. Copper soap of Groundnut oil — CG_{15}
2. Copper soap of Mustard oil — CM_{15}
3. Copper soap of Sesame oil — CSe_{15}
4. Copper soap of Soyabean oil — CSo_{15}

C. From treated oils for 60 minutes-
1. Copper soap of Groundnut oil — CG_{60}
2. Copper soap of Mustard oil — CM_{60}
3. Copper soap of Sesame oil — CSe_{60}
4. Copper soap of Soyabean oil — CSo_{60}

Purification of Solvent (Benzene)

Benzene (B.D.H.) was dehydrated by storage over sodium wire for 2-3 days and refluxing for about twenty hours. It was then distilled and the redistillation was carried out azeotropically with ethanol (B.P. -80°C)

Determination of Molecular Weights of Copper Soaps

Molecular weights of Copper soaps are determined from saponification equivalent. The saponification equivalent or saponification value is a measure of the average chain length of the fatty acid which make up a fat. The saponification equivalent (S.E) is the amount of potassium hydroxide whilst the saponification value (S.V) is the number of milligrams of KOH required to hydrolyse one gram of material, the two being related by the expression:

$$S.E = 56100/S.V$$

So S.E may be taken as average molecular weight of oil. Values of S.E are determined by experiments and from these values, average molecular weights of Copper soaps are calculated.

Reactions during Heating of the Oils

(1) Autoxidation: Oxidation by atmospheric oxygen conveniently described as autoxidation is of great importance. As autoxidation proceeds, peroxidic compounds are formed, there is a decrease in unsaturation and after prolonged reaction, a great variety of products are isolable including dihydroxy, epoxy and keto-hydroxy compounds. In autoxidation, the main reaction occurs between oxygen and the unsaturated centre present in the oil.

Bach (1897) and Engler (1897-1900) independently suggested that the first reaction was between molecular oxygen and an ethylene bond with formation of a peroxide which like hydrogen peroxide, was capable of oxidising other compounds. Fahrion (1909), Ellies (1932) and Morrell (1931) further suggested that the initially formed peroxide changes by intramolecular rearrangement to a tautomeric enediol- ketohydroxide system.

Staudinger (1925) believed that the moloxide was the primary product of reaction and this rearranged to the peroxide. Farmer confirmed that the primary product of autoxidation of nonconjugated unsaturated acids or esters are hydroperoxides in which the double bond remains intact.

In autoxidation of methyl oleate, early investigators working under varying conditions, isolated dihydroxy stearic acids, as well as nonanoic, octanoic, azelaic, suberic and oxalic acids and some polymeric products. Linoleate hydroperoxide has been isolated in autoxidation of methyl linoleate. The chief product of autoxidation of methyl linolenate is a methyl octadecatrienoatemonohydroperoxide.

Thermal Polymerisation

When the esters of di and tri ethenoid acids are heated above 200°C, they undergo certain changes. Paschke, Jackson and Wheeler (1952) from their study of the thermal polymerisation of non conjugated and conjugated octadecadienoates have concluded that the first step in the polymerisation of the nonconjugated dienes is isomerisation to the conjugated esters and that after configurational change to the trans–trans diene, this enters into Diels Alder condensation with conjugated or nonconjugated diene, preferably the latter since this is present in greater proportions.

Trimers are also formed and probably result from interaction of the dimer with a second molecule of conjugated diene The conjugated isomers[3] react more quickly since condensation occurs directly and is independent of the slow, rate determining, thermal conjugation reaction. Alternatively, it has been suggested that reaction occurs between one molecule of diene isomerised to a conjugated form and the reactive CH_2 group of a second linoleate molecule to give a dimer which, initially at least, is acyclic and is more unsaturated than the monocyclic dimer produced by Diels-Alder condensation.

From above described chemical reactions, which occur during heating of the oil, numerous decomposed or polymerised products may be formed. As a result, average molecular weight of oil changes after heating. It is apparent from results that maximum change in average molecular weight occurs in Soyabean oil. This fact is supported by several workers that the deterioration during frying is higher in the oils containing higher polyunsaturated fatty acids such as Soyabean oil.

SPECTRAL STUDIES

Electronic Absorption Spectra

In order to confirm the formation of Copper soaps derived from various oils, the electronic absorption spectra were recorded on a Perkin-Elmer-Lambda-28 spectrophotometer. These spectra give information concerning Copper-ligand binding. The electronic absorption spectra of all Copper soaps show one broad band at about 670-680 nm (14925-14706 cm-1) and a sharp band at about 280 nm (35714 cm^{-1}). One broad band may be attributed to $2E_g$?$2T_{2g}$ transitions arising from MLCT (metal-ligand charge transfer) absorption bands which confirms the formation of Copper soaps and proposes a distorted octahedral stereochemistry 5-10 around the metal ion. Absorption peaks (?<300nm) belong to or orbital transition of the ligand.

Infrared Spectral Analysis

In order to study the structure of Copper soaps derived from oils, the infrared spectra of these compounds in the present study were recorded in KBr disc by making use of Perkin Elmer infrared spectrometer. Some important characteristic absorption bands with relative intensities and assignments. The detailed infrared absorption spectral studies reveal that there are marked difference between the spectra of oils and that of corresponding Copper soap. In the IR spectra of sesame oil three distinct bands appear at 3008, 2925 and 2854 cm^{-1} due to = C-H stretching, -C-H symmetrical and –C-H antisymmetric stretching vibration respectively. Apart these, oils show characteristic absorption bands of esters (because oils are esters of long chain fatty acids). In IR spectra of oil, two bands are observed at 1745 and 1164 cm^{-1}. These bands may be assigned to C=O stretching and C-O stretching vibration of ester group.

In the spectra of Copper soaps, strong band in the region 2970-2840 cm^{-1} are due to C-H symmetrical and antisymmetrical stretching vibration of methyl and methylene group which is similar to oil. Gotoh and Takenaka have reported the similar results for the methyl group in acids of various chain lengths.

There is complete disappearance of the characteristic bands of esters in the spectra of soap molecules and appearance of two new absorption bands in the region 1580-1610 cm^{-1} and 1380-1400 cm^{-1}. These bands may be assigned to a symmetric and antisymmrtric vibration of carboxylate ion. These observations are in agreement with the frequencies assigned by Kagarise for phenyl stearic acid and by Mehrotra *et al.* for stearate soap.

The disappearance of the characteristic bands of esters and appearance of the bands of carboxylate ion indicate the formation of Copper soaps. Similar observations has also been reported for rubidium soaps by Mehrotra and Saroha. A number of progressive bands are observed for both oils and soaps in the region 1300-1120 cm^{-1}. Such progressive bands with medium or weak intensity are assigned to the wagging and twisting vibrations of the chain of successive methylene group of the soap molecule. Weak bands in the region 725-710 cm^{-1} may probably be due to methylene rocking vibrations of the straight carbon chain $-(CH_2)^-$.

The bands in the region 750-450 cm^{-1} in the infrared spectra of these soaps are due to metal to oxygen bond stretching vibration. These are called characteristic absorption of metal constituent of each soap molecule.

COMPARISON OF IR SPECTRA OF COPPER SOAPS DERIVED FROM UNTREATED AND TREATED OILS

In Copper soaps of untreated groundnut oils, there is no band in 3200-3600 cm^{-1} region. In the IR spectra of CG_{15}, appearance of a broad band at 3400 cm^{-1}, a medium band at 1625 cm^{-1} and a weak band at 1100 cm^{-1} may be due to the formation of enediol during heating the oil.

In the IR spectra of CM_{15} and CM_{60}, appearance of a broad medium band at about 3500 cm^{-1} and one band at 1612 cm^{-1} show the presence of enolic OH group which can be further supported by the existence of the OH deformation band at 1100 cm^{-1}.

In the IR spectra of CM_{60}, bands are present at 3444 cm^{-1}, 1743 cm^{-1} and 1114 cm^{-1} these bands may be due to formation of keto-hydroxide group formed during the autoxidation or these bands may be due to formation of carbonyl degradation products as the result of thermal abuse.

In the IR spectra of CSe_{60} also, bands are present at about 3500 cm^{-1} (very weak), 1750 cm^{-1} (strong), 1625 cm^{-1} (weak) and 1100 cm^{-1} (weak). Appearance of these bands may be due to formation of various autoxidised products such as enediol, keto-hydroxide or carbonyl degradation products.

In IR spectra of $CSo_{15}$and CSo_{60} bands are present at 3450 cm^{-1} and 1745 cm^{-1} which shows the formation of keto-hydroxide during the autoxidation reactions.

From comparison between IR spectra of Copper soaps of untreated oils and Copper soaps of treated oils, it is found that there is no band in 3200-3600 cm^{-1} region in Copper soaps derived from untreated oils. But in the IR spectra of copper soaps derived from treated oils, there are bands at about 3400-3500 cm^{-1}, 1750 cm^{-1}, 1625 cm^{-1}, 1100 cm^{-1}. These bands may be due to formation of various autoxidised products such as enediol, keto-hydroxide or carbonyl degradation products.

Table 2.: Fatty Acid Composition of Oils Used for Copper Soap Synthesis

Name of oil	% Fatty Acids					
	16:0	18:0	18:1	18:2	18:3	Other Acids
Groundnut Oil	10	4	61	18	-	C_{20}-C_{24} 7%
Mustard Oil	2	1	25	18	10	C_{20}-C_{22} 41%
Sesame Oil	8	4	45	41	-	-
Soyabean Oil	12	4	24	51	9	-

BIOCIDAL

Recently, the deeper understanding of the role of metal ion in bio-system has led to the awareness that metal complexing is useful in the treatment of bacterial, fungicidal and viral diseases. Most of the antimicrobial agents are obviously organic compounds, which behave as good chelating agent. Their pathogenic activity is enhanced on complexing with various transition and toxic metals. The biological effect of these derivatives depends on the nature and structure of ligands and their metal complexes and also on the presence of particular element.

Many Copper compounds are employed as pesticides either alone (as Cu (I) oxide and Cu (II) sulfate) or in mixtures. Examples of the latter are the pesticide Cupronil which contains 35% Cu (II) carbonate hydroxide and 15% zinc N,N-chloride hydroxide and 15% zineb (zinc ethylene-bis-dithiocarbamate); Bordeaux mixture-a fungicide prepared by reacting Cu(II) sulfate with hydrated lime; and Burgundy mixture-a fungicide similar to Bordeaux mixture but containing sodium carbonate instead of lime.

Berends *et al.* synthesised and evaluated the biological activity of Copper complexes with tridentate benzimidazolyl ligands. Many Copper thiosemicarbazone complexes are found to have significant antitubercular, fungicidal and anti-tumoractivities. The use of Copper linoleate as heavy duty wood preservative and many other biological activities of Copper metal containing surfactants also has been studied.

Formulated proprietary brands of cuprous oxide are extensively employed as fungicides and seed dressings. Copper oxychloride has a number of applications, by far the most important being as an agricultural fungicide for which purpose it is extensively employed in formulated form as dusts, wettable powders and pastes.

Small quantities of Copper soaps such as Copper stearate, Copper oleate and Copper abietate (from resins), are employed mainly for rot-proofing textiles, ropes, etc. The main applications of Copper sulfate are in the production of proprietary wood preservatives and agricultural fungicides.

Copper naphthenate is a widely used, broad-spectrum wood preservative. It has several properties which make it a highly valued commodity, including effective control of decay fungi and excellent control or mitigation of wood destroying insects, including termites, beetles carpenter ants and other host organisms. In the United States, the Environmental Protection Agency also classifies Copper naphthenate as a general use (unrestricted) pesticide.

Only limited data are found in the literature describing the preservative efficacy of Copper soaps of other carboxylic acids. Metal soaps of naturally occurring plant-based acids such as oleic, stearic, and tall oil acids were inferior to naphthenates when used to protect cellulosic material (Marsh, 1944). Hilditch (1983) observed that Copper and zinc soaps of "acypetacs", their term for synthetic acyclic branched carboxylic acids, were also slightly less effective than the corresponding naphthenates in ground contact studies. Metal soaps of synthetic acids are frequent substitutes for naphthenate soaps in paint driers and other applications because of their lower cost and higher metal content.

All the above studies suggest that the Copper metal play a vital role in fungicidal activities. Various edible oils are widely used, easily available and economic. These facts led us to synthesis Copper soaps of some oils and their treated oils remaining after frying, to study their micellar characteristics and role of copper metal in fungicidal activities for exploring their applications and other possible uses in various industries and agriculture. For this purpose, we have chosen some fungicidal activities of the synthesised Copper soaps against easily available fungi *Alternaria alternata*and *Aspergillus niger*.

The details of these studies have been described under the following two headings:

1. Experimental
2. Results and Discussion

EXPERIMENTAL

The general laboratory techniques followed in the course of this investigation are as suggested by Booth and Hawks worth.

1. Sterilisation of Glasswares: Glasswares used in our study were of pyrex brand. The glasswares viz. test tubes, conical flasks, pipettes (micro and macro), glass rods and petridishes were thoroughly washed after rinsing with chromic acid each time before sampling. The petriplates and other glassware were then sterilised in hot air oven at 160 °C for 24 hours before use.

2. Culture Media Used: The cultured medium used for the growth of the organism in the present study was P.D.A. The following media was used in the present study

Potatoes-200 gm

Dextrose-20 gm

Agar-20 gm

Distill water-1000 ml

200 gm of potatoes were cleaned, cut into pieces and boiled in about 1000 ml of tap water for 2 hours. Then, the contents were strained using muslin cloth. To this extract, 20 gm of dextrose, 20 gm of agar were added and made up to 1000 ml in graduated flask, before sterilizing the medium.

3. Preparation of Sample Solutions: All the Copper soaps derived from untreated and treated oils were tested for anti-fungal activity. The method of preparation of the soaps and complexes has been described in Chapter (II). The calculated amount of the soap was weighted in a standard flask and the solutions containing different concentration (1000 and 10000 ppm) of soaps in benzene were prepared.

4. Test Organism: In the present study, following two test organism are used:

A. Alternaria alternata

B. Aspergillus niger

The above organism were isolated from their natural habitat and then purified, characterized and identified.

5. Fungicidal Testing: 1 ml of the soap solution was aseptically transferred into sterile petriplates. Into these plates, 20 ml of P.D.A. was poured and was mixed with soap solution by rotating the petriplates in clockwise and anticlockwise direction 3-4 times and was allowed to solidify.

After the solidification of the above medium, single hypha / spore of test organism was aseptically transferred in the centre of the petriplates. The plates were incubated at 30 ?1°C for 3 days. After the period of incubation, the plates were observed for the growth of fungus in different concentration of the soap solution used in the present study. The data were statistically analysed according to the following formula:

$$\% \text{ Inhibition} = (C-T)*100/C$$

Where C = diameter of fungal colony in control plates after 3 days

T = diameter of fungal colony in test plate after 3 days

Results and Discussion

Copper soaps derived from untreated and treated oils have been screened for their antifungicidal activity against *Alternaria-alternata* and *Aspergillus-niger* at 1000 ppm and 10000 ppm by Agar-plate technique. Copper soaps showed moderate activities against both the fungi.

A perusal of Tables (2.2-2.4) reveals that all the Copper soaps have significant fungitoxicity at 10000 ppm but their toxicity decreases markedly on dilution (at 1000 ppm). From the Tables, it is apparent that their efficiency increases with their concentration. Thus it is evident that concentration plays a vital role in increasing the degree of inhibition. Fungicidal screening data revealed that at lower concentration the inhibition of growth is less as compared to higher concentration.

From comparison of the results for both the fungi, it is found that all Copper soaps are more potent (more toxic) against *Aspergillus niger* than against *Alternaria- alternata* i.e. inhibition of growth is higher for *Aspergillus niger* than inhibition of growth for *Alternaria alternata.*

A perusal of the Table 2.2 shows that CM is the least fungitoxic (% inhibition lowest) whereas CSo is the most toxic against both fungi. The activity (toxicity) of Copper soaps derived from untreated oils are found to increase in the order:

$$CSo > CSe > CG > CM$$

For Copper soaps derived from treated oils for 15 minutes, the results are same as Copper soaps derived from untreated oils. CM_{15} is the least active and CSo_{15} is the most active against both fungi. The order of activity of Copper soaps derived from treated oils for 15 minutes is as follows:

$$CSo_{15} > CSe_{15} > CG_{15} > CM_{15}$$

For Copper soaps derived from treated oils for 60 minutes, CM_{60} is the least active but difference in activity of these Copper soaps is not so high and order of activity is as follows:

$$CSo_{60} > CSe_{60} > CG_{60} > CM_{60}$$

From comparison of Copper soaps derived from untreated and treated sample of oil, it is found that fungitoxicity increases with the increase of time of heating for oils i.e.

$$CG_{60} > CG_{15} > CG$$

$$CM_{60} > CM_{15} > CM$$

$$CSe_{60} > CSe_{15} > CSe$$

$$CSo_{60} > CSo_{15} > CSo$$

Table 2.2: Antifungal Activity of Copper (Ii) Soaps Derived From Untreated Oils

Name of the Soap	Average % inhibition after 3 days			
	Alternaria alternata		Aspergilusniger	
	Concentration in ppm		Concentration in ppm	
	1000	10000	1000	10000
CG	3.33	30.00	25.86	36.20
CM	0.00	16.66	20.68	32.75
CSe	13.33	23.33	27.58	37.93
CSo	16.66	31.66	31.03	41.37

Table 2.3: Antifungal Activity of Copper (II) Soaps Derived from Treated Oils for 15 Minutes

Name of the Soap	Average % inhibition after 3 days			
	Alternaria alternata		As per gilusniger	
	Concentration in ppm		Concentration in ppm	
	1000	10000	1000	10000
CG_{15}	13.46	32.69	31.66	75.00
CM_{15}	5.76	26.92	26.66	70.00
CSe_{15}	15.38	46.15	43.43	76.66
CSo_{15}	23.07	50.30	50.00	78.33

Table 2.4: Antifungal Activity of Copper (II) Soaps Derived from Treated Oils for 60 Minutes

Name of the Soap	Average % inhibition after 3 days			
	Alternaria alternata		Aspergilusniger	
	Concentration in ppm		Concentration in ppm	
	1000	10000	1000	10000
CG_{60}	13.79	52.17	34.48	76.66
CM_{60}	3.44	50.00	27.58	73.33
CS_{e60}	6.89	54.34	48.27	78.33
CSo_{60}	17.24	54.34	51.72	80.00

REFERENCES

Agnihotri N.K., Singh V.K. and Singh H.B. : *Bibliographic Citation, Talanta- Oxford, India, 45:2, 331-341, (1998).*

Anacker E.W. : *J. Colloid Sci., 8, 402, (1953).*

Anilin,B and Soda-Fabrik A.G. : *Ger.1, 152, 816, (1963).*

Arens C.L. et. al. : *Biochem. J., 37, 1, (1943).*

Asset G. et.al. : *Lipids, 34, 39, (1999).*

Aulerio A.Z., Zambonelli A., Binanchi A., Catellani P.L. and Bitti S. : *Informatore Agrario, 54:45, 89-90, (1998).*

Ayers W.C. : *Anal. Chim. Acta, 15, 77-83, (1956).*

Banerjee B.C. and Palit S.R. : *J. Indian Chem. Soc., 27, 385-94, (1950).*

Barclay G.A. and Kennard C.H.L. : *J. Indian Chem. Soc., 3289, (1961).*

Bartleson D.J. and Hughes C.E. : *U.S. 2, 660, 542, (1951).*

Bespyatov M.P. and Palstyanoi V.I. : *Maslob, Zhir prom., 28 (6), 14-17, (1962).*

Bisewell B.C. : *U.S.2, 873,178, (1959).*

Blenis P.V., Nadeav L.B., Knowles N.R. and Logue G. : *Bibliographic Citation, Hort- Science, 32(6), 1077-1084, (1997).*

Buick T.A., Stall W.M., Kostewicz S.R. and Smith K. : *Bibliographic Citation, Hort- Science, U.S.A. 25:11, 1407-1408, (1990).*

Chatterjee B.K. and Palit S.R. : *J. Indian Chem. Soc., 39, 571 (1962).*

Conradie D., Turner P., Conradie W.E., Pendlebury J. and Pizzi T. : *Bibliographic Citation, Div. of Forest Science and Technology, Stockholm (Swedon), 22p, (1995)*

Crop. K. : *KokaiTokkyoKohoJp, 59, 193,129 18 Apr. (1983) C. A. 102, 168691z, (1985).*

Demchenko P.A. : *DopovidiAkad. Nauk, Ukrain USSR, 496-6 (1959), Masloboino- Zhirovaya Prom. 25(10), 22, (1959), Ibid 28(2), 23, (1962), Kolloid-Zhur23, 36-9, (1961), Ukrain. Khim. Zhur, 23, 46-8, 203-5, (1962). KolloidZh., 24(1), 11-14, (1962). J.Phys. Chem., 36, 1401-18, 1672-84, 2455-73, (1932).*

Demes H., Gaudchau M. and Burow R.F. : *Bibliographic Citation, Pesticide- Science, Germany, 38:2-3, 278-280, (1993).*

Dobry A. : *J. Phys. Chem. 58, 576, (1954).*

Duren FabrikChemisch, G.M.B.H. : *Ger.1, 062, 664 (1959).*

Dyakonov I.A., Vitenberg A.G. and Komendantov : *Zhur. Org. Khim., 1(7) 1183-8, (1964).*

ESSO Research and Engg. Co. : *Fr. 1, 381, 305 [Cl. C. 109], (1964).*

Fakuda H. and Tsurugi J. : *Nippon GomuKyokaishi, 34, 16-22, (1961).*

Figgis B.N. and Martin R.L. : *J. Indian Chem. Soc., 35, 37 (1956).*

Filov V. A., Bandman A. L. and Ivin B.A. : *"Harmful Chemical Substances" Vol-1, 66.Eills Horwood, Lmtd, Eng. (1988).*

Fisel S. : *Acad, rep. popular Romine Filialalaji StudicCareetaxi Stiint., 7(2),13-17 (1956); 6(3/4) 295-326, (1955).*

Foex G., and Karantases J. *Compt. Rend, 237, 982, (1953).*

Fremy E. : *Ann, 36, 44, (1840).*

Fuben F. and Bayer A.G. : *Ger. 1, 172, 686, (C1.CO7C) 1964.*

Gad : *Arch. Anat. Physiol., 181 (1978).*

Gebhardt H.L. : *Foundary74, 110-12, 198, 200, 202, 204, 206, (1946).*

Ghasy S.E., Samra S.E., Mahdy A.F.M. and Morsy S.M. : *Environmental Technology, 25(11), 1221-1231, (2004).*

Gilmour A. and Pink R.C. : *J. Indian Chem. Soc., 2198, (1953).*

Goff M.D., Sumack R.L., Tilt K.M. and Hagan A.K. : *Bibliographic Citation, J. of Arboriculture, U.S.A. 22:5, 201-205, (1996).*

Goll M. : *U.S.2, 494, 941, (1950).*

Grant R.F. : *Can. J. Chem., 42(4), 951, (1964).*

Greaves H., Adams N. and McGarthy D.F. : *Div Build Res CSIRO Melbourne, Australia Holzforchung36 (5) 225-31, (1982).*

Guha B.C. *Proc. Roy. Soc., A 206, 353, (1951).*

Gunstone F.D. : *An Introduction to the Chemistry of Fats and Fatty Acids, (Chapmann and Hall Ltd London) 1958.*

Hartley G.S. : *"Paraffin Chain Salts" Herman et.Cie, Paris, (1936).*

Hattiandi G.S., Vold M.I. and Vold R.D. *Ind. Eng. Chem., 41, 2320-4, (1949).*

Heckmann K, Gotz K.G. *et al.* : *Discussion Faraday Soc., 25, 71, (1958).*

Heller W. and Clevens H.B. : *J. Chem. Phys., 14, 567, (1946).*

Herron R.C. and Pink R.C. : *J. Indian Chem. Soc., 3948-52, (1956).*

Hilditch T.P. : *J. Soc. Chem. Ind., 58, 233, (1939).*
HiliditchE.A.and Sparks C.R. : *Rec Annu. Conv. Br. Wood Preserv Assoc, 71-72, (1983).*
Imperial Chemical Industries Ltd. : *Brit. 652, 947, (1951).*
Inoue H. and Nakagawa T. : *J. Phys. Chem., 70, 1108, (1966).*
Jain A.K. and Singh R.P.B. : *J. Colloid Interface Sci., 77 (1), 274, (1980).*
Japan Rayon Co. Ltd., : *Japan 26, 571, (1963)*
Jaycock M.J. and Ottewill R.H. : *IVth International Congress of Surface Activity, Brussels, 1964 Gordon and Breach, New York, N.Y. in press, Paper B/IV 8.*
Kishita M., Inoue M. and Kubo M. : *Nippon Kagaku Kaishi, 84, 758-59, (1963).*
Koeing A. E. : *J. Am. Chem. Soc., 36, 951, (1914).*
Kokot R. and Martin R.L. *Inorg. Chem. 3(9), 1306-12, (1964).*
Kolthoff I.M. and Stricks W. : *J. Phys. Colloid Chem., 52, 915-41, (1948), 53, 424, (1949).*
Kolthoff I.M. and Strieks W. : *J. Phys. Colloid Chem., 52, 915-41, (1948), 53, 424, (1949).*
Kreshech G.C., Hamari E., Devenport G. and Schenarga H.A. : *J. Am. Chemists Soc., 88, 246, (1966).*
Kriza A., Spinu C. and Pleniceanu M. : *J. Indian Chem. Soc. 76, 82, (2000).*
Kuhn M.J., Sheldon A.F. and Silverman M. : *U.S.2, 790, 734, (1957).*
Laurier L. Schramm , Elaine N. Stasiuk and D. GerrardMarangoni : *Annu. Rep. Prog. Chem., Sec. C, 99, 3 – 48, (2003)*
Lawrence A.S.C. : *Trans. Faraday Soc., 35,70,2-6 (1939) Ann. Reports (Chem. Soc. London) 37,102 (1940), J. Phys. Colloid Chem., 52, 1504, (1948).*
Levy J. : *Fatty-acids; Their Ind. Appl. 200-20 (1968).*
Leyland B.N. and Stanford R.L. : *Trans. Inst. Rubber Ind. 35, 25-44 (1959).*
Lindan G. : *Naturwiss, 20,396, (1932).*
Luzzati V. and Hussanf. : *J. Cell. Biol., 12, 207, (1962).*
Mahapatra B. B. and Ray Puspa. : *J. Indian Chem. Soc., 79, 536,(2002).*
Malik A.K., Kaul K.N., Lark B.S., and Rao A.L.J. : *Bibliographic Citation, Pesticide- Science, India, 53:1, 104-106, (1998).*
Malik W. U. and Ahemed S. I. : *Indian J. Chem., 2 (4), 168-9, (1964).*
Malik W. U. and Haque R. : *J. Am. Oil Chemists Soc., 41(6), 411-13, (1964).*
Malik W. U. and Haque R. : *J. Analyt. Chem., 189, 179-82 (1962).*
Malik W.U. and Ahemad S.I. : *J. Polarog. Soc., 12(2), 50-58, (1966).*
Marsh B.P. : *Ind. Eng. Chem. 36, 176-81, (1944).*
Martin R.L. and Waterman H. : *J. Indian Chem. Soc., 2545-51, (1957).*
Martin R.L. and Whitelay A. *J. Indian Chem. Soc., 1394-1402, (1952).*
Mattiello J.J. : *Protective and Decorative Coatings, vol. 1 Wiley, New York, (1941).*
Matuura R. : *Nippon Kagaku Kaishi., 82,1624, (1961).*
Matuura R. and Nagasue K. : *Mem. Fac. Sci. Kyusha Univ. Ser. C_3, 49-54, (1958).*
Mc Bain J.W., Morrill R.C. Jr. and Soldate A.M. : *Adv. Colloid. Sci., P.128, (1941).*
Mc. Bain J.W. and Laing. M.E. : *J. Am. Chem. Soc., 58, 2610, (1936).*
Mc. Bain J.W. and Morrill R.C. Jr. : *Ind. Eng. Chem. 34,915, (1942).*
Mc. Bain J.W. and Morrill R.C. Jr. : *J. Am. Chem. Soc. 63, 670, (1941).*

Mc.Bain J.W. and Green A.A. : *J. Am. Chem. Soc. 68, 1731-36, (1946)*

McBain J.W. : *Frontiers in Colloid Chemistry, Vol. VIII, Inter Science Publishers Inc. (1950).*

McBain J.W. and Huff H.M. : *J. Colloid Sci., 4, 383, (1949).*

McBain J.W. and Johnson K.E. : *J. Am. Chem. Soc., 66, 9-13, (1944).*

McBain J.W. and Morrill R.C Jr. : *J. Phys. Chem., 46,10-19, (1942).*

McBain J.W.andMc Hon H. : *J. Am. Chem. Soc., 70, 3838, (1948).*

Mehrotra K.N. and Jain Mamta. : *Indian J. Chem. 31(A), 452-456, (1992).*

Mehrotra K.N., Mehta V.P. and Nagar T.N. : *J. Prakt. Chem. 312, (1970).*

Mehrotra K.N., Mehta V.P. and Nagar T.N. : *J. Prakt. Chem. 313, Heft 4, 607-613, (1971).*

Mehrotra R.C. and Rai A.K. : *J. Inrog. Nuclear Chem., 21 (3/4), 311-14, (1961).*

Mehrotra R.C. and Rai A.K. *J. Inorg. Nucl. Chem. 21 (3/4), 311-14, (1961).*

Mehta V.P., Hasan M. and Mathur S.P. : *An. Quim. 74, 1016, (1978).*

Mehta V.P., Hasan M., Mathur S.P. and Rai G.L. : *Tenside Surf. Det., 16, 2, (1979).*

Mehta V.P., Talesera P.R. and Sharma Rashmi. : *Indian J. Chem., 39(A), 383-87, (2001).*

Mehta V.P., Talesera P.R. and Sharma Rashmi. : *Indian J. Chem., 40(A), 399-402, (2001).*

Metallargical Chemists Ltd. : *Brit 960 013, (CI.A.Oln) (1964).*

Meyer B. and Meltz K.D. : *Dairy Industries International, 64:4, 37, 39, 41, (1999).*

MijnLieff P.F., and Ditmarsch R. : *Nature, 208, 889, (1965).*

Moncrieff R.W. : *Textile Mfr., 89, 340-1, (1963).*

Moran K. : *Proceedings International Fertiliser Society, 545, 1-24, (2004).*

Mukherjee G. N. and Das A. : *J. Indian Chem. Soc., 77, 78, (2001).*

Mukherjee G.N. and Chakraborty P. K.: *J. Indian Chem. Soc., 79, 137, (2002).*

Nakagawa T. and Inoue H. : *IVth International Congress of Surface Acitivity, Brussels, 1964,Gorden and Breach, New York, N-Y In Press, Paper B/IV 11.*

Nelson S.M. and Pink R.C. : *J. Indian Chem. Soc., 1744-50, (1952).*

Nikitin, A. : *U.S.2, 467, 491, (1949).*

Noble R.W., Scalane T.J. and Eisher A. : *J. Am. Oil Chem. Soc., 35, 31-2, (1962).*

Noller C.R. : *J. Am. Chem. Soc., 56,1563, (1934).*

Ooshika V. : *J. Colloid Sci., 9, 254, (1954).*

Patel R.N., Kumar Subodh and Pandeya K.B.: *Indian J. Chem. 39A, 1124, (2000).*

Pedersen L.H. : *Acta Chem. Scand. 4, 487-507 (1950).*

Philips G.A. and Peter A.S. : *IIIrd International Congress of Surface Activity, Colongne, Verlagder, Universtatsdruckerei, Mainz, GMBH, Vol. I, P 239, 1960.*

Playfair L. : *Ann, 37,152, (1841).*

Popov A., Yanishlieva N. and Iuanova B. : *Maslo-Sapuena, Prom. Byal, 6(4), 13-19, (1967).*

Rafalski L. and Zawadzki J. : *Pol. P L 144, 961, 2 Aug (1985) C. A. 112,1211535 Mar- Apr (1990).*

Raphael R.A. : *Nature, 165, 235, (1950).*

Ratomahenina A., Galzy P., Graitte J. and Pina M. : *Riv. Ital. Sostanze Grasse [Eng.] 60, (11), 673, (1985).*

Reddy K.H., Reddy P.S. and Bahu P.R. : *Transition Met. Chem., 25, 154, (2000).*

Reed P. D. : *J. Am. Perfumer Aromat, 76 (3), 49-50, (1961).*

Relph C.L. : *J. Colloid Interface Sci. 21(3), 266, (1966).*

Riedel Detlaen A.G. : *Ger. 949, 101, (1956).*

Sacc. : *Ann, 51, 213, (1844).*

Sahid H.S.,Asjad H.S. and Mustaf. : *J. Sci. Ind. Res. Pakisthan, 10(3) 197-20, (1967).*

Samsonova O.A. : *TekStil Prom (1/2), 15-18, (1943).*

Sarricolea M. L., Villa- Elizaga I. and Lopez J. : *Bibliographic Citation, Biology of the Neonate, Spain, 63:1, 14-25, (1993).*

Sarricolea M.L., Villa- Elizaga I. and Montreal I. : *Bibliographic Citation, Revista-Espanola-de-Fisiologia, Spain, 49:1, 49-54, (1993).*

Satake I. and Matuura R. : *Chem. Fac. Sci., Kyushu Univ. Ser.* C_5. *1, 13-20, (1962).*

Schiller H. : *U.S.2, 364,391, (1944).*

Schulman J.H. and Riley D.P. : *J. Colloid Sci., 3, 383-405, (1948).*

Shinoda K. : *Bull. Chem. Soc. Jpn, 26, 101, (1953).*

Shinowara G.Y. : *J. Biol. Chem., 134, 331, (1940).*

Singh H., Srivastava V.K., Shukla S.N. and Upadhayaya M.K. : *Indian J. Chem. 31(A), 472-474, (1992).*

Singh, Verma S.B., Jordan J. and Sossna R. : *Ger. Offen D.E., 3, 703, 258 [Cl. 4 Feb. (1987) C. A. 110,10119z, Jan (1989).*

Smit Z.K. Indjic D., Vojinovic M. M. and Orbovic B. : *46th International Symposium on Crop Protection, Gent, Belgium, 3rd May, 59:2b, 625-637, (1994).*

Soyez J.L. : *Brighton Crop Protection Conference, Pests and Diseases, France, Vol. 1, 451- 456, (1992).*

Sparks C.S. : *Rec. Annu. Conv. Br. Wood preservAssoc, 48-51, (1978).*

Stockenius W. : *J. Cell. Biol., 12, 221, (1962).*

Stouthamer B. and Vlugte J.C. : *J. Am. Oil Chemists Soc., 42(7), 646-52 (1965).*

Thirumalaikumar M., Sivakolunthu S., MuthusubramanianS.andSivasubramanian S. : *Bull. Soc. Chim. Fr. 138, 207, (1999).*

Tilt K., Goff W.D. and Hagan A.K. : *Bibliographic Citation, J. of Arboriculture, Magnolia, 30:2, 22-29, (1995).*

Varkonj B. and Szell T. : *Acta Univ. Szegadiensis Acta Phys. Et.Chem., 5, 73, (1959).*

Verma R.P. and Goel H. : *Acoustica, 80,183, (1994).*

Verma R.P., Gour S.N. and Chaudhry O.P. : *Tenside Surf. Det. 24(6), 429, (1992).*

Villa-Elizaga I., Sarricolea M. L. and Lopez J. : *Bibliographic Citation, 8thIntenational Symposium on Trace Elements in Man and Animals, Spain, 23, 558-561, (1993)*

Voelcker A. : *Ann, 64, 342, (1848).*

Von Hann F.V. : *Kolloid, 2,62,202, (1932).*

Winsor P.A. : *Trans. Faraday Soc., 44,376,382,387,390, (1948).*

Wolff J.P. : *Olegineucu, 5, 20-3, (1950).*

Yoko Kurodo. : *Nippon Kagaku Kaishi., 86, 560, (1965).*

Yokolshii H. and Yogi S. : *Bunseki Kagaku, 17(1), 17-7, (1968).*

Yokovldev V.M., Pershina N.Y., Bekrenev A.N. and Masalkina C. N. : *Polytechnic Ins. Samara U.S.S.R., SU 1, 715-835 (CICIOMI 73/00), (1992) Appl. 4, 747, 084, 08 jan (1990).*

Zahradnivk J., Schmidt L. and Havranek A. : *ListyCukrov83(9), 193-7 (1967) [czech].*

Product Development and Waste Recycling **Pages 36-42**
Edited by: Pawan Kumar 'Bharti'
ISBN: 978-93-86841-94-0
Edition: 2019
Published by: Discovery Publishing House Pvt. Ltd., New Delhi (India)

3 Development of Biodegradable Packaging Film from Lantana camara - Invasive Plant Species

[1]Pawan Kumar Bharti

ABSTRACT

The aim of this paper is to determine the feasibility of Lantana camara in the development of biodegradable cellulose film. This perennial weed has not been used in any beneficial activity for many years worldwide. A few of interests have been shown for this plant in last few years in India and aboard. At the same time Lantana camara is one of the most notorious weeds in India. When introduced to terrestrial ecosystem it spreads very quickly due to its high growth potential. Therefore lantana tends to eliminate all other living organisms in surrounding. A development approach is given about potential usage of Lantana camara for cellulosic film preparation.

Keywords: Lantana camara, invasive weed, Cellulose, Biodegradable packaging film, cellophane

Introduction

Lantana camara is a low, erect or subscandent, vigorous shrub which can grow to 2 - 4 meters in height. The leaf is ovate or ovate oblong, 2 - 10 cm long and 2 - 6 cm wide, arranged in opposite pairs. Leaves are bright green, rough, finely hairy, with serrate margins and emit a pungent odour when crushed. The stem in cultivated varieties is often non-thorny and in weedy varieties with recurved prickles. It is woody, square in cross section, hairy when young, cylindrical and up to 15 cm thick as it grows older. Lantana is able to climb to 15 m with the support of other vegetation. Flower heads contain 20 - 40 flowers, usually 2.5 cm across; the colour varies from white, cream or yellow to orange pink, purple and red. Flowering occurs between August and March, or all year round if adequate moisture and light are available. Pollinators include lepidopteran species and thrips. The fruit is a greenish blue-black colour, 5 - 7 mm in diameter, drupaceous, shining, with two nutlets; seed setting takes place between September to May with 1 - 20 seeds on each flower head. Mature

[1] R & D Division, Shriram Institute for Industrial Research, 19, University Road, Delhi-110007, India

plants produce up to 12,000 seeds annually. Seed germination occurs when sufficient moisture is present; germination is reduced by low light conditions. The root system is very strong with a main taproot and a mat of many shallow side roots.

The diverse and broad geographic distribution of lantana is a reflection of its wide ecological tolerance. It occurs in diverse habitats and on a variety of soil types. Lantana generally grows best in open, un-shaded conditions such as wastelands, the edges of rain forests, on beachfronts, in agricultural areas, grasslands, riparian zones, scrub/shrub lands, urban areas, wetlands and forests recovering from fire or logging.

Major composition of Lantana plant is as follow:

Holocellulose	–	71.34%
α-Cellulose	–	64.91%
Pentosans	–	13.0%
Lignin	–	27.25%
Ash	–	1.8%

Lantana camara (Verbenaceae family), a fast-growing weed with encroached large areas worldwide, is rich in lignocellulosic material. Lantana camera is a rugged evergreen shrub growing to 1.8 m high. Stems are square in profile, with small prickles. The leaves are arranged in opposite pairs .They are broadly oval, rough with short hairs, with finely toothed edges. When crushed they have a strong smell. Flowers are a mixture of cream, pink or orange numerous small rounded heads, often in two colours, yellow and red. Fruits are fleshy berries in clusters, green ripening to black.

Distribution of Lantana

Lantana camara has been ranked as the highest impacting invasive species and is among the 100 worlds worst invasive alien species, because it posses great potential to escape cultivation and have deleterious effect on species richness. In India it was introduced in early nineteenth century as an ornamental plant, but now it is growing densely throughout India (Sharma *et al.,* 2005).

The species has made itself indispensable in most parts of India. It was introduced in 1809 as an ornamental plant by the British in Calcutta Botanical Garden. Voyaging two centuries of its establishment in India, at present it is considered to be extremely adaptable and prolific. Thus, it has its indiscriminate spread and presence in almost all regions of India including farm, pasture, fallow land and forest except the Thar Desert and its surroundings (Dobhal *et al.,* 2011). Not only is the geographic range of *Lantana camara* still expanding in many regions of India, but the density of infestations within its range is increasing and has been recognized as a future threat to ecosystems.

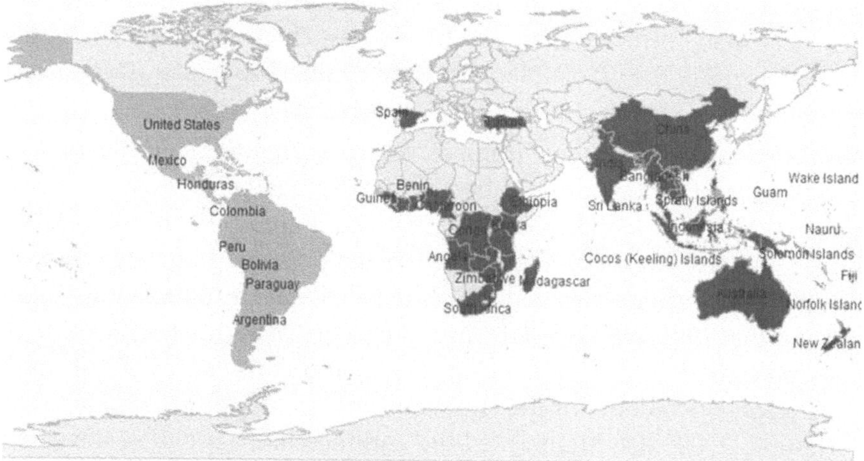

Fig. 3.1: *Lantana camara* native (light grey) and introduced (dark grey) regions (Day *et al.,*, 2003)

Lantana has become the most problematic weed in many tropical and subtropical terrestrial habitats worldwide. Lantana forms thick shrub like colonies and caused problems for Horticulture, agriculture, biodiversity, shelter for dangerous wild animals like leopards. Hence, its proper utilization and eradication is immediately required.

Lantana species are widely spread weeds in warm climates. Lantana camara is poisonous to stocks and humans. In India, it is a weed of national significance and must continuously be suppressed and destroyed.

Lantana camara becomes a threat to environment, agriculture soil and other flora and fauna due to its phenomenal growth rate. There are various technologies that have already been adopted to eradication of lantana but the benefits are temporary and sometimes costly too.

Historical Resume

International Status

As attempts to control the weed have caused high costs and labour requirements, leading to nothing but temporary removal of the Lantana, considerable research effort has been directed towards exploration of various ways of unlocking value in the otherwise troublesome weed. A number of possible uses of the plant, some of which have been developed and others are still in their infancy have been suggested.

In many parts of the world the plant has been used to treat a wide variety of disorders, in the folk medicine especially for tumors and cancer. A tea prepared from the leaves and flowers is taken against fever, influenza and stomach ache. With other preparations of the plant fever, cold, rheumatism, asthma and high blood pressure are treated. In Central and South America the leaves were made into a poultice to treat sores, chicken pox and measles. In Ghana infusions of the whole plant are used against bronchitis. The powdered root in milk was given to children for stomach ache.

In Asian countries leaves are used for cuts, rheumatism, ulcers, and as a vermifuge. Decoctions are applied externally against leprosy and scabies (Ghisberti, 2000). Pass and Steward (1984) highlighted the administration of activated charcoal for the treatment of lantana poisoning of sheep and cattle. Fourie *et al.,* (1987) demonstrated the acute toxicity of Lantana camara in cattle. Ganai and Iha (1991) explained the immunsuppression due to chronic toxicity of Lantana camara in sheep. Pan *et al.,* (1992) and Pan *et al.,* (1993) studied on the chemical constituents of the roots and leaves of Lantana camara. Deena and Thoppil (2000) also highlighted the antimicrobial activity of the essential oil of Lantana camara. Bouda *et al.,* (2001) highlighted the effects of essential oils from leaves of Ageratum conyzoides, Lantana camara and Chromolaena odorata onthe mortality of Sitophilus zea mais (Coleoptera, Curculionidae). Ali-Emmanuel *et al.,* (2003) performed the treatment of bovine dermatophilosis with Senna alata, Lantana camara and Mitracarpus scaber leaf extracts. De Mello *et al.,* (2003) explained the effects of Lantana camara on rat fertility. Abdel-Hady*et al.,* (2005) analysed the chemical composition and insecticidal activity of the volatile oils of leaves and flowers of Lantana camara L. cultivated in Egypt.

National Status

Possible utilization of the Lantana is being performed in antibacterial and toxicological studies in India. In India, the leaves of the plant are boiled for tea and the decoction is a remedy against cough. The decoction of the whole plant is given as treatment against tetanus, rheumatism, malaria and ataxia of abdominal viscera. It is used as a lotion for wounds, too. Pounded leaves are applied to cuts, ulcers and swellings (Verma and Verma, 2006). Sharma (1984) made a review on the biochemical effects of Lantana camara toxicity. Akhter *et al.,* (1990) showed the skin and liver toxicity in experimental Lantana camara poisoning in albino rats. Dua *et al.,* (1996) highlighted the repellency of Lantana camara (Verbenaceae) flowers against Aedes mosquitoes. Garg *et al.,* (1997) explained the antilymphocytic and immunosuppressive effects of Lantana camara leaves in rats. Misra and Laatsch (2000) analysed some triterpenoids, essential oil and photooxidative lactonization of oleanolic acid from Lantana camara. Sagar *et al.,* (2005) evaluated the antimotility effect of Lantana camara L.var aculeate constituents on neostigmine induced gastrointestinal transit in mice.

Objectives

- To find strategies for turning the invasive weed into worthy resources.
- To separate the lignin and find out cellulose from Lantana plants.
- To produce biodegradable packaging film.
- To develop a strategy to convert the problem into useful resources with the help of proper technology and management.

Methodology

The strategy for the present work includes the following specific work elements as described in the following points:

1. Invasive weed Lantana will be collected from its natural habitats.
2. Lantana plants will be chopped and homogenized in order to achieve a well mix material.
3. Performing delignifications, Cellulose will be extracted from Lantana grass
4. Xanthation will be performed for making cellulose Xanthate.
5. Casting and coating of biodegradable film will be executed.

Schematic representation of methodology is given below:

Step 1: Delignification

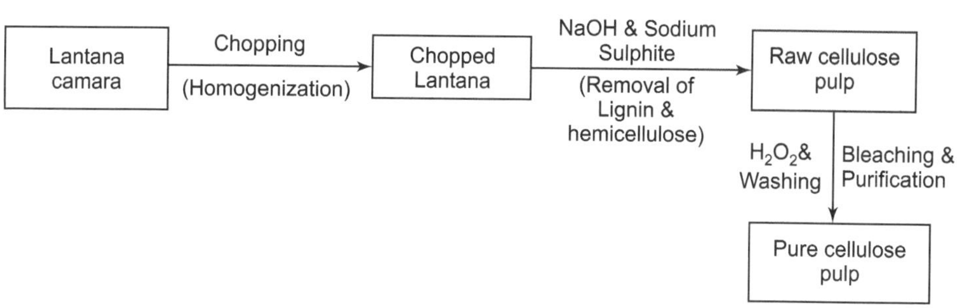

Step 2: Viscose Formation

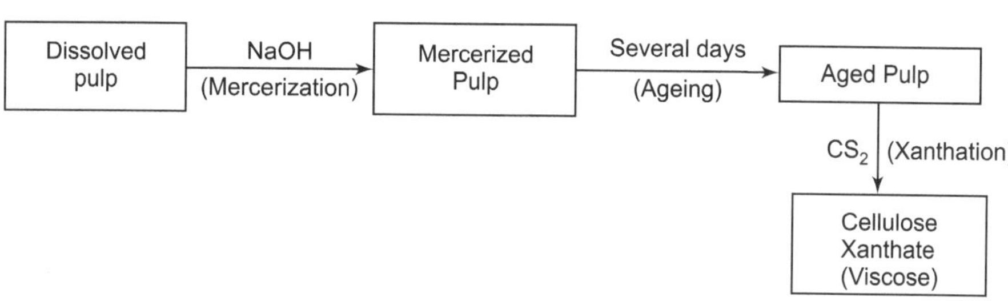

Step 3: Casting of cellulose film

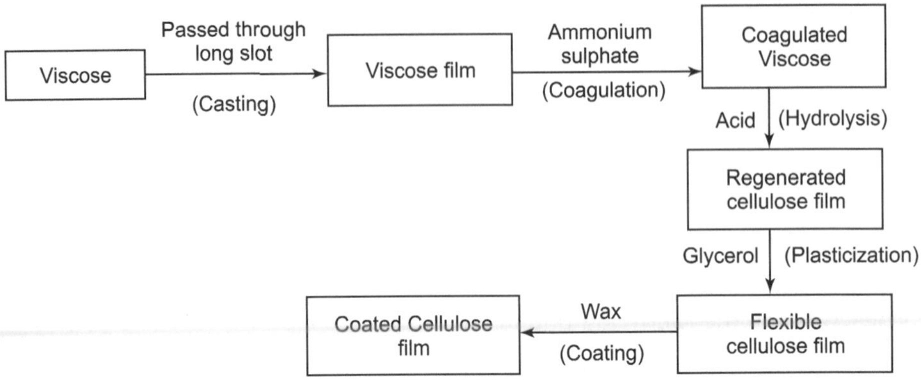

Significance of the Work

All plastic and polythene films like polythene, PPE, PTFE, PVC, etc. are petrochemical oriented and due to the increasing demand of petroleum products, it will not be available in near future. On the other hand, petrochemical based films are not degradable and the all types of existing films pollute the environment in several ways. It is necessary to find out the alternative of petroleum based packaging film. In this context, a biodegradable film derived from natural material will be appreciated. Furthermore, Lantana grass has no use to mankind rather it is detrimental as a useless weed to degrade the terrestrial ecosystem. Hence, it will be the best solution to degenerate the weeds and in lieu to develop some useful product from it like biodegradable packaging film.

Conclusion

Industries working in the field of biodegradable films can utilize the results of the proposed work. Proposed product biodegradable cellulosic film will be eco-friendly and will not create pollution and hence, conserve the environment. As raw material is Lantana grass, so it will help to save the trees. People can use this biodegradable sheet and can throw it anywhere. This biodegradable film will be beneficial for current consumers of recent and advanced market.

Raw material used for the development of biodegradable sheets, will be a useless invasive plant species, which is available in plenty. Therefore the developed material would be cheaper. The developed technology will be scaled-up before commercialization. Initially the development process will be executed at laboratory scale.

REFERENCES

Abdel-Hady, Abdei-Halim AS, Al-Ghadban AM (2005) Chemical Composition and Insecticidal Activity of the Volatile Oils of Leaves and Flowers of L. camara L. Cultivated in Egypt. *J Egypt Soc Parasitol* 35,2: 687-98 PubMed 16083076.

Akhter MH, Mathur M, Bhide NK (1990) Skin and Liver Toxicity in Experimental L. Camara Poisoning in albino Rats. *Indian J Physiol Pharmacol* 34,1: 16-6.

Ali-Emmanuel N, Moudachirou M, Akakpo JA, Quetin-Leclerc J (2003) Treatment of Bovine Dermatophilosis with Senna alata, Lantana camara and Mitracarpus scaber Leaf Extracts, *J Ethnopharmacol* 86,2-3: 167-71.

Bouda H, Tapondjou LA, Fontem DA, Gumedzoe MY (2001) Effects of Essential Oils from Leaves of Ageratum conyzoides, Lantana camara and Chromolaena odorata on the Mortality of Sitophilus zea mais (Coleoptera, Curculionidae). *J Stored Prod. Res.* 37,2: 103-9 PubMed 11124347.

Day MD, Wiley CJ, Playford J, Zalucki MP. (2003) Lantana: Current Management, Status and Future Prospects. Australian Centre for International Agricultural Research, 5: 1- 20.

De Mello FB, Jacubus D, de Carvallo KC, de Mello JR (2003) Effects of L. camara on Rat Fertility. *Vet Hum Toxicol*, 45,1: 20-1 PubMed 12583691.

Deena MJ, Thoppil JE (2000) Antimicrobial Activity of the Essential Oil of L. camara. *Fitoter* 71: 453-5

Dobhal PK, Kohli RK, Batish DR. (2011) Impact of *Lantana camara* L. invasion on Riparian Vegetation of Nayar Region in Garhwal Himalayas (Uttarakhand, India). Journal of Ecology and the Natural Environment, 3 (1), 11-22.

Dua VK, Gupta NC, Pandey AC, Sharma VP (1996) Repellency of L. camara (Verbenaceae) Flowers against Aedes Mosquitoes. *J Am Mosqu Contr Assoc* 12,3: 406-408 PubMed 8887218

Fourie N, van der Lugt JJ, Newsholme SJ, Nel PW (1987) Acute L. camara Toxicity in Cattle. *J S Afr Vet Assoc*, 58,4: 173-8 PubMed 3508461.

Ganai GN, Iha GJ (1991) Immunsuppression Due to Chronic L. camara Toxicity in Sheep. *Indian J Exp Biol*, 29,8: 762-6 PubMed 1769720.

Garg SK, Shah MA, Garg KM *et al.*, (1997) Antilymphocytic and Immunosuppressive Effects of L. Camara Leaves in Rats, *Indian J Exp Biol*, 35,12: 1315-8.

Ghisberti EL (2000) Lantana camara L.(Verbenaceae) Fitoterapia 71: 467-86.

Misra L, Laatsch H (2000) Triterpenoids, Essential Oil and Photooxidative Lactonization of Oleanolic Acid from L. camara, *Phytochem*, 54:969-74.

Pan WD, Li YJ Mai LT *et al.*,(1992) Studies on the Chemical Constituents of the Roots of L. camara Yao Xue Xue Bao 28,1 PubMed 8328269.

Pan WD, Mai LT, Li YJ *et al.*, (1993) Studies on the Chemical Constituents of the Leaves of L. camara Yao Xue Xue Bao 28, 1:3 5-9 PubMed 8328268.

Pass MA, Steward C (1984) Administration of Activated Charcoal for the Treatment of Lantana Poisoning of Sheep and Cattle. *J Appl Toxicol*, 4,5: 267-9.

Sagar L, Sehgal R, Ojha S (2005) Evaluation of Antimotility effect of L.camara L.var aculeate Constituents on Neostigmine Induced Gastrointestinal Transit in mice BMC Complement Altern Med 5: 18 Pub Med 16168064.

Sharma OP (1984) Review of the Biochemical Effects of L. camara Toxicity, *Vet Hum Toxicol*, 26,6: 488-93.

Sharma GP, Raghubanshi AS, Singh JS. (2005) Lantana Invasion: An Overview. *Weed Biology Management*, 5: 157–167.

Verma RK, Verma SK (2006) Phytochemical and Termiticidal Studies of L. camara var Aculeata Leaves, *Fitoterapia* 77, 6: 466-8.

Product Development and Waste Recycling **Pages 43-50**
Edited by: Pawan Kumar 'Bharti'
ISBN: 978-93-86841-94-0
Edition: 2019
Published by: Discovery Publishing House Pvt. Ltd., New Delhi (India)

4 Utilization of E-Waste Black Powder in Making Concrete Blocks for Pavements

[1]Pawan Kumar Bharti

ABSTRACT

In the present context, electronic waste is one of the emerging global issues and must required proper attention at global as well as local level. Moradabad is now biggest hub of e-waste recycling in India and handling almost 50% PCBs waste of the country with involvement of almost 2 Lakh people.

A field visit was undertaken at Moradabad E-waste dumping site; sampling & preliminary characterization of e-waste black powder done at Lab scale. The condition of Moradabad ecosystem is really need urgent attention and hence there is an immediate need of an eco-friendly technology for environmental protection. People are openly dumping ash of PCBs after executing recycling activities. This black powder ash is creating problem to terrestrial and aquatic ecosystem of the vicinity. Thus, there is a need to make an integrated strategy to combat against e-waste pollution as well as site reclamation/restoration in association with suitable local authorities or community.

Key words: E-waste, Informal recycling, Black powder, Environmental Pollution.

Introduction

Electronic waste or e-waste is described the discarded electrical or electronic devices. Electronic waste contains harmful components such as lead, cadmium, beryllium, or brominated flame retardants. Crude & unscientific recycling of e-waste involves risk to health of workers and also leads to emissions of toxic materials such as heavy metals. Informal processing of e-waste in developing countries can lead to emission of pollutants, which can have adverse effects on human health and environment.

Electronic waste or E-Waste includes computers, office electronic equipment, entertainment device electronics, mobile phones, television sets, and refrigerators. This includes used electronics which are destined for reuse, resale, salvage, recycling, or disposal. Others are re-usables and secondary scrap

[1] R & D Division, Shriram Institute for Industrial Research, 19, University Road, Delhi-110007, India

(copper, steel, plastic, etc.) to be 'commodities', and reserve the term 'waste' for residue or material which is dumped by the buyer rather than recycled, including residue from reuse and recycling operations, because loads of surplus electronics are frequently commingled (good, recyclable, and non-recyclable), several public policy advocates apply the term 'e-waste' broadly to all surplus electronics. Cathode Ray Tubes (CRTs) are considered one of the hardest types to recycle.

Current Disposal

The problem of e-waste disposal and safe recycling is escalating rapidly through increased production of electronics in developing countries because of the beneficial economic incentives that it provides. The total amount of e-waste produced has reached approximately 41 million ton and is increasing at a rate of 3-5% every year.

Global Scenario

In the world, about 50 million metric tonnes (Mt) of e-waste is generated annually in 2016. This is close to 4,500 Eiffel Towers each year. The amount of e-waste is expected to increase to 55 million metric tonnes, by 2021. Of those 44.7 Mt, approx. 1.7 Mt are discarded into the residual waste in developed countries, and are also incinerated or land-filled. Around 10 Mt of e-waste are to be collected and recycled, which corresponds to 20% of all the e-waste generated. The USA is ranked first in e-waste generation, generating 11.7 million tonnes of e-waste annually. China is ranked second with 6.1 million tonnes of e-waste every year.

Indian Scenario

India is ranked as the fifth largest generator of electronic waste in the world, with an estimated 1.85 million tonnes generated annually as on 2016. Globally, the number is an astounding 40 to 50 million tonnes annually. India accounts for roughly 4% of e-waste generated annually.

The 70% e-waste is being generated by ten states in India. 50% of PCBs are being dismantle in Moradabad only, where approx. 2 Lakh peoples are involve in e-waste recycling. Informal e-waste recyclers are recovering 70% of precious metals and materials using crude technology (Burning/washing), while dumping remaining 30% in the form of black carbon.

Scenario at Moradabad

The UP district of Moradabad has for last one decade in recycling of e-waste in India in unscientific ways. It generates around 9 tonnes of hazardous waste daily, and around 50,000 people are involved in it. Most of the recycling is illegal. Location map of Moradabad district is given as Fig. 4.1 (A-B). As per the Centre for Science and Environment (CSE) report on Moradabad's e-waste recycling industry in city the situation is alarming. The e-waste workers may face serious health hazards, and the industry poses a serious threat to the environment.

The country does not even have soil contamination norms or standards. There is a need to develop them to measure and lower the level of pollution in cities like Moradabad. There is also a need to monitor e-waste related activities in Moradabad.

It is found that zinc levels were 15 times more than that the prescribed limits. Copper levels, were five times higher in the soil samples collected near river Ramganga. Chromium level was twice the standard, while cadmium was 1.3 times.

According to the study, the results were similar for water samples taken from Ramganga where mercury levels were found to be eight times higher. Traces of arsenic were found too. CSE collected samples from Nawabpura, Karula, Daswaghat and Rehmat Nagar localities, where a vast majority of the population is involved in handling e-waste, and Bhojpur, a neighbouring village which is also a major e-waste handling centre. Open dumping site for e-waste black powder and collected black powder samples are shown in Fig. 4.2 (A-B).

With huge amounts of e-waste being dismantled and recycled in the city, black powder is generated during recycling of e-waste are needed to deal with the problem. The study said that the soil and water of Moradabad contain heavy metals, which are dangerous to the environment and can cause serious ailments, including cancer. High levels of mercury and arsenic can lead to chronic poisoning. Tests to detect such poisoning are usually expensive and nobody gets them done. Mercury enters the food chain through bio-accumulation in fish and other aquatic life forms. It is a known neurotoxin and interferes with the proper functioning of the brain and the nervous system. However, ailments caused by heavy metal pollution go unreported or undetected. High levels of zinc, cobalt and nickel do not have any reported clinical problems, but they may lead to sub-clinical problems which cannot be detected on the basis of symptoms, but persist.

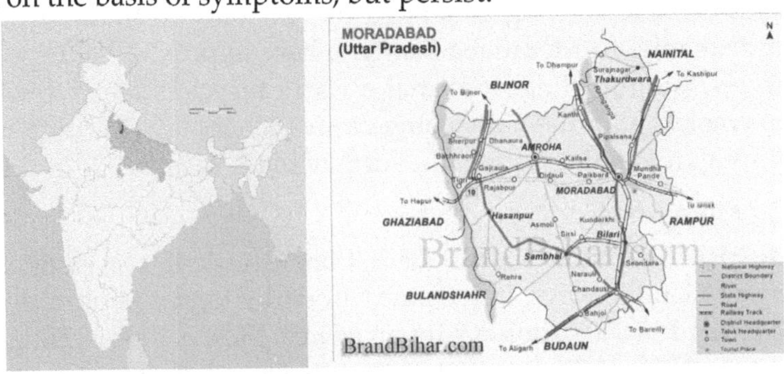

A B

Fig. 4.1 (A-B): Map of Moradabad district (Source: www.brandbharat.com)

A B

Fig. 4.2 (A-B): Dumping site and black powder sample

The health hazard was also highlighted in a report the district pollution control board had shared with the central government last year. In fact, then UP chief secretary had ordered a complete ban on e-waste recycling in Moradabad, Ghaziabad and Hapur last year, but nothing much came of it.

There have been several incidents in the city where residents have had to rush out of their houses choking on toxic fumes. In many cases, such incidents have led to hospitalization of people and police raids on illegal e-waste recycling dens. In 2014, more than 50 cases of illegal e-waste recycling were registered under Mughalpura and Nagfani police stations and more than a hundred offenders were put in jail.

Recycling of E-waste

Only 6% e-waste is recycled in India, out of which 95% is recycled through informal sector. In an environmental friendly manner, all e-waste should be recycled in formal recycling facilities with high technology. The formal e-waste facilities are costly to operate, especially in India, informal recycling are prevalent. The informal e-waste sector extract the valuable materials of the e-waste using crude recycling and disposal methods usually without any safety equipment or the assistance of technology. The workers in these communities depend on the extraction of the valuable metals from e-waste for their livelihood. The valuable materials are removed and the remaining parts of the e-waste are burned, buried or discharged into water for easy disposal. These crude processes used in the informal sectors lead to environmental contamination because the processes emit toxic chemicals from the e-waste into the surrounding.

The most common operation is open burning to remove valuable metals from PCBs and other e-waste. During the process, it releases toxic chemicals such as PAHs into the air and water environment. The improper incineration and the burning of e-waste to recover metals is also carried out and lead to emission of dioxins which are extremely toxic compounds. The open acid leaching are also used to recover metals from the electrical components. The spent acid from treatment process is dumped into the surroundings, which creates environmental hazard. The pollutants can be exposed to the environment from e-waste being physically dismantled, buried or dumped into the environment. E-waste informal processing sites can be located near agricultural fields and other cropland where heavy metals and other pollutants can penetrate into the soil where food is grown.

Environmental Impacts

The processes of dismantling and disposing of electronic waste in developing countries led to a number of environmental impacts as illustrated in the graphic. Liquid and atmospheric releases end up in bodies of water, groundwater, soil, and air and therefore in land and sea animals – both domesticated and wild, in crops eaten by both animals and human, and in drinking water. These may be as follows:

- Airborne dioxins – one type found at 100 times levels previously measured
- Levels of carcinogens in duck ponds and rice paddies exceeded international standards for agricultural areas and cadmium, copper, nickel and lead levels in rice paddies were above international standards
- Heavy metals found in road dust – lead over 300 times that of a control village's road dust and copper over 100 times

The major impacts of the processing of different e-waste components on environment are given in Table 4.1.

Table 4.1: The Environmental Impact of the Processing of Different e-waste Components

S.No.	E-Waste	Process Used	Potential Environmental Hazard
1	Cathode Ray Tubes	Dismantling and dumping	Lead, barium and other heavy metals leaching into the water and release of toxicants
2	Printed Circuit Board (PCBs)	De-soldering; open burning and acid baths.	Air emissions and emissions of glass dust, tin, lead, dioxin, beryllium cadmium and mercury
3	Chips and other gold plated components	Chemical treatment and burning of chips	PAHs, heavy metals, brominated flame retardants into water. Tin and lead contamination of water. Air emissions of dioxins, heavy metals and PAHs
4	Printers, keyboards, monitors, etc.	Shredding	Emissions of dioxins, heavy metals and hydrocarbons
5	Wires & Cables	Open burning to remove copper	PAHs released into air, water and soil.

Issues and Challenges

One of the major challenges is itself recycling of the electronic wastes. The e-waste contains precious metals as gold, silver, platinum, etc. and also metals such as copper, iron, aluminum, etc. Presently, e-waste is processed by burning and acid leaching to recover copper and metals. The conventional method employed is shredding and separation but the recycling efficiency is low. Alternative methods such as cryogenic decomposition have been studied for printed circuit board recycling, and some other methods are still under investigation. Properly disposing of or reusing electronics can help prevent health problems, reduce greenhouse-gas emissions, and create jobs. Reuse and refurbishing offer a more environmentally friendly and socially conscious alternative to downcycling processes. Hazardous and Non-hazardous substances present in e-waste are given in Table 4.2.

Table 2: Hazardous and Non-hazardous Substances in e-waste

S.No.	Category	Elements/compound
1.	Hazardous substances	Americium, Lead, Mercury, Cadmium, Hexavalent chromium, Sulphur, Brominated Flame Retardants (BFRs), Perfluorooctanoic acid (PFOA), Beryllium oxide
2.	Non-hazardous substances	Aluminium, Copper, Germanium, Gold, Lithium, Nickel, Silicon, Tin, Zinc,

Solutions

The existing policies that developing countries have created so far have not been effective in reducing the amount of informal recycling because there is an overall lack of governance and enforcement resources in these areas. Formal facilities have not been able to compete with the informal recycling. An incentive system will most likely be needed to have the informal recyclers be more willing to bring their collected e-waste to the formal facilities where it will be recycled without resulting in negative impacts to the environment and human health. Additionally, investment in the resources necessary to provide enforcement and supervision for the existing and potential new policies that will be put in place should be implemented. For example, the restriction of e-waste importation needs to be controlled better in order to decrease the amount of e-waste being transported to these informal recycling areas. Considering future mitigation methods, one primary option is for manufacturers and producers to become more involved in implementing take-back systems to recycle their electronic items properly.

For the existing problems in the informal sector of India, a few issues must be resolved in an integrated manner. Proper training should be provided to e-waste dealers, dismantlers, recyclers and appropriate awareness programmes must be organized for them. It will help out to make the recycling method better and technology oriented.

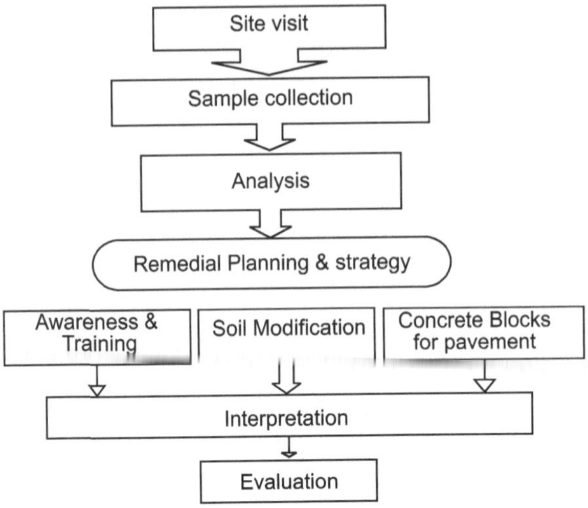

Fig. 4.3: Flow Chart of Integrated Strategy to Combat e-waste Pollution

Utilization of e-waste slag/ black powder must be carried out in some useful applications for the betterment of society. The applications may be material development, concrete blocks for pavements, etc. to make sure the leaching of hazardous metals out of it. The task can be jointly carried out by Nagar Palika, SDM, UPSPCB, local community and other research body. A flow chart of integrated strategy to combat e-waste pollution is given in Fig. 4.3.

One another big issue is the reclamation of infected site due to the e-waste ash contamination. Soil modification is the prime concern in this regard. Top soil modification is required for soil affected by black carbon slag of burnt e-waste. Either top soil removal or replacement by new healthy soil or soil amendment using sand, lime & compost/green manure is the possible solutions. Biotechnological approaches (using Bacteria/Super Bug, Macrophytes, Grass or woody plants) may be a good option for soil reclamation of contaminated sites. The approach must be designed in such a way, so that the solution of the problem is resolved to a great extent.

Conclusions

E-waste is generated at a rapid rate in almost all developing countries including India. This e-waste disposal & recycling issue needs to be addressed scientifically to reduce the harmful effects of the toxic chemicals in e-waste that have an environmental and human health impact. The e-waste recycling should be carried out in a sustainable manner. It is advised to adopt the above given integrated strategy to combat e-waste pollution as well as site reclamation/ restoration in association with suitable local authorities or community.

REFERENCES

An, D, Yang, Y, Chai, X, Xi, B, Dong, L, 2015. Mitigating Pollution of Hazardous Materials from WEEE of China: Portfolio Selection for a Sustainable Future Based on Multi-criteria Decision Making. Res. Conser. and Recyc. 105: 198-210.

Bharti, P.K., R.K. Singh and A.K. Tyagi 2018. E-waste Generation and Recycling: Problems and Solutions. Science Reporter *(Communicated)*.

Bharti, P.K., R.K. Singh, Raju Joshi, Shambhu Thakur and A.K. Tyagi 2018. Metal Constituents of E-Waste Black Powder and their Potential Utilization. *Current Science (Accepted)*. Sthiannopkao, S., Wong, M.H., 2013. Handling e-waste in Developed and Developing Countries: Initiatives, Practices and Consequences. Sci. of the Tot. Environ. 463: 1147-1153.

Baldé, C.P., Forti V., Gray, V., Kuehr, R., Stegmann, P. 2017. The Global E-waste Monitor – 2017, United Nations University (UNU), International Telecommunication Union (ITU) & International Solid Waste Association (ISWA), Bonn/Geneva/Vienna. pp. 116.

CSE, 2015. Recommendations to Address the Issues of Informal Sector Involved in E-Waste Handling: Moradabad, Uttar Pradesh, Centre for Science and Environment, pp. 1-16.

Garlapati, V.K., 2016. E-waste in India and Developed Countries: Management, Recycling, Business and Biotechnological Initiatives. Renew. and Sustain. Ener. Rev. 54: 874-881.

Kumar, A, Holuszko, M, Espinosa, D.C.R., 2017. E-waste: An Overview on Generation, Collection, Legislation and Recycling Practices. Res. Conser. and Recyc. 122: 32-42.

Perkins, B.D., Nxele, S., 2014. E-waste: A Global Hazard, Annals of Global Health. Articl. and Rev. 80: 286-295.

Park, J.K., Hoerning, L., Watry, S., Burgett, T., Matthias, S., 2017. Effects of Electronic Waste on Developing Countries. Adv. Recycling Waste Manag. 2: 128. doi:10.4172/2475-7675.1000128.Song, Q., Li, J., 2014. A Systematic Review of the Human Body Burden of e-waste Exposure in China. Environ. Int. 68: 82-93.

Terazono, A., Oguchi, M., Yoshida, A., Medina, R.P., Ballesteros, F.C., 2016. Metal Recovery and Environmental Impact by Informal e-waste Recycling Sites in Philippines. Sustain. Throu. Innov. Prod. Lif. Cyc. Des., pp. 197-213.

Wikipedia, 2018. https://en.wikipedia.org/wiki/Electronic_waste as Accessed on 08-02-2018.

Zhang, W.H., Wu, Y.X., Simonnot, M.O., 2012. Soil Contamination Due to e-waste Disposal and Recycling Activities: A Review with Special Focus on China. Pedos. 22: 434-455.

Zhao, G., Wang, Z., Zhou, H., Zhao, Q., 2009. Burdens of PBBs, PBDEs, and PCBs in Tissues of the Cancer Patients in the e-waste Disassembly Sites in Zhejiang, China. Sci. of Tot Environ. 407: 4831-4837.

Product Development and Waste Recycling **Pages 51-57**
Edited by: Pawan Kumar 'Bharti'
ISBN: 978-93-86841-94-0
Edition: 2019
Published by: Discovery Publishing House Pvt. Ltd., New Delhi (India)

5

Integrated Approach of Utilizing Water Hyacinth to Develop Valuable Products

Microcrystalline Cellulose, Biogas and Vermicompost

[1]Pawan Kumar Bharti

Introduction

Water hyacinth is a monocotyledon aquatic macrophyte of family Pontederiaceae. Its scientific name is *Eichhornia crassipes* (Martias) solms. Water hyacinth was originated in Amazon basin and distributed throughout the tropics due to its attractive purple flower. Mature plants consist of roots, rhizomes, stolon, leaves and inflorescence. Its leaves are thick, waxy and glossy with bulbous and spongy stalk. The inflorescence is spike of 8-10 flowers. The flowers are purplish blue. Each flower has 6 petals, the upper most petals with a yellow blue bordered central splotch. Its shoots consist of branched, stoloniferous rhizome. Roots are adventitious, fibrous and dark in colour. Water hyacinth reproduces both sexually and vegetatively. However, sexual reproduction is limited. Vegetative reproduction occurs by stolon under favorable condition.

Water hyacinth is a well known cleaner of polluted water & different pollutants (like heavy metals) are deposited in its root. So roots are generally removed in case where water hyacinth is collected from polluted water. Major composition of water hyacinth plant is as follow:

Cellulose – 20%
Hemicellulose – 33%
Lignin – 10 %
Ash – 20%
N – 03 %

Water hyacinth has become the most problematic weed in many tropical and subtropical fresh water habitats worldwide. Water hyacinth forms thick mat over the water body and caused problems for fishing, biodiversity, river or canal transportation, irrigation, causing siltation followed by flooding and become the labour room for many vector borne diseases. Hence, its proper disposal and utilization is immediately required so that we can significantly

1 Scientist Shriram Institute for Industrial Research 19, University Road, Delhi, 110007

contribute towards the 'Swachh Bharat Mission' of our Prime Minister Shri Narendra Modi.

Water hyacinth is an aquatic weed growing in fresh water lakes, rivers, ponds etc. It was originated from South America and distributed throughout the tropics. But it appears as a potential problem in our state as well as other areas by creating blockages in ponds, canals, Rivers etc and become a threat to other aquatic flora and fauna due to its phenomenal growth rate. There are various technologies that have already been adopted to reduce the hazards of water hyacinth but the benefits are temporary and sometimes costly too.

Review of Current Monitoring Situation/Work Done so Far

International Status

As attempts to control the weed have caused high costs and labour requirements, leading to nothing but temporary removal of the water hyacinths, considerable research effort has been directed towards exploration of various ways of unlocking value in the otherwise troublesome weed.

A number of possible uses of the plant, some of which have been developed and others are still in their infancy have been suggested. These include possible utilization of the weed as a phytoremediation agent (Sajn *et al.*, 2005), for power, alcohol and biogas production (Mshandete *et al.*, 2004; Ali *et al.*, 2004), as a compost (Szczeck, 1999), and for animal fodder/ fish feed (Aboud *et al.*, 2005).

Water hyacinth, among other aquatic macrophytes, has been shown to possess a great potential to remove pollutants when being used as a biological filtration system. It contains many polyfunctional metal-binding sites for both cationic and anionic metal complexes The weed could remove several heavy metals and other pollutants (Pinto *et al.*, 1987; Delgado *et al.*, 1993; Zaranyika *et al.*, 1994; Mahamadi and Nharingo, 2007, 2010a, 2010b).

Recorded achievements triggered efforts directed towards the utilization of water hyacinth in phytoremediation.

Schneider et al. (1995) studied the feasibility of dried water hyacinth roots for the removal of Pb^{2+}, Cu^{2+}, Cd^{2+} and Zn^{2+} ions from aqueous solution.

Beside these, Klass and Ghosh (1981) demonstrated the methane production by anaerobic digestion of water hyacinth *(Echhornia crassipes)*. Kikuchi *et al.* (1997) used water hyacinth (*Eichhornia crassipes*) as an indicator to show the absence of *Anopheles suncaicus* larvae in aquatic ecosystem.

Gunnarsson and Petersen (2007) highlighted the water hyacinths as a resource in agriculture and energy production. Sornvoraweat and Kongkiattikajorn (2010) explained separated hydrolysis and fermentation of water hyacinth leaves for ethanol production.

National Status

In India, possible utilization of the water hyacinth have been suggested as a biosorbent for toxic metals (Malik, 2007), Other potential uses of the weed include its use as pulp material for producing greaseproof paper (Goswami and Saikia, 1994) and the production of fiberboards for a variety of end uses such as bituminized board for low-cost roofing material, indoor partitioning, etc. Formulations of water hyacinth-based medicines to treat certain diseases have been reported in India (Oudhia, 1999a, b).

Some other uses of water hyacinth were also reported in India and some of them are given here. Sharma (1971) explained the eradication and utilization of water hyacinth in various applications. Reddy and Sutton (1984) used water hyacinths for water quality improvement and biomass production. Patel *et al.,* (1993) highlighted the thermo-chemical pretreatment of water hyacinth for improved bio-methanation.

Chanakya *et al.,* (1993) explained the solid phase biogas production with garbage or water hyacinth. Goswami and Saikia (1994) suggested the water hyacinth as a potential source of raw material for greaseproof paper at labscale. Sahu *et al.,* (2002) find out the efficacy of water hyacinth compost in nursery pond for larval rearing of Indian major carp, *Labeo robitta.* Sannigrahi *et al.,* (2002) emphasized on large scale utilization of water hyacinth (*Eichhornia crassipes)* as raw material for vermin-composting and surface mulching in vegetable cultivation. Singhal and Rai (2003) carried out biogas production from water hyacinth and channel grass used for phytoremediation of industrial effluents. Kadirvelu *et al.,* (2004) pointed out the separation of mercury (II) from aqueous solution by adsorption onto an activated carbon prepared from *Eichhornia crassipes.* Hasan *et al.,* (2010) optimized the water hyacinth biomass (WHB) for the biosorption of hexavalent chromium. Hussain *et al.,* (2010) explained the phytoremediation technologies for Ni^{++} removal by water hyacinth. Lata and Veenapani (2011) highlighted the response of water hyacinth manure on Growth attributes and yields in *Brassica juncea.*

Gaps in Existing Situation and Need for Study

The institutions have vast experiences to develop wealth from the waste materials. Municipal solid waste was converted in to compost and biogas to utilize its calorific value in domestic consumption. Wastewater was also utilized in various applications after an appropriate treatment. Besides, plastic waste was converted into plastic board composites, filler material in road construction.

Water hyacinth is dangerous invasive weed species and is not being utilized in any form in the country. It is a matter of great importance to utilize this aquatic weed in some useful applications. The outcomes of proposed projects will give benefits to human society as well as will conserve the environment.

Objective

1. To extract cellulose from water hyacinth and prepare microcrystalline cellulose (MCC).
2. To produce biogas from the waste generated in delignification process of above extraction.
3. To convert the biomass from the biogas plant into vermin-compost as opposed to synthetic fertilizer.

Scope of Work

One of the major anticipated products of the proposed project is microcrystalline cellulose (MCC), which will be used in eco-friendly applications. Biogas will be used as pollution free kitchen fuel alternative. Third product of the proposed work is vermin-compost, which may be a good manure alternative in green farming.

The aim of this work is to determine the feasibility of water hyacinth in multiple applications. This floating perennial plant has been used in aquatic systems for waste water purification for many years worldwide. A lot of interests have been shown for this plant in last few years in India and aboard. Water hyacinth is very efficient in removing vast range of pollutants, from suspended materials, BOD, nutrients, organic matter to heavy metals and pathogens. At the same time *Eichhornia crassipes* (known as water hyacinth) is one of the most notorious weeds worldwide. When introduced to aquatic ecosystem it spreads very quickly due to its high reproduction potential. Therefore water hyacinth tends to eliminate all other living organisms in surroundings. An integrated approach has been proposed in the study to undertake the development of some valuable products like microcrystalline cellulose and production of biogas & vermin-compost using water hyacinth as the raw material.

Methodology

The strategy of the work includes the specific work elements as described in the following points:

1. Water hyacinth plants will be chopped and homogenized in order to achieve a well mix material.
2. Delignification of water hyacinth.
3. Extraction of Cellulose.
4. Treatment of cellulose to make it microcrystalline.
5. Testing and characterization of developed MCC.
6. Spent liquid from delignification will be used in biogas production in biogas plant.
7. The chopped hyacinth plants will be placed in acid phase fermentor to extract volatile fatty acids (VFA). This VFA extract will be used in the biogas plant.

8. Remaining spent from the fermentor will be used in making vermin-compost.
9. A portion of chopped hyacinth mixed with cow dung slurry will be utilized to make compost using vermin-technology.

Schematic Representation of Methodology is Given Below

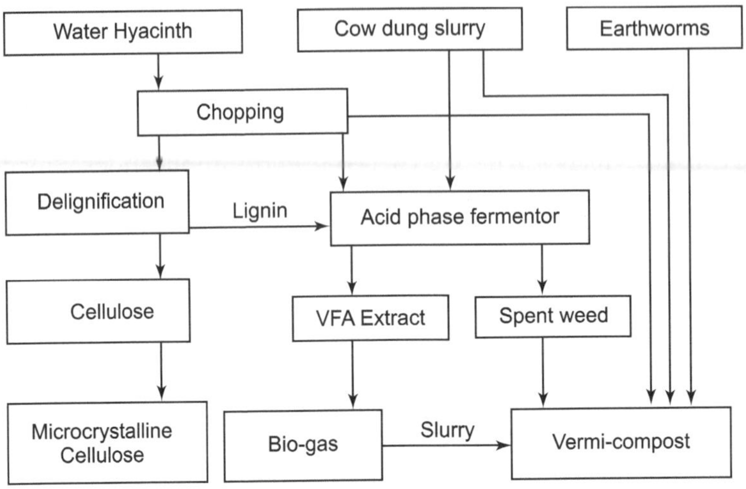

Outcome/deliverables of the Work

The work from the proposed studies would lead to development of degradable cellulose film for the packaging application. Besides this, biogas from spent materials and vermin-compost from water hyacinth residue parts are also the important outcome of the proposed study.

All plastic and polythene films like polythene, PPE, PTFE, PVC, etc. are petrochemical oriented and due to the increasing demand of petroleum products, it will not be available in near future. On the other hand, petrochemical based films are not degradable and the all types of existing films pollute the environment in several ways. It is necessary to find out the alternative of petroleum based packaging film. In this context, a biodegradable film derived from natural material will be appreciated. Furthermore, water hyacinth has no use to mankind rather it is detrimental as a useless weed to degrade the aquatic ecosystem. Hence, it will be the best solution to degenerate the weeds and in lieu to develop some useful product from it like MCC, biogas and vermi-compost.

REFERENCES

Aboud AAO, Kidunda RS, Osarya J (2005). Potential of Water Hyacinth (Eicchornia crassipes) in Ruminant Nutrition in Tanzania. Livest. Res. Rural Dev. 5: 17.

Ali N, Chaudhary BL, Khandelwal SK (2004). Better Use of Water Hyacinth for Fuel, Manure and Pollution Free Environment. Indian J. Environ. Prot., 24: 297–303.

Chanakya, H.N., Borgaonkar, S., Meena, G. and Jagadish, K.S. (1993). Solidphase Biogas Production with Garbage or Water Hyacinth. *Bioresour. Technol.* 46: 227–231.

Delgado M, Bigeriego M, Guardiola E (1993). Uptake of Zn, Cr and Cd by Water Hyacinths. Water Res., 27: 269–272.

Goswami T, Saikia CN (1994). Water Hyacinth—a Potential Source of Raw Material for Greaseproof Paper. Bioresour. Technol., 50: 235– 238.

Gunnarsson, C.C., Petersen, C.M. (2007). Water Hyacinths as a Resource in Agriculture and Energy Production: A Literature Review. *Waste Manage.* 27: 117–129.

Hasan SH, Ranjan D. and Talat M (2010). Water Hyacinth Biomass (WHB) for the Biosorption of Hexavalent Chromium: Optimization of Process Parameters. *Biol. Res.,* 5(2): 563-575.

Hussain ST, Mahmood T. and Malik SA (2010). Phytoremediation Technologies for Ni++ by Water Hyacinth. *Afr. J. Biotechnol.,* 9(50): 8648-8660.

Kadirvelu K, Kanmani P, Senthilkumar P. and Subburam V (2004). Separation of Mercury (II) from Aqueous Solution by Adsorption onto an Activated Carbon Prepared from *Eichhornia crassipes. Adsorp. Sci. Technol.,* 22, 207–222.

Kikuchi, T., Takagi, M., Tokuhisa, E., Suzuki, T., Panjaitan, W., Yasuno, M. (1997). Water hyacinth (*Eichhornia crassipes*) as an Indicator to Show the Absence of *Anopheles suncaicus* larvae. *Med. Entomol. Zool.* 48(1): 11–18.

Klass, D.L. and Ghosh, S. (1981). Methane Production by Anaerobic Digestion of Water Hyacinth (*Echhornia crassipes*). In: Klass, D.L., Emert, G.H. (Eds.), Fuel from Biomass and Wastes. *Ann. Arbor Science Publication Inc,* MI, USA, pp. 129–148.

Lata, N. and Veenapani, D. (2011). Response of Water Hyacinth Manure on Growth Attributes and Yields in *Brassica Juncea.* Journal of Central European Agriculture, 12(2), p.336-343 DOI: 10.5513/JCEA01/12.2.921.

Mahamadi C, Nharingo T (2007). Modelling the Kinetics and Equilibrium Properties of Cadmium Biosorption by River Green Alga and Water Hyacinth Weed. Toxicol. Environ. Chem., 89(2): 297-305.

Mahamadi C, Nharingo T (2010a). Utilization of Water Hyacinth Weed (Eichhornia crassipes) for the Removal of Pb(II), Cd(II) and Zn(II) from Aquatic Environments: An Adsorption Isotherm Study. Environ. Technol., 31(11): 1221-1228.

Mahamadi C, Nharingo T (2010b). Competitive Adsorption of Pb(II), Cd(II) and Zn (II) Ions onto *Eichhornia Crassipes* in Binary and Ternary systems. Bioresour. Technol., 101(3): 859-864.

Malik A (2007). Environmental Challenge *vis a vis* Opportunity: The Case of Water Hyacinth. Environ. Int., 33: 122-138.

Mshandete A, Kivaisi A, Rubindamayugi M, Mattiasson BO (2004). Anaerobic Batch Codigestion of Sisal Pulp and Fish Wastes. Bioresour. Technol., 95: 19–24.

Oudhia P (1999a). Medicinal Weeds in Rice Fields of Chhattisgarh (India). Int. Rice Res. Notes 24: 40.

Oudhia P (1999b). Studies on Allelopathy and Medicinal Weeds in Chickpea Fields. Int Chickpea Pigeonpea Newsl. 6: 29–33.

Patel, V., Desai, M. and Madamwar, D. (1993). Thermochemical Pretreatment of Water Hyacinth for Improved Biomethanation. *Appl. Biochem. Biotechnol.* 42: 67–74.

Pinto CLR, Caconia A, Souza MM (1987). Utilization of Water Hyacinth for Removal and Recovery of Silver from Industrial Wastewater. Water Sci. Technol., 19: 89–101.

Reddy, K.R. and Sutton, D.L. (1984). Water Hyacinths for Water Quality Improvement and Biomass Production. *J. Environ. Quality* 13, 1-8.

Sahu, A.K., Sahoo, S. K., and Giri, S. S. (2002). Efficacy of Water Hyacinth Compost in Nursery Pond for Larval Rearing of Indian Major Carp, *Labeo robitta. Bioresource Technology* 85: 309 – 311.

Sajn SA, Bulc TG, Vrhovsek D (2005). Comparison of Nutrient Cycling in a Surfaceflow Constructed Wetland and in a Facultative Pond Treating Secondary Effluent. Water Sci. Technol., 51: 291–298.

Sannigrahi, A. K., Chakrabortty, B. and Borah, B. C. (2002). Large Scale Utilization of Water Hyacinth (*Eichhornia crassipes)* as Raw Material for Vermi Composting and Surface Mulching in Vegetable Cultivation. *Ecology Environment Conservation* 8: 269 – 271.

Schneider IAH, Rubio J, Misra M, Smith RW (1995). Eichhornia Crassipes as Biosorbent for Heavy Metal Ions. Min. Eng., 8: 979–988.

Sharma, A. (1971). Eradication and Utilization of Water Hyacinth: A Review. *Curr. Sci.* 40: 51–55.

Singhal, V. and Rai, J.P.N. (2003). Biogas Production from Water Hyacinth and Channel Grass Used for Phytoremediation of Industrial Effluents. *Bioresource Technology* 86, 221-225.

Sornvoraweat, B. and Kongkiattikajorn, J. (2010). Separated Hydrolysis and Fermentation of Water Hyacinth Leaves for Ethanol Production, *KKU Res. J.* 15 (9): 794-802.

Szczeck MM (1999). Suppressiveness of Vermicompost against Fusarium wilt of Tomato. J. Phytopathol. Phytopathologische Zeitschrift 47: 155–161.

Zaranyika MF, Mutoko F, Murahwa H (1994). Uptake of Zn, Co, Fe and Cr by Water Hyacinth *(Eichhornia crassipes)* in Lake Chivero, Zimbabwe. Sci. Total Environ., 153: 117–121.

Product Development and Waste Recycling **Pages 58-66**
Edited by: Pawan Kumar 'Bharti'
ISBN: 978-93-86841-94-0
Edition: 2019
Published by: Discovery Publishing House Pvt. Ltd., New Delhi (India)

6 Development of Herbal Mosquito Repellent from Weed Plant Motha (*Cyperus rotundus*)

[1]Pawan Kumar 'Bharti'

ABSTRACT

The aim of this work is to determine the feasibility of weed plant Motha (*Cyperus rotendus*) in the development of herbal mosquito repellent. This common weed has not been used in any beneficial activity for many years in India. A few of interests should be initiated for this plant in India and aboard.

At the same time Motha is one of the most common and notorious weeds in India. When introduced to agriculture fields or any terrestrial ecosystem it spreads quickly due to its high growth potential and networking system of nodules. Therefore Motha tends to inhibit the growth of all other crop plants in surrounding. A development approach will be given about potential usage of Motha weed for herbal mosquito repellent development.

Keywords: Motha plant, agriculture weed, mosquito repellent, *Cyperus rotundus*.

Introduction

Today, the environmental safety of an insecticide is considered to be of paramount importance. An insecticide does not have to cause high mortalities on non-targeted organisms in order to be acceptable. Anti-feeding and growth inhibiting molecules reduce damages produced even without killing the pest.

Some plants known to contain toxic molecules can play a useful role in the control of vectors. Several wild plants extracts or isolated active compounds have been shown to act as potent acute or chronic insecticides, anti-feeding and insect growth regulators against a variety of insect species including mosquitoes.

Although insect-borne diseases currently represent a greater health problem in tropical and subtropical climates, no part of the world is immune to their risks. Mosquitoes have become the most important single group of insects well-known for their public health importance, since they act as the vector for many tropical and subtropical diseases such as dengue fever, yellow

[1] R & D Division, Shriram Institute for Industrial Research, 19, University Road, Delhi, India

fever, malaria, filariasis and encephalitis of different types including, Japanese encephalitis.

Anopheles stephensi, Aedes aegypti and *Culex quinquefasciatus* are the major urban vectors of malaria, dengue and lymphatic filariasis, respectively. Thus, one of the approaches for control of these mosquito-borne diseases is the interruption of disease transmission by killing or preventing mosquitoes from biting human beings. Herbal products with proven potential as repellents can play an important role in the interruption of the transmission of mosquito-borne diseases at the individual as well as at the community level. However, the discovery, development and use of synthetic organic chemicals with persistent residual action not only overshadowed the use of herbal products against mosquitoes but also became the major weapon for mosquito control by repeated use of these synthetic insecticides for mosquito populations. It has also resulted in the development of resistance of mosquito to synthetic insecticides, undesirable effects on non-target organisms and fostered environmental and human health concern.

This has necessitated the need for search and development of environmentally safe, biodegradable, low cost, indigenous methods for vector control, which can be used with minimum care by individuals and communities in specific situations. Phytochemicals obtained from plants with proven mosquito control potential can be used as an alternative to synthetic insecticides or along with other insecticides under the integrated vector control. Plant products can be used either as insecticides for killing larvae or adult mosquitoes or as repellents for protection against mosquito bites, depending on the type of activity they possess.

Plant products can be obtained either from the whole plant or from a specific part (leaves, stembark, roots and fruits) by extraction with different types of solvents such as ethanol, methanol, hexane, petroleum ether, chloroform, among other products, depending on the polarity of the phytochemicals.

Cyperus rotundus is indigenous to India, but now it is found in tropical, subtropical and temperate regions from Asia, South Africa, South America, etc. Different phytochemical studies on *Cyperus rotundus* revealed the presence of alkaloids, flavonoids, tannins, starch, glycosides, furochromones, monoterpenes, sesquiterpenes, sitosterol, a fatty oil containing a neutral waxy substance, glycerol, linolenic, myristic and stearic acids.

The major compounds isolated from essential oil are: α-cyperone, cyperene, cyperotundone, cyperol, β-selinene, β-caryophyllene, valerenal, sugeonyl acetate, α-copaene, patchoulene, trans-pinocarveol, patchoulenenone, aristrol-9-en-3-one, selina-4, 11 diene, aristrol-9-en-8-one, kobusone, sugetriol, isokobusone, isocyperol, sugeonol and sitosterol (Oladipupo and Oyedeji, 2009; Sonwa and Konig, 2001)).

α-Pinene, 1, 8-cineole, α-Cyperone, cyperene are some well known compounds having excellent repellency against mosquitoes. α-Cyperone and cyperene are the major components of essential oil of Motha plant (*Cyperus rotundus*). Literature suggests that *Cyperus rotundus* have an enough efficiency to repel few insects like mosquitoes, cockroaches, etc. (Oladipupo and Oyedeji, 2009).

α-Pinene has been shown to possess repellent activity against many insects, such as mosquitoes, cockroaches, stored product insects and common tick. 1, 8-Cineole has showed strong repellent activity against several insects, e.g. stored product insects. 1, 8-Cineole was effective against mosquitoes *Culex pipiens molestus* bites offering complete protection for 2 h. No attract activity of 1, 8-cineole to insects was found so far. The literature suggested that α-pinene and 1, 8-cineole may have potential to develop as new natural repellents in the control of mosquitoes (Dhillon *et al.*, 1993).

Literature showed the tuber extracts of *Cyperus rotundus* to be more effective for repellency of all the mosquito vectors even at low dose. The extract can be applied as an effective personal protective measure against mosquito bites.

The isolation and identification of the bioactive compounds in the essential oil of *Cyperus rotundus* is of utmost importance so that its potential application in controlling mosquitoes can be fully exploited.

Owing to the adverse effects of synthetic insecticides, there has been increasing need to search for natural and environment friendly insecticides of plant origin as agents of control of vector. This study will be aimed to investigate the repellent activity of Motha grass against mosquitoes. Despite the large number of plant extracts tested against mosquitoes by many authors, the present study dealt with extract from a weed plant species namely, *Cyperus rotundus* tested against mosquitoes.

Rationale of the Study Supported by Cited Literature

Although insect-borne diseases currently represent a greater health problem in tropical and subtropical climates, no part of the world is immune to their risks. Mosquitoes have become the most important single group of insects well known for their public health importance, since they act as the vector for many tropical and subtropical diseases such as dengue fever, yellow fever, malaria, filariasis and encephalitis of different types including, Japanese encephalitis (Hubalek and Haluzka, 1999).

Anopheles stephensi, Aedes aegypti and *Culex quinquefasciatus* are the major urban vectors of malaria, dengue and lymphatic filariasis, respectively. Thus, one of the approaches for control of these mosquito-borne diseases is the interruption of disease transmission by killing or preventing mosquitoes from biting human beings.

Herbal products with proven potential as repellents can play an important role in the interruption of the transmission of mosquito-borne diseases at the individual as well as at the community level. However, the discovery, development and use of synthetic organic chemicals with persistent residual action not only overshadowed the use of herbal products against mosquitoes but also became the major weapon for mosquito control by repeated use of these synthetic insecticides for mosquito populations. It has also resulted in the development of resistance of mosquito to synthetic insecticides, undesirable effects on non-target organisms and fostered environmental and human health concern (Fanello *et al.,* 1999).

Many synthetic insecticides are being used for mosquitoes and various insects continuously since last few decades. These insecticides are a group of pesticide and can have many side effects due to their accumulation in food chain or in environmental components.

Phytochemicals obtained from plants with proven mosquito control potential can be used as an alternative to synthetic insecticides or along with other insecticides under the integrated vector control. Owing to the adverse effects of synthetic insecticides, there has been increasing need to search for natural and environment friendly insecticides of plant origin as agents of control of vector i.e. mosquitoes (Egunyomi *et al.,* 2010). This study aimed to develop an herbal mosquito repellent and to investigate the repellent activity of Motha weed plant.

Current Status of Research and Development in the Subject

Various researchers from India and abroad have worked or are engaged in experimental work on different body parts of Motha weed (*Cyperus rotundus* Linn.). Various effects of essential oils extracted from the tubers of *C. rotundus* were studied.

Ovicidal and larvicidal activity, Insect repellency activity, Insecticidal activity,Antimicrobial activity, Antimutagenic and radical scavenging activity, Antimalarial activity, Antispasmodic activity, Anticonvulsant and antioxidant activity, Antibacterial activity, Antiplatelet activity, Lipid lowering activity, Wound healing activity was studied by many national and International researchers.

National Status

Kapadia *et al.,* (1967) emphasized on Sesquiterpenoids from Essential oil of *Cyperus rotundus*. Kalsi *et al.,* (1969) and Singh *et al.,* (1970) made a pharmacological study and some chemical studies on the essential oil from *Cyperus rotundus.* Gupta *et al.,* (1971) conducted pharmacological studies to isolate the active constituents from *Cyperus rotundus* possessing anti-inflammatory, anti-pyretic and analgesic activities.

Sharma *et al.*, (1993) explained preliminary mosquito repellent action of neem (*Azadirachta indica*) oil. Ansari and Razdan (1995) highlighted relative efficacy of various oils in repelling mosquitoes. Dua *et al.*, (1996) showed repellency of Lantana camara flowers against Aedes mosquitoes.

Sharma (2001) suggested some health hazards of mosquito repellents and safe alternatives to use against mosquitoes. Das *et al.*, (2003) made an evaluation of botanicals as repellents against mosquitoes. Ansari *et al.*, (2005) showed some larvicidal and mosquito repellent activities of Pine (Pinus longifolia, Family: Pinaceae) oil. Singh *et al.*, (2009) performed an evaluation of Hexane Extract of Tuber of Root of *Cyperus rotundus* Linn (Cyperaceae) for Repellency against Mosquito Vectors.

Dua *et al.*, (2010) explained some adulticidal activity of essential oil of Lantana camara leaves against mosquitoes. Mandal (2011) showed repellent activity of Eucalyptus and Azadirachta indica seed oil against the filarial mosquito Culex quinquefasciatus Say (Diptera: Culicidae) in India. Pal *et al.*, (2011) analysed the chemical composition and mosquito repellent activity of the Essential Oil of *Plectranthus incanus* Link. Bisht *et al.*, (2011) evaluated the chemical composition and antimicrobial activity of essential oil of tubers of *Cyperus rotundus* Linn. collected from Dehradun (Uttarakhand). Patel *et al.*, (2012) made a review on various mosquito repellent methods. Singh *et al.*, (2012a) discussed the toxicity of a plant based mosquito repellent/killer. Singh (2012b) made an overview on phyto-pharmacotherapeutics of *Cyperus rotundus* Linn. (Motha). Sivapalan (2013) prepared a review on medicinal uses and pharmacological activities of *Cyperus rotundus* Linn. Vijisaral and Subramanian (2014) carried out GC – MS analysis of ethanol extract of *Cyperus rotundus* leaves. Samraj *et al.*, (2014) gave an update on Siddha herb Korai (*Cyperus Rotundus* L.). Prasad (2014) emphasized on analysis of antimicrobial compounds in *Cyperus rotundus* and *Azadirachta indica* against human pathogens. Imam *et al.*, (2014) described the incredible benefits of motha (*Cyperus rotundus*).

International Status

Akperbekova (1967) described the characteristic feature of the chemical composition of the *Cyperus rotundus* root stock. Harborne *et al.*, (1982) find out some Flavonoids in leaves and inflorescences of Australian Cyperus species. Collins *et al.*, (1993) executed an assessment of the efficacy of Quwenling as a mosquito repellent. Thebtaranonth *et al.*, (1995) focused on antimalarial sesquiterpenes extracted from tubers of *Cyperus rotundus* and the structure of 10, 12-peroxycalamenene, Asesquiterpenes endoperoxide. Jantan *et al.*, (1999) carried out an evaluation of smoke from mosquito coils containing Malaysian plants against Aedes aegypti.

Sonwa and Konig (2001) conducted a chemical study of the essential oil of *Cyperus rotundus*. Tawatsin *et al.*, (2001) explained the repellency of volatile oils from plants against three mosquito vectors. Jirovetz *et al.*, (2004) made a comparative analysis of the essential oil and SPME-headspace aroma compounds of Cyperus rotundus L. roots/tubers from South-India using GC, GC-MS and olfactometry. Caroline (2005) focused on plant-based mosquito repellents and highlighted on making a careful choice. Odalo *et al.*, (2005) showed the repellency of essential oils of some plants from the Kenyan coast against *Anopheles gambiae*. Zoghbi *et al.*, (2008) explained the comparison of the main components of the essential oils of "priprioca": *Cyperus articulatus* var. *articulatus* L., *C. articulatus* var. *nodosus* L., *C. prolixus* Kunth and *C. rotundus* L. Oladipupo and Adebola (2009) analysed the chemical composition of the essential oils of *Cyperus rotundus* L. from South Africa.

Dekker *et al.*, (2011) carried out the identification of mosquito repellent odours from *Ocimum forskolei*. Soumaya *et al.*, (2013) carried out pharmacological, antioxidant, genotoxic studies and modulation of rat splenocyte functions by *Cyperus rotundus* extracts. Imam and Sumi (2014) explained the evaluation of antinociceptive activity of hydromethanol extract of *Cyperus rotundus* in mice.

A preliminary relevant work has been done by many researchers from India and abroad. *Cyperus rotundus* L. is being used in few investigations in many parts of the World..

Objectives

- Collection of weed plant Motha from its natural habitat.
- To distillate the Motha to extract the essence of plant
- To make a mosquito repellent product
- To evaluate the efficiency and performance of developed product

Experimental Design

First Year

- Literature survey covering various aspects of development of herbal mosquito repellent including extraction of essence of plant, characterization, etc.
- Procurement of lab scale distillation assembly to extract the essence of selected plant.
- Procurement of raw materials required for preparation of mosquito repellent product for human use.

Second Year

- Distillation of Motha plant including its various parts like leaves, roots, florets, etc.
- Collection and preservation of plant extract from distillation assembly.
- Development of mosquito repellent product.
- Repellency test of product against mosquitoes.

Third Year

- Toxicological studies of the developed mosquito repellent product viz. acute systemic toxicity, toxicity to oral mucosa, implantation and sensitization.
- The developed mosquito repellent will be patentable and will have characteristics suitable to indigenous requirements.
- Data interpretation and Final report preparation.

REFERENCES

Akperbekova, B.A. (1967): Characteristic Feature of the Chemical Composition of the *Cyperus rotundus* Root Stock. *Farmatsiya,* 16(3): 36-41.

Ansari M. A. and R. K. Razdan (1995): Relative Efficacy of Various Oils in Repelling Mosquitoes. *Indian Journal of Malariology,* 32 (3): 104–111.

Ansari M.A., P.K. Mittal, R.K. Razdan & U. Sreehari (2005): Larvicidal and Mosquito Repellent Activities of Pine (Pinus longifolia, Family: Pinaceae) oil. *J. Vect. Borne Dis.* 42: 95–99.

Bisht Anupam, G.R.S. Bisht, Mamta Singh, Richa Gupta and Vinod Singh (2011): Chemical compsition and Antimicrobial Activity of Essential oil of tubers of *Cyperus rotundus* Linn. Collected from Dehradun (Uttarakhand). *International Journal of Research in Pharmaceutical and Biomedical Sciences,* 2(2): 661-665.

Caroline Cox (2005): Plant-Based Mosquito Repellents: Making a Careful Choice. *Journal of Pesticide Reform,* 25(3): 6-7.

Collins D. A., J. N. Brady, and C. F. Curtis (1993): Assessment of the Efficacy of Quwenling as a Mosquito Repellent. *Phytotherapy Research,* 7(1): 17–20.

Das N.G., I. Baruah, P.K. Talukdar & S.C. Das (2003): Evaluation of Botanicals as Repellents against Mosquitoes. *J. Vect. Borne Dis.* 40: 49–53.

Dekker Teun, Rickard Ignell, Maedot Ghebru, Robert Glinwood and Richard Hopkins (2011): Identification of Mosquito Repellent Odours from *Ocimum forskolei. Parasites & Vectors.* 4: 183.

Dhillon, R.S.; Singh, S.; Kundra, S. and Basra, A.S. (1993): Studies on the Chemical Composition and Biological Activity of Essential Oil from *Cyperus rotundus* Linn. *Plant Growth Regul.,* 13: 89-93.

Dua V.K., A.C. Pandey & A.P. Dash (2010): Adulticidal Activity of Essential Oil of Lantana camara Leaves Against Mosquitoes. *Indian J. Med. Res.* 131: 434-439.

Dua V.K., Gupta N.C., Pandey A.C., Sharma V.P. (1996): Repellency of Lantana camara Flowers against Aedes Mosquitoes. *Journal of Am. Mosquito Control Assoc.* 12: 406–408.

Egunyomi A., Gbadamosi I.T. and Osiname K.O. (2010): Comparative Effectiveness of Ethnobotanical Mosquito Repellents Used in Ibadan, Nigeria. *Journal of Applied Biosciences* 36: 2383- 2388.

Fanello C., Kolaczinski J.H., Conway D.J., Carnevale P., Curtis C.F. (1999): The Kdr pyrethroid Resistance Gene in Anopheles Gambiae: Tests of Nonpyrethroid Insecticides and a New Detection Method for the Gene. *Parasitologia* 41: 323 –326.

Gupta MB, Palit TK, Singh N, Bhargava KP. (1971): Pharmacological Studies to Isolate the Active Constituents from *Cyperus rotundus* Possessing Anti-inflammatory, Anti-pyretic and Analgesic Activities. *Indian Journal of Medical Research;* 59: 76–82.

Harborne, JB.; Williams, C.A.; Wilson, K.L. (1982): Flavonoids in Leaves and Inflorescences of Australian Cyperus species. *Phytochemistry,* 21: 2491-2507.

Hubalek Z. and Halouzka J. (1999): West Nile Fever – A Reemerging Mosquito-borne Viral Disease in Europe. *Infectious Diseases.* 5(5): 643 - 650.

Imam H, Z, Sofi G, Seikh A, Lone A. (2014): The Incredible Benefits of Nagarmotha (*Cyperus rotundus*). *Int. J. Nutr. Pharmacol. Neurol. Dis.;* 4(1): 23-27.

Imam M.Z. and Sumi C.D. (2014): Evaluation of Antinociceptive Activity of Hydromethanol Extract of *Cyperus rotundus* in mice. BMC Complementary and Alternative Medicine, 14: 83. doi:10.1186/1472-6882-14-83.

Jantan I., Z.M. Zaki, A.R. Ahmad and R. Ahmad (1999): Evaluation of Smoke from Mosquito Coils Containing Malaysian Plants against Aedes aegypti, *Fitoterapia,* 70 (3): 237-243.

Jirovetz, L.; Wobus, A.; Buchbauer, G.; Shafi, M.P.; Thampi, P.T. (2004): Comparative Analysis of the Essential Oil and SPME-headspace Aroma Compounds of Cyperus rotundus L. roots/tubers from South-India using GC, GC-MS and Olfactometry. *J. Essent. Oil-Bearing Plants,* 7: 100-106.

Kalsi, P.S.Z.; Ganhoi, M. L. and Bhatia, I. S. (1969): Chemical studies on the essential oil from *Cyperus rotundus. J. Res. Punjab Agri. Univ.* 6(2): 383-387.

Kapadia, V.H.; Naik, V.G.; Wadia, M.S.; Dev, S. (1967): Sesquiterpenoids from Essential oil of *Cyperus rotundus. Tetrahedron Lett.,* 46-61.

Mandal, Shyamapada (2011): Repellent Activity of Eucalyptus and Azadirachta Indica Seed Oil Against the Filarial Mosquito Culex Quinquefasciatus Say (Diptera: Culicidae) in India. *Asian Pacific Journal of Tropical Biomedicine.* S109-S112

Odalo J.O., M.O. Omolo, H. Malebo, J. Angira, P.M. Njeru, I.O. Ndiege and A. Hassanadali (2005): Repellency of Essential Oils of Some Plants from the Kenyan Coast against *Anopheles gambiae. Acta Tropica,* 95 (3): 210-218.

Oladipupo A. Lawal and Adebola O. Oyedeji (2009): Chemical Composition of the Essential Oils of *Cyperus rotundus* L. from South Africa. *Molecules,* 14: 2909-2917; doi:10.3390/ molecules14082909.

Pal, Mahesh, Anil Kumar, Shri Krishna Tewari (2011): Chemical Composition and Mosquito Repellent Activity of the Essential Oil of *Plectranthus incanus* Link. *FACTA UNIVERSITATIS,* Series: Physics, Chemistry and Technology Vol. 9, No 1, 2011, pp. 57 – 64. DOI: 10.2298/FUPCT1101057P

Patel E.K., A. Gupta and R.J. Oswal (2012): A Review On: Mosquito Repellent Methods. *International Journal of Pharmaceutical, Chemical and Biological Sciences.* 2(3): 310-317.

Prasad M.P. (2014): Analysis of Antimicrobial Compounds in *Cyperus rotundus* and *Azadirachta indica* against Human Pathogens. *Int. J. Curr. Microb. App. Sci.,* 3(3): 206-210.

Samraj K., S.Thillaivanan and K.Kanagavalli (2014): An Update on Siddha Herb Korai (*Cyperus Rotundus* L.): A Review. *International Journal of Pharmacognosy,* 1(4): 233-242.

Sharma V. P., M. A. Ansari, and R. K. Razdan (1993): Mosquito Repellent Action of Neem (*Azadirachta indica*) oil. *American Mosquito Control Association Journal,* 9: 359–360.

Sharma, V.P. (2001): Health Hazards of Mosquito Repellents and Safe Alternatives, *Current Science,* 80 (3): 341-343.

Singh Bhoopendra, Prakash Raj Singh, Manoj Kumar Mohanty (2012): Toxicity of a Plant Based Mosquito Repellent/Killer. *Interdiscip Toxicol.* 5(4): 184–191.

Singh N., V. K. Kulshrestha, M. B. Gupta, and K. P. Bhargava (1970): A Pharmacological Study of *Cyperus rotundus, Indian Journal of Medical Research,* 58: 103–109.

Singh S. P., K. Raghavendra, and A. P. Dash (2009): Evaluation of Hexane Extract of Tuber of Root of Cyperus Rotundus Linn (Cyperaceae) for Repellency against Mosquito Vectors. *Journal of Parasitology Research.* Article ID 908085, pp: 1-5. doi:10.1155/2009/908085.

Singh, N; Pandey, B.R.; Verma, P.; Bhalla, M and Gilca, M. (2012): Phyto-pharmacotherapeutics of *Cyperus rotundus* Linn. (Motha): An overview. *Indian Journal of Natural Products and Resources*, 3(4): 467-476.

Sivapalan S.R. (2013): Medicinal Uses and Pharmacological Activities of *Cyperus rotundus* Linn - A Review. *Int. J. Sci. Res. Pub.*, 3:1–8.

Sonwa, M.M. and Konig, W.A. (2001): Chemical Study of the Essential Oil of *Cyperus rotundus. Phytochemistry*, 58(5): 799-810.

Soumaya K.J., Dhekra M., Fadwa C., Zied G., Ilef L., Kamel G., Leila C.G. (2013): Pharmacological, Antioxidant, Genotoxic Studies and Modulation of Rat Splenocyte Functions by *Cyperus rotundus* Extracts. *BMC Compl. Alt. Med.*, 13: 28.

Tawatsin A., S. D. Wratten, R. R. Scott, U. Thavara and Y. Techadamrongsin (2001): Repellency of Volatile Oils from Plants against Three Mosquito Vectors. *Journal of Vector Ecology*, 26 (1): 76–82.

Thebtaranonth, C.; Thebtaranonth, Y.; Wanauppaphamkul, C.; Yuthavong, Y. (1995): Antimalarial Sesquiterpenes from Tubers of *Cyperus rotundus*. Structure of 10, 12-peroxycalamenene, Asesquiterpenes endoperoxide. *Phytochemistry*, 40: 125-128.

Vijisaral Elezabeth. D and Subramanian Arumugam (2014): GC – MS Analysis of Ethanol Extract of *Cyperus rotundus* Leaves. *Int. J. Curr. Biotechnol.*, 2(1): 19-23.

Zoghbi, M.D.G.B.; Andrade, E.H.A.; Carreira, L.M.M. and Rocha, E.A.S. (2008): Comparison of the Main Components of the Essential Oils of "priprioca": *Cyperus articulatus* var. *articulatus* L., *C. articulatus* var. *nodosus* L., *C. prolixus* Kunth and *C. rotundus* L. *J. Essent. Oil Res.* 20: 42-46.

Product Development and Waste Recycling **Pages 67-73**
Edited by: Pawan Kumar 'Bharti'
ISBN: 978-93-86841-94-0
Edition: 2019
Published by: Discovery Publishing House Pvt. Ltd., New Delhi (India)

7 Impact of Sulphur Pollutants on Polyvinyl Chloride (PVC) Products

[1]Pawan Kumar 'Bharti', [2]Anil Kumar Singh and [3]R. K. Singh

ABSTRACT

A study was undertaken to investigate the colour development of sulphur pollutants on the PVC products and its raw material used. A number of findings were observed and recommendations were made to avoid such problems originating by sulphur pollutant exposure. Hydrogen sulphide was found one of the major pollutants that can harm the properties of PVC by causing colour development on product surface. The pollutant gas creates tanning and thus destroy the value and appearance of final PVC products.

Key words: PVC, H_2S gas, Colour development, Tanning problem.

INTRODUCTION

Polyvinyl chloride also known as polyvinyl or vinyl, commonly abbreviated PVC. It is the third-most widely used synthetic plastic used, after polyethylene (PE) and polypropylene (PP).

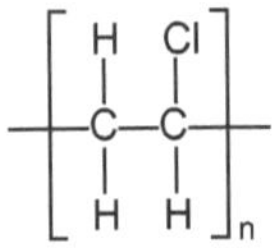

Fig. 7.1: Chemical structure of PVC monomer

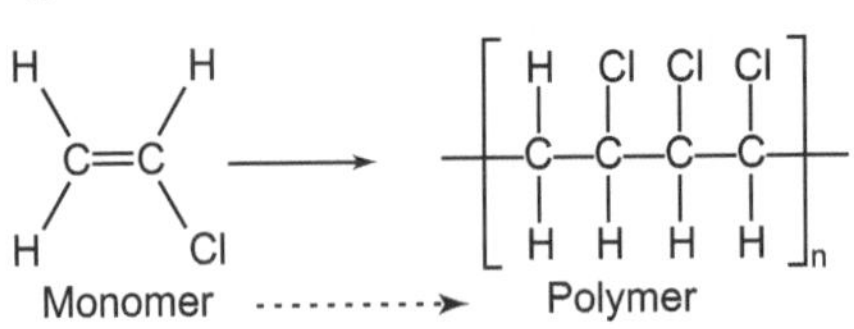

Fig. 7.2: PVC monomer and Polymer

PVC resin is made from the polymerisation of vinyl chloride monomer (VCM). It is manufactured commercially by bulk, suspension and emulsion polymerization techniques. PVC is a versatile polymer but it suffers from low thermal stability and poor impact strength. This problem can be overcome to

[1,3]R & D Division, Shriram Institute for Industrial Research, 19, University Road, Delhi, India

great extent by mixing PVC with various ingredients or grafting with suitable monomers. It can be formulated to a flexible or rigid material to make opaque or transparent materials. It can also be formulated to non-flammable and non-toxic material. Versatility of PVC is also due to the fact that PVC compound can be processed by many techniques such as extrusion, injection moulding, compression moulding, blow moulding, dip moulding etc. PVC moulded materials are widely used in diverse applications in various sectors such as film, packaging, foot wear, tubings, pipes etc.

Table 7.1: Properties of PVC Resin

S.No.	Properties	Value
1	Chemical formula	$(C_2H_3Cl)_n$
2	Notch test	2-5 kJ/m^2
3	Glass Transition Temperature	82 °C
4	Heat of combustion	17.95 MJ/kg
5	Specific heat (c)	0.9 kJ
6	Water absorption %	0.04-0.4
7	Dielectric Breakdown Voltage	40 MV

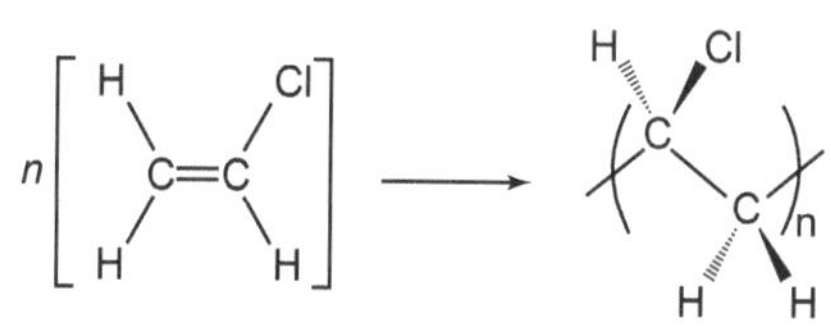

Fig. 7.3: Polymerization of vinyl chloride monomer (VCM)

Materials Used for Making PVC Products

A number of materials are used to make PVC product. The major raw materials used for making PVC products are as follow (given in Table 7.2):

Table 7.2: Raw Materials Used for making PVC Compounds

S.No.	Particulars	Ingredients
1	Polymer Resin	PVC Resin
2	Primary Plasticiser	Di Octyl Phthlate (DOP) Di Butyl Phthlate (DBP)
3	Secondary Plasticiser	Epoxidiesed Soyabean Oil (ESO) Chlorinated Paraffin Wax (CPW)
4	Stabilizer	Tri Basic Lead Sulphate (TBLS)Di Basic Lead Pthalate (DBLP) Di Basic Lead Stearate (DBLS)
5	Pigment	Titanium Dioxide (TiO_2)
6	Lubricant	Stearic Acid
7	Filler	Calcium carbonate, Talc

H_2S Gas Formation

Hydrogen sulfide is a gas with the formula H_2S. It is a colorless chalcogen hydride gas with the odor of rotten eggs. It is very poisonous, corrosive and flammable. Hydrogen sulfide is produced from the microbial breakdown of organic matter in the absence of oxygen gas such as in swamps and sewers. This process is known as anaerobic digestion which is done by sulfate-reducing microorganisms. Sulfate-reducing bacteria generate low-oxygen conditions by using sulfates to oxidize organic compounds or hydrogen; this produces hydrogen sulfide as a waste product. H_2S also occurs in volcanic gases, natural gas and in some sources of well water.

Hydrogen sulfide is commonly obtained by its separation from sour gas, which is natural gas with high content of H_2S. It can also be produced by treating hydrogen with molten elemental sulfur at about 450 °C.

A standard lab preparation is to treat ferrous sulphide with a strong hydrochloric acid in a Kipp generator:

$$FeS + 2\,HCl \rightarrow FeCl_2 + H_2S$$

Many metal and nonmetal sulfides, e.g. aluminium sulfide, phosphorus pentasulfide, silicon disulfide liberate hydrogen sulfide upon exposure to water:

$$6\,H_2O + Al_2S_3 \rightarrow 3\,H_2S + 2\,Al(OH)_3$$

This gas is also produced by heating sulfur with solid organic compounds and by reducing sulfurated organic compounds with hydrogen.

Table 7.3: Properties of H_2S Gas

S.No.	Properties	Value
1.	Chemical formula	H_2S
2.	Molar mass	34.08 g·mol^{-1}
3.	Appearance	Colorless gas
4.	Odor	Rotten eggs
5.	Density	1.363 g dm^{-3}
6.	Melting point	–82 °C
7.	Boiling point	–60 °C
8.	Solubility in water	4 g dm^{-3} (at 20 °C)
9.	Vapor pressure	1740 kPa (at 21 °C)
10.	Acidity (pKa)	7.0
11.	Magnetic susceptibility (χ)	$-25.5 \cdot 10^{-6}$ cm^3/mol
12.	Refractive index (n_D)	1.000644 (0 °C)
13.	Flash point	–82.4 °C

Colour Development on PVC Products

The compounds responsible for staining of PVC products are used in standard formulation. They may be present itself as its regular components or may also be present as impurities in many additives. Whenever these components come in contact with external surface or atmospheric pollutants, may result in problem of sulphur staining. Further, they also are encountered in the internal component of materials with which PVC compound may come into during mixing, processing and storage.

The factors that may be responsible for producing localized stains or give overall discolorations in PVC are as follows:

- Metal component of PVC compound interact with sulphur compounds to create metallic sulphide, resulting in a visible coloration of the PVC material. The metals are lead, cadmium, antimony and tin. Basic equations of colour development of PVC products is as follow:
  - $Pb + H_2S \rightarrow$ Lead sulphide (Brown Black)
  - $Cd + H_2S \rightarrow$ Cadmium sulphide (Yellow)
  - $Ca + H_2S \rightarrow$ Calcium sulphide (Milky hazy)
  - $Ba + H_2S \rightarrow$ Barium sulphide (White)
- Lead salts or compounds are widely used for stabilizing PVC compounds. They have excellent heat stability and is suitable for processing of PVC at higher temperature. They have been used in opaque, flexible, rigid and foamed applications. The other advantages of the use of lead stabilization are low cost, good thermal stability, light stabilization and low stabilizer volatility for PVC compounds. Further, they are also used for reduction in heat distortion temperature in PVC compounds.
- Examples of commonly used lead based stabilizers are:
  - Tri Basic Lead Sulphate (TBLS),
  - Di Basic Lead Sterate (DBLS),
  - Di Basic Lead Phosphite (DBLP),
  - Lead Sterate (PbSt) etc.
- Plasticized PVC compounds develop colour/stain in environments containing sulphide gases even in very low concentration. The amount of stain formation is dependent on relative humidity, ambient temperature, gas concentration and the length of time the PVC compound is exposed to the gases. The most common type is due the reaction of hydrogen sulphide or ammonium sulphide with certain metallic compounds in the PVC formulation.

Effect of H_2S Gas on Colour/Stain Development in Raw Materials of PVC Product

The effects of H_2S on change in colour of the raw materials used in PVC compound were studied in detail. The results are presented in Table 3. The results indicate that the change in colour was found to be dependent on the metal component used in manufacture of PVC product.

It shows that the brown colour change was observed for lead based stabilizer. The Ba-Cd liquid stabilizer also changed to light yellow colour. Moreover, TBLS, DBLS and DBLP used to make PVC product changed from white to brown colour. It was suggested that PVC compound should be formulated to make stain free white products.

Table 7.3: Effect of H_2S gas on Raw Materials used in PVC Product

S.No.	Compound	Observation
1.	PVC resin	No effect/No clour change
2.	DOP (Di Octyl Pthalate)	No effect
3.	ESO (Epoxidiezed Soyabean Oil)	No effect
4.	$CaCO_3$	No effect
5.	Lead Based Stabilizer (TBLS, DBLS)	Dark brown colour developed
6.	Stearic acid	No effect
7.	TiO_2 (Titanium Dioxide)	No effect
8.	Optical brightener	No effect
9.	Pigment	No effect
10.	Ba-Cd Stabilizer	Light yellow colour developed

Effect of H_2S Gas on Colour Development in PVC Compounds

The effects of H_2S on change in colour of the PVC compound were studied in detail. PVC compounds changed from white to brown colour on hydrogen sulphide gas exposure. It was suggested that PVC compound should be packed to make stain free white product.

Table 7.4: Effect of Packaging Material

S.No.	Packaging	Observation
1	PVC compound (Lead based)	Brown colour
2	PVC compound (Polythene packed)	Brown colour
3	PVC compound (Metalized multilayer packed)	No effect/No clour change

Observations

The findings of the study with regard to colour/ stain development in PVC products are as under:

1. Brown colour development in PVC products is surface phenomenon and is mainly due to metal sulphide staining.
2. Cadmium or lead containing stabilizers, lubricants or pigments are used in manufacture of PVC compound/granules which may lead to formation of metal sulphides (brown-black colour) when interact with hydrogen sulphide.
3. The change in color of PVC compounds when exposure to hydrogen sulphide gas clearly showed that the metal containing compound (Pb or Cd) is responsible for change in color are used in these compounds.

Conclusion and Recommendations

A number of findings were observed and the following recommendations are suggested on the basis of present study:

1. Avoid the use of Pb and Cd based additives in manufacturing of PVC granules & products.
2. Use of polyethylene based packaging may be avoided for the packaging of PVC products.
3. Use metalized multilayer packaging for the products made of PVC compounds before putting into inner box to avoid direct contact of materials i.e. product with inner packaging box.
4. It is advised to carry out environmental monitoring at processing, PVC manufacturing and storage site to ensure the absence of sulphur containing compound/gases in the premises.

REFERENCES

Cohen, G.F. (1975): Industrial Preparation of Poly(vinyl chloride). Environmental Health Perspectives. 11 (5): 3-7.

Cowfer, J.A., Magistro, A.J. (1985): Vinyl Polymers: Vinyl Chloride. In: Kirk-Othmer Concise Encyclopedia of Chemical Technology. New York, NY: John Wiley and Sons, Inc., 1229-1233.

CPSC (1997): CPSC staff report on Lead and Cadmium in Children's Polyvinylchloride (PVC) Products. U.S. Consumer Product Safety Commission. Washington, D.C. November 21, 1997.

DEPA (1995): Environmental Aspects of PVC, Danish Environmental Protection Agency (DEPA), Environmental Project No. 313.

DEFRA (2001): Life Cycle Assessment of Polyvinyl Chloride and Alternatives. Final Report. Prepared by Entec UK Limited (September 2000), London, England for the Chemicals and Biotechnology Division of the Department of the Environment, Transport and the Regions (DTSR) and Provided by the Department for Environment, Food and Rural Affairs (DEFRA) (March 2001). http://www.defra.gov.uk/environment/consult/pvc/01.htm.

EC (2000): Green Paper: Environmental Issues of PVC. European Commission (EC). July 2000. Brussels. (COM (2000)469,26/7/2000).

ECVM (2004): Science: PVC Recycling in Europe. European Council of Vinyl Manufacturers. Found at: http://www.ecvm.org.

EPA (2000): National Emission Standards for Hazardous Air Pollutants. United States Environmental Protection Agency (EPA). (Code of Federal Regulations, Subpart J, 67FR45 885).

EPA (2000): Proposed Air Toxics Standards for Polyvinyl Chloride and Copolymers Production Facilities. Technology Transfer Network Air Toxics web site. United States Environmental Protection Agency (EPA). December 4, 2000.

http://www.epa.gov/ttn/atw/pvc/pvc_fs.html.

https://en.wikipedia.org/wiki/Polyvinyl_chloride

http://www.calrecycle.ca.gov/publications/Documents/GreenBuilding%5C43106016.pdf

Hjertberg T. and Gevert T. (1995): Evaluation of Possible Degradation of Pipes and Cable Insulation of PVC: Results Obtained Samples Collected After 25 Years Use. Report prepared for: HydroPlast, Stenungsund. Gothenburg, Sweden.

Hydro (1995): Norse Hydro. PVC and the Environment'96. Oslo. ISBN 82-90861-32-X.

Svalander, J.R. (1996): Presentation Materials on Pursuing New Horizons: Taking PVC Beyond the Millennium. PVC '96 New Perspectives Conference. Brighton, UK.

SEPA (1994): Sample reports 610s09 and 0610s017: PVC Suspension/PVC Plastic and PVC Suspension Used to Make PVC. Stockholm: Swedish Environmental Protection Agency.

UBA (1992): Environmental Damage by PVC: An Overview. German Federal Office of the Environment. Berlin: Umweltbundesamt.

Product Development and Waste Recycling **Pages 74-79**
Edited by: Pawan Kumar 'Bharti'
ISBN: 978-93-86841-94-0
Edition: 2019
Published by: Discovery Publishing House Pvt. Ltd., New Delhi (India)

8 Development of Gel Based Perfume Formulation for Automobiles

[1]Pawan Kumar 'Bharti', [2]Anil Kumar Singh and [3]R. K. Singh

Introduction

Fragrances have been used to mask odors. A variety of compounds have been used over the past two decades for their abilities to create pleasant aromas or eliminate unpleasant odors.

The modern air freshener was introduced in 1948. It was based on pressurized spray using a chlorofluorocarbon (CFC) propellant. The product delivered a fine mist of aroma compounds that would remain suspended in the air for an extended period of time. This type of product became the standard air freshener. In the 1950s, many companies began to add chemicals that counteract odors to their fragrance formulas. These chemicals are intended to neutralize or destroy odors, unsaturated esters, pre-polymers and long-chain aldehydes.

In the 1980s, the air freshener market shifted away from aerosols, due to concerns over the destruction of the ozone layer by CFCs. Many other air freshener methods e.g. gel, soaking papers, coated cloths, heat release products and filters, etc. have become popular.

History

Fragrance compounds have been used since antiquity to freshen air and mask odors. For example, the ancient Egyptians were known to use musks and other natural materials to scent their tombs. Over the last 2,000 years a variety of compounds, including numerous spices and floral extracts, have been used for their ability to impart a pleasant aroma. However, it was not until 1948 that the first modern air freshener was introduced. This product, using technology developed by the military to dispense insecticides, was a pressurized spray containing about 1% perfume, 24% alcohol or other solvents, and 75% chlorofluorocarbon (CFC) propellant. This was able to deliver a fine mist of fragrance that remained suspended in the air for a long period of time. This format of the product became the standard in the industry and sales grew

[1,3] R&D Division, Shriram Institute for Industrial Research 19, University Road, Delhi – 110007

tremendously. In the early 1950s, many companies began to add odor-counteractant chemicals to their formulas. These were chemicals that were intended to actually destroy or neutralize offensive odors, as opposed to simply masking them with fragrance. Perfumery houses showed these active chemicals were capable of reducing a variety of unpleasant odors, such as cigarette smoke, urine and fecal odors, cooking smells, and amine odors typically associated with fish. Compounds used for this purpose included various unsaturated esters, longchain aldehydes and a few pre-polymers.

Over the next 25 years, aerosol air freshener formulas were modified to improve performance and reduce formula costs. But by the 1970s, the market significantly shifted away from aerosols, due to concerns about destruction of the ozone layer by chlorofluoro-carbons (CFCs). While reformulation by the aerosol industry has kept this product form from disappearing completely, alternate air freshener delivery forms have become increasingly popular. In the 1990s, a resurgence in potpourri and candles lead to a host of new air freshening products. For example, Kalib Enterprises Ltd.'s Potpourri, which contains a blend of dry spices and herbs, uses a battery-operated fan to circulate fragrance throughout the room. Arizona Natural Resources Inc.'s Crystal Candle division has introduced candles that kill odors, as well as aromatherapy candles that have specific therapeutic uses.

One of the most innovative, and popular, new formats is Glade Plug-Ins, manufactured by S. C. Johnson of Racine, Wisconsin. Plug-Ins use heat generated by electricity to spread fragrance through the air. It consists of a tiny plastic tray containing a gel-like fragrance concentrate. The consumer simply peels a multilayer barrier film from the top of the tray, leaving a permanent membrane layer that allows the fragrance to diffuse into the air. The tray is inserted into a warmer unit, which then is plugged into an electrical outlet. As the warmer unit heats up, fragrance permeates at a controlled rate through the film membrane, dispersing into the air.

Objectives

- Analysis of standard commercial reference samples (market) for their chemical composition, polymer content solid content, perfume content, solvent content, stability at different temperature, etc.
- Sourcing and procurement of chemicals based on the analysis of reference samples.
- Development of gel based perfume formulation for automobile using suitable polymer/ resin, pigment, perfumes, surfactants, diluents, etc.
- Optimization of the best formulation based on experimentations.
- Consolidation of results and preparation of final technical report.

Evaluation of Reference Sample of Perfume Gel

A study was undertaken for evaluating the reference sample of perfume gel provided by sponsor. The reference sample was for the following variables:

- Volatile/Nonvolatile content
- Solubility
- Ash Content
- Identification of nature of polymer
- Thermal stability etc.

Total Volatiles/ Non-Volatiles

Study for determination of volatile content was carried out in a laboratory oven at 105 ± 2°C. The total volatiles and non-volatiles in the sample were calculated by weight differential method. The results of the reference sample are given as below:

S. No.	Temp (°C)	Volatile (%)	Nonvolatile (%)
1.	105 ± 2°C	8	92

Solubility

Solubility of reference sample was carried out for different solvents at room temperature. The results of the reference sample are given as below:

S.No.	Name of solvent	Status
1.	Water	Soluble
2.	Ethanol	Insoluble
3.	Iso-Propyl Alcohol (IPA)	Insoluble
4.	Mineral oil	Insoluble
5.	Castor oil	Insoluble

Estimation of Total Ash Content

Estimation of ash content in reference sample was done at 800 °C for 4 hrs. It was observed that the ash content in the reference sample is 0.6%. The results for ash content is also summarized is following table as under:

S. No.	Temp (°C)	Ash content (%)
1.	800°C	0.6

Identification of Nature of Polymer and Other Constituents

For the identification of nature of polymer, FTIR studies were done. An FTIR spectrum of reference sample was matched with the library of FTIR. It has been observed that the nature of polymer of reference sample is matching with

Low Density Polyethylene (LDPE), Sodium Stearate, Magnesium Stearate, Sodium Laurate, Microcrystaline wax, Polymide resin, Ethylene-Propylene Copolymer, Candelilla wax, Carnuba Wax, Polyethylene, etc. The maximum resemblance of polymer of reference sample is with the LDPE in the FTIR library. The results IR of reference sample is attached as an Annexure-I.

Thermal Stability Studies

Thermal stability of the reference samples was carried out by Thermogravimetric Analysis (TGA). The TGA studies showed that the maximum thermal degradation temperature of reference sample is between 100 °C to 220 °C. At 500°C only 5% ash was found. The TGA thermogram of the reference sample is attached as an Annexure-II.

Preparation of Perfume Gel

Procedure for making perfume gel formulation

Procedure for making car perfume gel using different ingredients is listed in Table 8.1. In hot water (70-80°C) Tween-80 was added and stirred for 5 min; followed by addition of perfume and total composition was mixed for 5 minutes. Ethanol was added in the above composition and mixed for 5 minute under string. Further, formaldehyde was also added to avoid any kind of microbial contamination of developed perfume gel. In above mixture, appropriate amount of gelatin was added and properly mixed. Add Carrageenan and Sodium polyacrylate and mix it properly.

Table 8.1: Composition of Perfume Gel

S.No.	Materials	Wt. (g)	Supplier
1	Water	800	Distilled water
2	Tween – 80	32	Merk Life Sciences
3	Perfume	80	Supplied by Sponsor
4	Ethanol (LR)	80	Zliesher Nobel
5	Formaldehyde (37-41%, w/v solution)	5	SDFCL Ltd
6	Gelatin (Bacteriological)	80	Fisher Scientific
7	Carrageenan (Kappa)	16	Titan Biotech ltd.
8	Sodium Polyacrylate	1.6	Otto
	Total Wt.	**1094.6**	

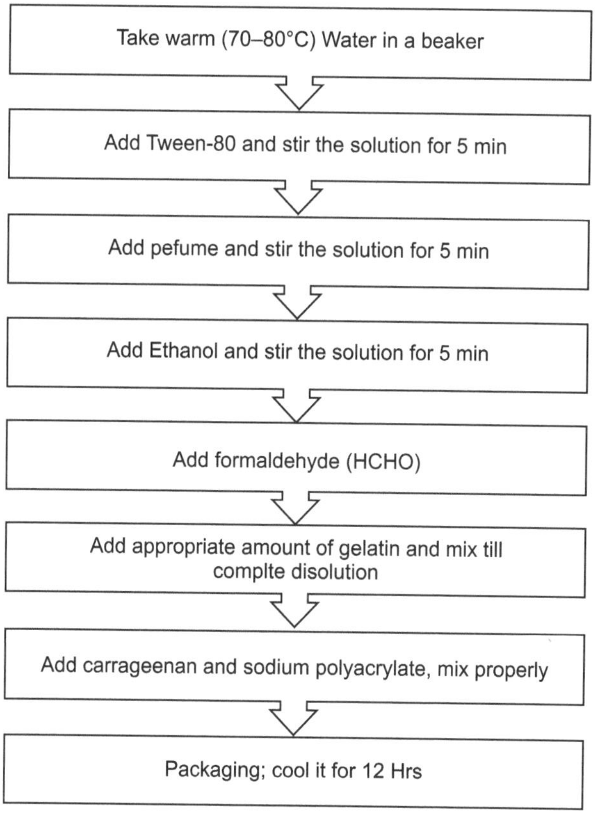

Fig. 8.1: Procedure for making perfume gel formulation

Characterization of Developed Perfume Gel Formulation

Characterization of developed perfume gel formulation has been done against reference (market) sample and results are summarized in Table 8.2.

Table 8.2: Characterization of Developed Perfume Gel Sample

S.No.	Properties	SRI developed	Reference (market) sample
1.	Volatile content @ 105°C	10%	8%
2.	Non-volatile content @ 105°C	90%	92%
3.	Stability at 60°C after 3 days	Stable	Stable
4.	Drying of upper surface at 60°C after 3 days	No	No
5.	Perfume fragrance efficiency	5-10 miters	5-10 miters
6.	Composition stability	Stable	stable

Conclusion

A sample of car perfume gel was developed and evaluated vis-à-vis the reference sample provided by sponsor. The developed sample matched in performance of the reference sample.

REFERENCES

Anonis, D. (1970) Perfumes and Creams. DCI, 107(3), 44–48, 164–166.

Behan, J.M. and Perring, K.D. (1987) Perfume Interactions with Sodium Dodecyl Sulphate Solutions. Intl. J. Cos. Sci., 9, 261–268.

Blakeway, J.M. et al. (1979) Studies in Perfume Solubilization. Int. J. Cos. Sci., 1, 1–15.

Bonadeo, I. et al. (1980) Hydrophilic Properties of Aromatics. Int. J. Cos. Sci., 2, 215–229.

Carles, J., A. Method of Creation in Perfumery, Reserches, 11 Dec. 1961, pp. 8–25; 12 Dec.1962, pp. 18–29; 13 Dec. 1963, pp. 92–103.

Dellas, J.G. and Lenoci, Vito, G. (1980) The EST Principle: Maintaining a Fragrance Accord in Diverse Media. Cos. Tech., 2(2), 33–35.

Denis. (2010). Air Freshener Formula. Yogyakarta: Faculty of Agriculture University of Gadjah Mada. Pg. 17-19.

Fitrah, N.A. (2013). Air Freshener Gel Formulations Using Carrageenan, Glucomannan and Perfume Oils. Bogor: Faculty of Agriculture Bogor Institute of Agriculture. Pg.5-11.

Friberg, S. et al. (1999) Stability Factors and Vapor Pressure in a Model Fragrance Emulsion System, JSCC, 50(4), 203–219.

Friberg, S., Mandell, L. and Larsson, M. (1969) Mesomorphous Phases, a Factor of Importance for the Properties of Emulsions. J. Colloid Int. Sci., 29(1), 155–156.

Herman, S.J. (1994) Fragrancing Emulsions. C&T, 109(8), 71–75.

Herman, S.J. (2002) Fragrance Applications: A Survival Guide. Allured, Carol Stream, II.

Johnson, R.L. and Morrison, D.S. (1999) Non-aqueous Controlled Release Pest and Air Care Gel Composition. US Pat. 5 871 765.

Joulain, D., Racine, P. and Maire, F. (1989) Agent Neutralizing Bad Smells from Excretions and Excrements of Animals. US Pat. 4840792.

Lanzet, M. (1960) Air Treating Gel and Method of Preparing the Same. US Pat. 2927055.

Meder, M. A Primer on Perfuming Polymers, Perf. & Flav., 11(1) Feb/Mar 1986: Part II, 12(6) Dec. 1987/Jan. 1988.

Mookherjee, B.D. et al. (1998) Fragrance Emission from the skin. C&T, 113 (7), 53–60.

Munden, D.R. (1988) Effect of Perfumes on the Viscosity of Surfactant Systems. C&T, 103(5), 65–67.

Patel, G.C., Patel, M.M. (2009). Preliminary Evaluation of Sesbania Seed Gum Mucilage as Gelling Agent. International Journal of PharmTech Research. Vol.1. No.3.Pg. 840-843.

Rosemary Hutagaol (2017): Formulation of air Freshener Gel with Carrageenan as Gelling Agent, Lemon Oil as Fragrance and Patchouli Oil as Binder. International Journal of ChemTech Research, Vol.10 No.4, pp 207-212,

Sagarin, E. and Balsam, M. (1956) The Behavior of Perfume Materials in Thioglycolate Hairwaving Preparations. JSCC, 6, 480–486.

Web help:

http://www.madehow.com/Volume-6/Air-Freshener.html

https://www.perfumersworld.com/perfume-formulas

http://www.basenotes.net/huddlerarchive/376004

https://www.solverchem.com/articles/auto-care-products/auto-perfume-gel-formulation-properties/details

Product Development and Waste Recycling **Pages 80-101**
Edited by: Pawan Kumar 'Bharti'
ISBN: 978-93-86841-94-0
Edition: 2019
Published by: Discovery Publishing House Pvt. Ltd., New Delhi (India)

9 Waste Recycling and Fish Culture

[1]Siddhnath, [1*]Shiv Mohan Singh, [1]Ravikant Bharti, [2]Abdul Aziz, [3]Bhogeshwar Chirwatkar, [4]Bhagchand Chhaba, [5]Narinder Kaur

Introduction

Fisheries in India play a very important role in the daily life of people as more than 60-65% of the total animal protein intakes of Indian people come from fish. It is clear that India is a fish-eating community and that fish is an important food staple, second only to rice. The present fish production is 10.15 Mt with a contribution of 3.58 Mt from marine sector and 6.57 Mt from inland sector. The contribution of fisheries to GDP is 78,053 crores which are around 0.83 per cent of the total GDP. The sector contributes about 4.75 per cent to the agriculture GDP. The vibrancy of the sector could be identified from the fact that it has registered an eleven-fold increase in production over the past five decades. This reflects the importance of fisheries in the daily life of the people, as a source of employment and as a contribution to the national economy.

The development of aquaculture has been promoted as a means of responding to the urgent need to complement natural fisheries in order to meet the increasing demand. Fish can be grown in different systems by using feed or fertilizer supplied artificially or derived from natural resources.

The aquaculture systems used in India are:

- In cages, pens, ponds, and in rice fields,
- In monoculture or poly-culture,
- In integrated farming systems.

[1] Department of Fish Processing Technology, Faculty of Fishery Sciences, West Bengal University of Animal and Fishery Sciences, Kolkata (WB), India

[2] Department of Fisheries Economics and Statistics, Faculty of Fishery Sciences, West Bengal University of Animal and Fishery Sciences, Kolkata (WB), India

[3] Department of Fisheries Resource Management, Faculty of Fishery Sciences, West Bengal University of Animal and Fishery Sciences, Kolkata (WB), India

[4] Department of Aquatic Environment Management, Faculty of Fishery Sciences, West Bengal University of Animal and Fishery Sciences, Kolkata (WB), India

[5] Department of Aquatic Environment and Health Management, Central Institute of Fisheries Education, Mumbai (MS), India

In remote areas, people are poor not just in economic terms but also in access to resources. Thus there is a real need to develop appropriate technologies which can be adapted to local conditions and be both beneficial and sustainable. Farming systems which integrate the production of animals, crops, agro-forestry and fish is a way of optimizing the use of natural resources since it facilitates recycling of by-products and wastes thereby giving a higher overall production than would be generated from the sum of the individual sub-systems. The principle behind integrated farming is the maximum use of all available land and water resources using solar energy to drive the system, and with low external inputs.

In recent years, research on integrated farming systems has been strongly promoted in developing countries, as it has been recognized as one of the means of responding to problems of rural poverty, increase of population, air pollution, water pollution and environmental degradation. The Integrated Bio-System (IBS) puts special emphasis on the role of biodigesters as a key component in making farming systems more sustainable, because of the many positive impacts such as reducing emissions of carbon dioxide, better human and animal health through control of pathogens, reducing deforestation as the biogas replaces fuel wood and better nutrient recycling.

Waste Recycling in Aquaculture

Shortage of fertilizer in most Asian countries poses a constraint in food production. However, the amount of organic wastes available for recycling in Asia is immense, and if utilized effectively could play a tremendous role in food production. Moreover, animal wastes, agricultural wastes, and aqueous waste from industries are rich in nutrients, and when discharged into rivers or water bodies and land cause pollution of the environment.

The potential for using animal wastes in fish culture has been demonstrated by Chinese farmers who have used animal manure as the main fertilizer in fish culture since 1952 (Edwards, 1980). It was realized that about 72-79% of the nitrogen (N), 61-87% of the phosphorus (P) and 82-92% of the potassium (K) in the rations fed to animals are recovered in their excreta.

Wastewater-fed Aquaculture

The potential of wastewater- fed aquaculture has long been recognized in Asia, and the history of such systems goes back over several centuries. The traditional systems in China involve the collection of night soil (human excreta) and using it as a fertilizer for fish culture. However, the use of municipal wastewater (sewage) has developed rapidly since the 1950s. In 1985 the total area of waste water-fed aquaculture involving more than 30 sites in China was 8000ha with fish production of 30,000 tonnes annually, equal to 1.3% of the total freshwater aquaculture production of the country (Edwards, 1980). In Germany, scientists have studied the wastewater–fed aquaculture since the late 19th century, culminating in the construction of the 233 ha ponds complex in Munich. In India, wastewater fish culture began about 1930. The Calcutta wastewater fish-ponds system covers about 4 000 ha. The advantages of this system are not only the production of fish but also the improvement in water quality and reduction of pathogens in the sewage (Jana 1998).

Animal Manures in Fish Culture

Animal manures have been used for fish culture since a long time ago, in different ways such as in fresh, composted (aerobic and anaerobic) and fermented forms. The quantity and fertilizer quality of animals wastes vary according to species, size, and age, feed and water intake and environmental factors (Table 9.1).

Table 9.1: Fresh Manure Production and Characteristics

	Cow	Pig	Chicken	Duck
Production per adult, tonnes/yr	6-9	3-4	0.05	0.05
Dry matter (DM) in %	15-20	20-30	30-50	30-50
N as % of DM	1.2	1.9	3.5	2.3
P_2O_5 as % of DM	0.5	0.8	4.6	3.3
K_2O as % of DM	1.2	0.5	2.1	1.4
C/N ratio	25	14	18	18

Nitrogen in animal wastes may be in the form of organic compounds (eg: microbial protein), NH_3, NH_4, NO_3 and NO_2, the levels of which vary considerably. Gaseous NH_3 can easily be lost to the atmosphere, and handling can affect other losses of the various forms of N. In solid waste handling, losses of nitrogen may vary from 20% in deep pits to 55% in open feedlots, whereas in liquid handling, N losses range from 25% for anaerobic systems to 80% under aerobic conditions.

Addition of manures to the pond can increase fish production by two main pathways (Figure 9.1):

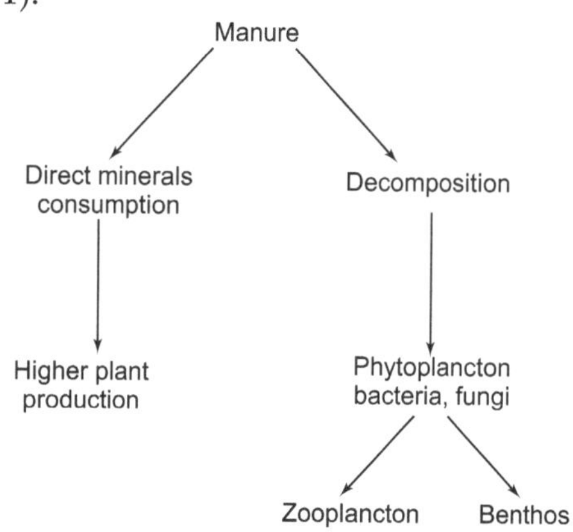

Fig. 9.1: Possible pathways for manure to increase fish production

Apart from regular small nutrient additions to the pond in order to maintain a stable ecosystem, stocking with a polyculture of fishes may also help stabilization. Phytoplankton and zooplankton numbers may be kept in better balance by the stocking of filter feeding fish.

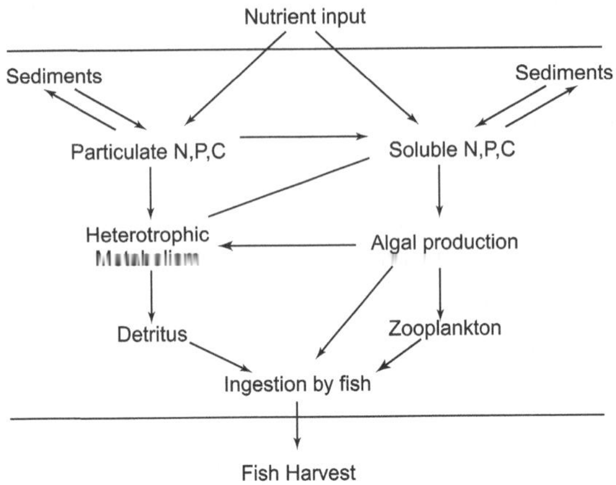

Fig. 9.2: Schematic diagram showing ecological pathways of fertilizer nutrients added to a culture pond (Source- Knud-Hansen *et al.*, 1998).

Manure Decomposition

The process by which nutrients are released from the manure through the action of bacteria and fungi is known as decomposition. Decomposition can occur either aerobically or anaerobically.

Aerobic decomposition is the desired process. Aerobic digestion of organic matter by bacteria frees 20-50% of the available carbon (C) in bacterial cells, and releases nutrients into the water in an available form for uptake by phytoplankton. Anaerobic decomposition occurs when there is no oxygen. This may happen when too much manure is added. Nutrients in an anaerobic layer are less accessible to bacteria and cannot be easily incorporated into the food web. Also nutrients are lost in the form of gases (CH_4, NH_3, and H_2S) which are also toxic to fish. Anaerobic composition is to be avoided by careful regulation of the manure loading. The recommended loading rates of manure from different animal species (Table 9.2) indicate that manure from chickens and ducks can be used in greater amounts than manure from pigs and will support better conversion rates (Table 9.3).

Table 9.2: Range of Manure Loadings Used in Fish Ponds

Animals	Animals/ha fish pond	Fresh manure(kg/ adult/day)	Maximum manure loading (kg/day/ha)
Pigs	30-300	5 (100 kg pig)	150
Meat chickens	1000-4000	0.15 (1.5 kg bird)	150 - 600
Meat ducks	750-3000	0.2 (2 kg bird)	150 - 600

Table 9.3: Conversion Ratios of Manure to Fish (kg Fresh Manure/kg Increase in Weight of Fish)

Cattle	35-45
Pig	20-30
Chicken	15-25
Duck	15-25

Biochemical Oxygen Demand (BOD)

The amount of oxygen required for the decomposition of a given waste in a specific time is termed its BOD (Biochemical oxygen demand). For the purposes of aquaculture, a 12 hour BOD ($BOD_{0.5}$) has often been found appropriate since decomposition has its most critical effect, in decreasing dissolved oxygen in the pond, during the night. The value, which is waste specific, is highly correlated to the amount of dry matter. Decomposition is also temperature dependent and thus low temperature will result in slower breakdown and hence higher BOD values. As a rough guide, rates of decomposition reduce by 50% for every 5°C temperature drop. The use of BOD values (Table 4) facilitates estimating safe levels of organic matter that can be added to ponds, ensuring the minimum dissolved oxygen for the fish.

The fresh manure needs higher BOD than composted, fermented manure and effluent from biodigester. For instance, BOD for biogas-effluent is about 60 % to 70% lower than fresh manures.

Table 9.4: The 24 hour Biochemical Oxygen Demand (BOD) for Various Inputs into Pond Culture of Fish

Material	BOD (g O_2/ kg/24 hr) at 30°C
Dry human wastes	35-50
Chicken manure	20-40
Duck manure	20
Terrestrial fodder	13.4
Pig manure	12
Field day manure	10
Submerged aquatic weed	8.6
Liquid cowshed manure	7
Floating aquatic weed	6.3
Emergent aquatic weed	5.4
Liquid calf manure	5
Human sewage	2.5-3

Chemical Oxygen Demand (COD)

Whereas the BOD value indicates the oxygen demand for respiration of micro-organisms acting on an organic substrate, the COD measures chemically the amount of oxygen required for the complete oxidation of a particular waste. However, the COD gives no information on the rate of oxidation of a particular waste and will not define, for example, the amount of oxygen taken up in 12 or 24 hours. If the wastes contain fractions that bacteria cannot readily oxidize, the COD value tends to overstate the effect of the wastes in the pond. A ratio of COD/ BOD will however give useful information on the longer term oxygen requirements from waste added to ponds, since it is an indication of the rate of decay and thus oxygen demand over time. Thus if the COD greatly exceeds BOD, the waste will be oxidized slowly and can be expected to take up oxygen beyond 12 or 24 hours. If the values are approximately similar, the waste will have negligible long term effect.

Pig Manure

Pig waste has been used for growing fish since a long time ago, in different ways such as in fresh, composted and fermented form. Its quality varies depending upon the form in which it is applied and on the type of feeds and the degree of digestion by the animals that produce it. Data on composition of pig excreta are given in Table 9.5. The C: N ratio is about 14:1 and the biochemical oxygen demand (BOD) at 3°C for 24 hours is about 12g/kg. The conversion of fresh pig manure to fish is about 25 kg / 1 kg of fish.

Table 9.5: The Composition of Pig Manure (%)

	Organic matter	N	P_2O_5	K_2O
Fresh pig manure	18	0.8	0.4	0.3
Pig urine	2	0.3	0.1	0.6
Air dried pig manure	33	2	1	2.5
Pig manure litter	34	0.5	0.2	0.6

Table 9.6: Pig Manure Production Rates

	Manure (kg/day)	Urine (litres/day)	Total (kg/day)
Weaning (30-60 d)	1-1.5	0.5-1	1.5-2.5
Fattening (60-220 d)	2.5-3	1.5-2	4-5
Sow 1 year or more	4-5	2.5-3.5	6.5-8.5

The effects of fresh pig manure and anaerobically fermented pig manure upon fish farming growing Silver carp, Bighead carp, Crucian carp and common carp. It was found that the total net weight increment of fish was 5% lower in the pond with anaerobically fermented pig manure (APM) than in ponds fed with fresh pig manure (FPM). APM ponds had higher NH_4^+-N and 21% higher biomass of plankton than in FPM ponds, with 21% more Cryptophyta and 31.7% less Cyanophyta. The net weight increment of silver carp and bighead carp was 13% higher in APM ponds than in FPM ponds. In FPM ponds, a lot of food detritus, which was not digested completely inside the manure residues together with bacteria on the surface of the detritus, were the feed for bottom feeder fish. Therefore, the net weight increment of Crucian carp and common carp was 21% higher in FPM ponds than in APM ponds.

Experiments conducted to study the effects of fresh and fermented pig manures on fish production in polyculture ponds (Silver carp, Bighead carp, common carp and Carassius spp). Six ponds were divided into three groups: fresh pig manure ponds (F_2), fermented pig manure ponds (F_1) and chemically fertilized ponds (C) with equal amounts of N and P as sole inputs. In the two experiments, the proportions by weight of fish from were 100: 156: 226 and 100: 294: 382, respectively for chemically fertilized ponds, fermented pig manure ponds and fresh pig manure ponds. Biological and chemical parameters showed that the fish did not feed only on natural food, but also directly utilized fresh pig manure. There were no signs of disease.

It can be concluded that fresh pig manure has high potential in fish culture, especially when used with inorganic fertilizer. But the application of manure should be considered in terms of the effects on water quality, particularly as it relates to oxygen depletion in the early morning, which is the main cause of fish death and slow growth.

Biodigesters

Biodigesters can have a positive impact in many areas, such as:

- The environment, by reducing emissions of carbon dioxide and methane
- Human health, through reduction in pathogen levels in the process of biodigestion
- Use of the gas for cooking, leading to reduced needs for fire wood, and less pressure on the forests
- Saving of plant nutrients

There are three main types of biodigester, which originated respectively in India (floating canopy), in China (the fixed dome) and in Taiwan (the plastic red tubular plug flow model). Modification was done into a simpler form by using tubular polyethylene film, which is cheaper and more appropriate than the other materials for poor farmers in developing countries.

Biodigesters as Sources of Nutrients

The quality of effluent derived from a biodigester depends on the quality of the manure and on the hydraulic retention time. The effluent contains all the plant nutrients present in the original manure. The effluent discharged from the digester may contain between 1 and 12% of solids and consists of refractory organic material, soluble organic salts, new cells formed during digestion and ash. The effluent can be separated into liquid and solid fractions; it can be dried or used in the fresh state. The components of the effluent which act as fertilizer are the soluble nutrients (especially ammonium salts), trace elements, insoluble nutrients and the organic material present in the solids fraction (humic materials). The pH is nearly neutral ranging from 6.8 to 7.5. The N concentration in effluent from pig manure is mainly a function of the level of N in the pig's diet and the dilution rate of the input material. A range of values from 290 to 470 mg/litre, with most of it present as ammonia

Effluent from the Biodigester has Potential in Aquaculture

In southern China, cultivation of fish in ponds is very common. Normally the fish are fed wheat bran pellets. However, it was reported some 20 years ago that biodigester effluent was being used as a fish supplement, increasing fish production and decreasing costs for feed.

When digester effluent is added to ponds, the nutrients stimulate the growth of both phytoplankton and zooplankton (daphnia and crustaceans), which the fish are able to harvest. The direct benefits to aquaculture may be realized both through the direct feed value of some components and its value as fertilizer to stimulate growth of plankton. Jones *et al.*, 2016 used effluent as feed in the pond. Thus digester effluent, in common with other organic wastes, supports fish growth by stimulating the natural food web rather than as a direct feed source.

In China, a biodigester of 10 m^3 capacity (to supply biogas to a family of 4-6 persons) produced approximately 10 m^3 of sludge and 14 m^3 of effluent per year. The slurry was used in the nursery ponds as well as for culture of market fish.

Anaerobically digested cow manure (mesophilic biodigester) was used in fish ponds for a polyculture of Tilapia, Common carp and Silver carp. The ponds were divided into three groups: the first group received concentrate pellets, the second liquid cow manure and the third, digested cow manure. The tilapia grew at the same rate in all three groups, but carp fed on pellets grew faster than those in the other two groups. The researchers were unable to determine the effects of the manure on each species in this experiment, though they indicated that tilapia was probably one of the species best suited to feeding on slurry. Dissolved oxygen was also measured in the early morning hours, and varied between 1 and 8 ppm, remaining at over 3 ppm for 80% of the time. No correlation was found between manure / feed treatment and dissolved oxygen. Primary production studies were conducted to estimate the effects of organic materials on the fish yield. Rates of photosynthesis were found to be only slightly higher in slurry-fed ponds than in chemically-fertilized ponds. In ponds fed with slurry plus feed, a higher proportion of zooplankton was found in the total plankton population than in non-manure ponds.

Growth rates of tilapia were examined with (a) high protein pellet diet (28% protein); (b) 50% low protein pellets (21% protein) + 50% wet untreated effluent; (c) 50% low protein pellets + 50% sun-dried effluent. The results of this study showed that digested slurry could replace 50% of the food in fish ponds, but that the different kinds of slurry were not equal in their effects. In a study of the influence of the liquid fraction of the digested slurry on tilapia culture, it was found that the low level of carbohydrates in the slurry was compensated by the production of algae, so balancing the ratio of metabolizable energy to protein in the fish diet. It was found that the liquid fraction of the slurry may be important in improving the oxygen level, raising primary production and the concentration of chlorophyll. Sun drying the effluent resulted in the loss of 18% of the nitrogen, mainly as ammonia in the volatile form.

Manure, when put in the fish pond, could be used to breed plankton in the water for feeding fish; the oxygen consumption was decreased, pH was nearly neutral, and there were no fish diseases. The colour of the water changed to a drab "tea" colour, which raised the absorption of heat from the sun. The temperature of water was thus raised and this contributed to better fish growth.

Study on the effects of fresh pig manure (FPM) and biogas fermentation liquid (BFL) on fish yield in a polyculture of seven species (Silver carp, Bighead carp, Chinese bream, Grass carp, Black carp, Common carp and Crucian carp). The results showed that the overall fish yield in the BFL ponds was 26.2% higher than in FPM ponds and all the species responded similarly, except for Bighead carp that grew the same on both treatments. Dissolved oxygen content was 43.5% higher in the BFL than in FPM ponds. The phytoplankton biomass was 31.6% higher in BFL ponds but zooplankton was relatively poorer. In water transparency and temperature there was no difference. The nutrients NH_4^+ and NO_2^- were higher in BFL ponds than in FPM ponds. Alkalinity was higher but the phosphate content was lower in BFL compared with FPM ponds

Thus it can be concluded that biodigester effluent supports fish growth by stimulating the natural food web rather than as a direct feed source. This should be most beneficial to fish such as plankton feeders.

Aquaculture Systems

In general, there are two forms of fish culture: monoculture and polyculture. Each system has its own important characteristics and the decision as to which system to use will depend on the purpose of the operation. Mostly, fish are raised in polyculture system for extensive and semi-intensive culture systems while monoculture is the choice for intensive systems.

Polyculture System

Polyculture is the practice of culturing more than one species of aquatic organism in the same pond. The motivating principle is that fish production in ponds may be maximized by raising a combination of species having different food habits. The mixture of fish gives better utilization of available natural food produced in a pond. Polyculture began in China more than 1000 years ago. The practice has spread throughout Southeast Asia, and into other parts of the world. This system is mostly used for growing fish in ponds by applying organic wastes or chemical fertilizer. Furthermore, the different groups of fish eat different feeds. Carnivorous fish prefer meat, herbivorous fish prefer plants and plankton and omnivorous fish will eat both. There will be competition among fish species within a polyculture if their feeding strategies are the same. Thus, before stocking the fish in the polyculture system, it is important to know their feeding characteristics.

In Chinese carp polyculture, at least four kinds of carp are stocked together in the pond system:

- a surface feeder (e.g. grass carp [*Ctenopharyngodon idella*]) that feeds mainly on higher aquatic plants,
- pelagic mid-water feeders one of which, the Silver carp (*H. molitrix*), prefers phytoplankton for food,
- the bighead carp (*A. nibilis*) which prefers zooplankton,
- a group of bottom feeding omnivores, which can include the common carp (*Cyprinus carpio*), the mud carp (*Cirrhina molitorella*) and black carp (*Mylopharyngodon piceus*).

Many polyculture systems use only two or three species but still achieve considerable improvements in yield over a single species culture. The stocking of Common carp, for instance, with one other species, such as Silver carp or Tilapia significantly increased yields (Stickney, 2017). Examples of polyculture stocking are given in Table 9.7.

Table 9.7: Examples of Polyculture Stocking (fish/ m^2)

Type of feeders	Bangladesh	China	India 1	India II
Herbivorous (macrophytes)	5	40	10	—
Surface (phytoplankton	50	8	20	30
Mid water (Zooplankton)	25	12	50	30-60
Bottom (detritus/omnivorous)	20	40	20	10-40

Herbivorous fish: grass carp, tawes (silver barb)
Surface feeders: silver carp, rohu;
Mid water feeders: bighead carp, catla
Bottom feeders: common carp, mrigal, mud carp

The pond depth in polyculture systems should be at least 2 m, the best is 2.5 – 3 m and the surface area about 3000 m^2 (Haque *et al.*, 2015). The deep pond is suitable for a polyculture of fish having distinct feeding habit like silver carp, bighead carp, grass carp, black carp, mud carp and common carp. If the water is too shallow the different strata are not deep enough to optimize polyculture or to rear large numbers of fish, and overheating and eutrophication problems can arise (Haque *et al.*, 2015). In principle, one species cannot efficiently use all the available food in a waste-fed pond, though stocking omnivorous and less specialized feeding fish is better than using those which are more selective in their diet.

Potential Problems in Polyculture

Polyculture is an effective way to maximize benefit from available natural food in a pond. But pond management becomes more difficult when stocking different fish species having specialized feeding habits in the same pond, because good fertilization and feeding practices must be followed. If inadequacy in the fingerling supply for polyculture is a constraint, at least one species should have general rather than specialized feeding behavior. This will allow more of the available natural food to be utilized.

Monoculture System

Monoculture is generally not as popular in extensive and semi- intensive cultivation systems as it is in intensive culture. In intensive culture the fish are confined in a small area, such as in cages and concrete ponds, and derive all their sustenance from high protein, processed feeds. In such cases, a specially developed feed is provided for a specific species of fish. Where fish are raised primarily on natural food sources, monoculture results in ineffective utilization of several levels of the pond's natural food chain.

Nevertheless, some of the highest yields observed in integrated systems have been achieved in monoculture. High yields of the Nile tilapia, *Oreochromis niloticus*, for instance, in waste-fed ponds, suggest such a system is practical. This species is particularly tolerant of poor water quality and this facilitates the use of higher waste loads than are possible in polyculture systems that include more sensitive fish.

Stocking Density

Stocking density is the number or weight of fish per unit area or volume of pond. Choice of a particular stocking density will depend on the system: extensive, semi-intensive or intensive. It varies considerably from system to system and according to several factors, including fish species, the desired size of fish at harvest, the initial weight of the stocked fish, the length of the growing period, the fish carrying capacity, the quality of the pond water and the level of management. Normally, the stocking density varies in the range of 1 to 5 fish/m^2 in a pond and from 20 to 100 fish/m^2 in the cage system. The stocking density varies in countries such as Thailand: 10, 000 to 20, 000 fish/ha, Bangladesh: 8000-20,000 fish/ha, China: 10,000 – 100, 000 fish/ha, India: 10,000 – 30,000 fish/ha and Vietnam: 40,000 – 50,000 fish/ha.

Stocking Types

There are different ways whereby stocking density can be changed during the growth cycle:

- Multi-stage stocking involves moving the fish as they grow to successively larger ponds, or to divide the lot of fish in one pond into several ponds of equal and large size, to accommodate their increasing size. Generally this is only used in large scale operations.
- Multi-size stocking involves the culturing of various sizes and ages of fish in order to better utilize all the available food in the pond. Marketable sized fish are harvested periodically.
- Mono-size stocking involves the stocking of the single size or age of fish. All fish are harvested at the same time. This is the simplest, but also the least productive management strategy.

Ecological Niches

Different species of fish have different feeding habits. Some are mainly herbivorous, feeding on the primary producers (Figure 9.2). These include species such as the silver carp, which filter phytoplankton from the surface waters. Other filter feeders (e.g. bighead carp, catla) trap larger plankton, mainly zooplankton. Zooplanktons are very small crustaceans which feed extensively on phytoplankton and bacteria. Big zooplankton such as copepods, macrocladocerans, feed on smaller zooplankton such as rotifers and protozoa. In a heavily stocked fish pond, the concentration and size of zooplankton may vary according to the feeding habits of the fish. The concentrations of smaller zooplankton will rise if fish which eat predominantly larger zooplankton are stocked. Similarly, concentrations of phytoplankton may rise and fall in relation to the densities of zooplankton that consume them.

The big macrophytes of the fringe community can be eaten by some herbivorous fish (grass carp, tawes-silver barb), but like land plants they tend to be fibrous so of lower nutritional value than phytoplankton. Some fish species (eg: Tilapia) consume large quantities of detritus together with protein-rich bacteria. Invertebrates (eg: snails, worms, insect larvae), which live in the benthic community may form a large proportion of the diet of omnivorous fish (eg: common carp) or more specialized feeders (eg: black carp). Finally, some fish are predominantly predators, feeding on larger insect larvae and smaller fish.

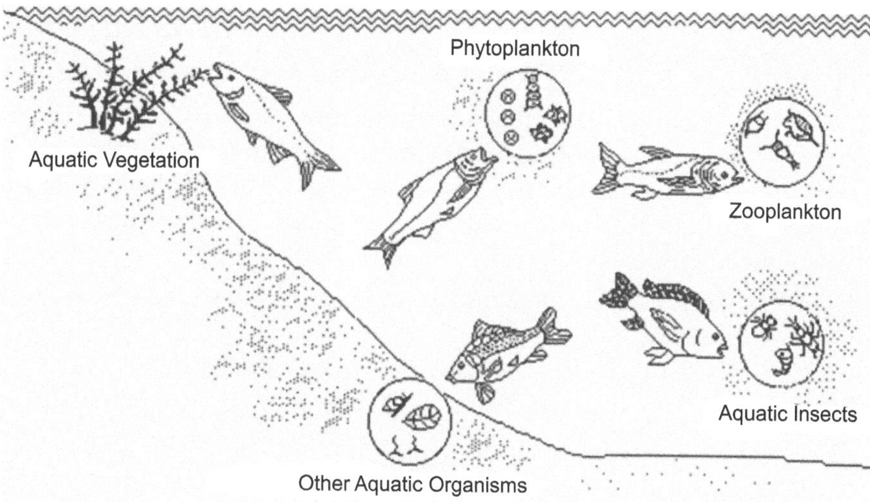

Fig. 9.3: Polyculture utilizes natural foods efficiently

Water Quality

The management of water quality is the single most important factor in productive fish farming. Water quality management is an ongoing, never ending process which requires a certain amount of diligence from the fish farmer. Daily monitoring of the pond's conditions and the fish behavior, along with accurate record keeping, allow the farmer to recognize and prevent deleterious environmental conditions in the pond and thereby maximize his production and profit. Water quality can be defined as the web of the chemical, biological and physical factors which constitute the water environment and influence the production of fish.

Oxygen

Maintenance of sufficient dissolved oxygen in the pond at all times is, without doubt, the most essential of the water quality management tasks performed by the fish farmer. There are two main sources of oxygen in water; diffusion from the atmosphere and through the photosynthesis of aquatic plants, mostly phytoplankton. The atmosphere contains nearly 21% oxygen gas, but solubility in water is low, so the greater amount of oxygen in the water comes from the process of photosynthesis. There are three main factors that influence level of dissolved oxygen in the pond; temperature, photosynthesis and respiration. This oxygen is used by plankton, fish and benthic organisms for respiration and for the decomposition of organic material. Oxygen solubility decreases with increasing temperature and increasing salinity. The magnitude of daily changes in oxygen concentration is influenced by phytoplankton density. Oxygen is lowest at sunrise, before photosynthesis becomes active, increases during the daylight hours to peak in late afternoon or early evening, and declines at night. Oxygen consumption rates by fish vary with water temperature, dissolved oxygen concentration, fish size, level of activity, time after feeding, and other factors. Metabolic rates vary by species and are limited by low oxygen conditions; small fish consume more oxygen per unit size than large fish of the same species. Critical oxygen demands for a given species are difficult to assess since there is such a broad spectrum of effects as oxygen levels change. In general, warm-water species tolerate lower oxygen conditions than cold water species.

Devi *et al.*, (2017) developed a dissolved oxygen (DO) scale for warm water fish

- DO < 0.3 mg/litre : Fish die after short-term exposure
- DO : 0.3 mg to 1mg/litre : Lethal for long- term exposure
- DO: 1 mg to 5mg/litre : Fish survive, but growth is slow for long-term exposure.
- DO – 5 mg/litre : minimum for warm water fish (fast growth)

Fish do not grow well when DO concentration remains below 25% of saturation for long periods (Tucker *et al.*, 2017). It is commonly accepted by aquaculture researchers and producers that fish perform better and are healthiest when DO concentrations are near saturation. Some authors recommend that the DO concentration in aquaculture systems be kept at about 90% of saturation, as a minimum at all times, for optimum performance.

Table 9.8: The Effect of Temperature on Oxygen Saturation of Water (Modified from Cassidy, 2018)

Temperature (°C)	Oxygen saturation (mg/litre)
10	10.9
15	9.76
20	8.84
25	8.11
30	7.53
35	7.04

pH

pH is important in aquaculture as a measure of the acidity of the water or soil. Fish can not survive in waters below pH 4 and above pH 11for long periods. The optimum pH for fish is between 6.5 and 9. Fish will grow poorly and reproduction will be affected at consistently higher or lower pH levels.

Carbon dioxide (CO_2) is very soluble and reacts with water to yield bicarbonate and hydrogen ions which lower the water pH. During photosynthesis, phytoplankton utilize CO_2 thereby removing it from the water and consequently raising the water pH. Conversely, phytoplankton respiration in the evening will increase the CO_2 content of the water and lower the pH. As a result of photosynthesis and respiration, the daily pH values will fluctuate, especially if the pond has a low total alkalinity. pH should be measured at dawn and in the afternoon to determine the extent of the fluctuation. The pH fluctuation in itself is not directly harmful to the fish. The pH of the water can be increased by adding lime to the pond. It can be decreased by the addition of alum ($AlSO_4$), which acts to decrease the total concentration of basic minerals in the water.

The pH of most natural waters ranges between 5 and 10 (Boyd, 2017) and it changes according to the influence of many factors such as acid rain, pollution, and CO_2 from the atmosphere and fish respiration. The decay of organic matter and oxidation of compounds in bottom sediments also alter pH in water bodies. In ponds, phytoplankton and other organic plants use up CO_2 during photosynthesis, so the pH of a water body rises during the day and drops at night. In poorly buffered pond waters the pH can be as low as 5 to 6 in the morning rising to 9 or more in the afternoon. In waters with high alkalinity, pH typically ranges from 7.5 to 8.0 at daylight and from 9 to 10 in the afternoon. According to Boyd (2017), in general, fish are intolerant to pH extremes outside of the range of 5 to 9.

Table 9.9: The Effects of pH on Warm-water Pond Fish

pH	Effect on fish
4	Acid death point
4 to 5	No reproduction
4 to 6.5	Slow growth
6.5 to 9	Desirable ranges for fish reproduction
9 to 10	Slow growth
– 11	Alkaline death point

pH can affect the fish in three ways:

- Large changes in pH tend to stress fish and reduce growth. These can be avoided by liming to increase bicarbonate concentrations and so buffer the water.
- Most cultured fish species prefer a pH of between 6.5 and 9. There are wild fish species that are adapted to live in waters of very low or high pH but these are not widely cultured.
- Acid waters (pH below 6.5) will not have good phytoplankton growth and so will not be very productive. Fresh waters with permanently high pH are not common and very little can be done to make them more suitable for fish culture except for the use of large quantities of alum or other acid producing compounds.

Nitrogenous Compounds

In aquaculture system, if all of oxygen demands are met, the second factor that becomes limiting is the accumulation of nitrogenous compounds. The major source of nitrogen (up to 90%) in an aquaculture system is from fish feeds and is produced through the normal metabolic processes of the fish. Ammonia also results from the decay of organic matter. Most of the nitrogen in organic matter exists as the amino acids in protein. The chemistry of nitrogen in ponds is very complex because of the many states in which nitrogen can exist: NH_3, NH_4^+, N_2, N_2O, NO, N_2O_3, N_2O_5, NO_2^-, and NO_3^- (Piedrahita *et al.*, 2017). The oxidative states of many of these compounds have little significance in aquaculture systems.

Table 9.10: The Major Forms of Nitrogen in Aquaculture Systems (Boyd, 2015)

Form	Notation	Comments
Nitrogen gas	N_2	Inert gas; transfers in and out from atmosphere; no significance.
Organic nitrogen	Org-N	Decays to release ammonia.
Un-ionized ammonia	NH_3	Highly toxic to aquatic animals; predominates at high pH levels.
Ionized ammonia	NH_4^+	Nontoxic to aquatic animals except at very high concentration; predominates at low pH levels.
Total ammonia	$NH_3 + NH_4^+$	Sum of unionized and ionized ammonia; typically measured in the test for ammonia; converted to nitrite by nitrifying bacteria.
Nitrite	NO_2^-	Highly toxic to aquatic animals; converted to nitrate by nitrifying bacteria.
Nitrate	NO_3^-	Nontoxic to aquatic animals except at very high concentrations; readily available to aquatic plants.

The main nitrogenous compounds of concern are gaseous nitrogen (N_2), un-ionized ammonia (NH_3), ionized ammonia (NH_4^+), nitrite (NO_2^-), and nitrate (NO_3^-). Molecular nitrogen gas (N_2) readily diffuses in and out of the aquaculture system. It is the major gas in the atmosphere, comprising about 78% of the total. Although N_2 is relatively soluble in water, equilibrium concentrations are higher than for O_2because N_2 is the principle gas in air. Similar to O_2 and CO_2, the equilibrium concentration for N_2 declines with increasing temperature and salinity. At normal fish culture temperature water contains about 10-20 mg/litre N_2 at equilibrium.

The Nitrogen Cycle

Ammonia is produced through the biological conversion of organic nitrogen through a process called ammonification (Figure 3). Ammonia is also produced as the major end product of protein catabolism and is excreted by fish and invertebrates (Weihrauch *et al.,* 2018). It is excreted primary as unionized ammonia (NH_3) through the gills. Ammonia is also produced through the decomposition of urea, fish feces, and uneaten feed.

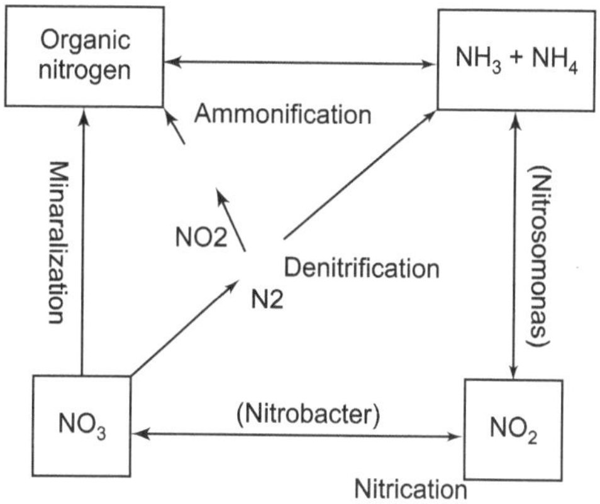

Fig. 9.4: The nitrogen cycle

Ammonia

Ammonia exists in two states, ionized ammonia also called the ammonium ion (NH_4^+) and un-ionized ammonia (NH_3). The sum of the two (NH_4^++ NH_3) is called total ammonia or simply ammonia. Total ammonia nitrogen NH_4^++ NH_3-N is often written as TAN. The toxicity of TAN is dependent on what fraction of the total is in un-ionized form since this is by far the more toxic of the two. In most environments NH_4^+-N predominates; however, the fraction present in this form is dependent on pH, temperature and salinity. Water pH has the strongest influence on the direction in which the equilibrium equation will shift.

$$NH_3 + H_2O = NH_4OH = NH_4^+ + OH^-$$

As pH lowers, the reaction will shift to the right and as pH is raised the reaction will shift to the left. Toxic concentrations of NH_3-N for short-term exposure vary between 0.6 and 2 mg/litre for many pond fish, and some effects can be seen at 0.1 to 0.3mg/litre (EL-SHEBLY and Gad, 2017)). Normally warm- water fish are more tolerant to ammonia than cold-water fish. To be safe, ammonia concentrations below 0.05 mg/litre as NH_3-N and 1.0 mg/litre as TAN are recommended for long-term exposure.

Nitrite

Nitrite (NO_2-N) is the ionized form of nitrous acid (HNO_2), and it can be as lethal as NH_3-N. Nitrite levels in fish ponds typically range from 0.5 to 5mg/litre, probably due to the reduction of nitrate in anaerobic mud or water (Verma *et al.,* 2010). Concentrations of both nitrite and nitrate show distinct seasonal patterns in fish ponds. They both are usually minimal in the summer months and increase in autumn, winter and spring. The toxicity of NO_2-N is due principally to its effects on oxygen transport and tissue damage.

Nitrate

Like nitrite, nitrate buildup occurs most in the autumn in pond systems when water temperature is lower. The nitrosomonas bacteria, which convert ammonia to nitrite, function at cool temperatures (16-20° C), but nitrobacter, which convert nitrite to nitrate, do not function well at temperature this low, hence nitrite will accumulate. Neither species functions well at temperatures below 16 ° C. Thus ammonia accumulates in ponds during the cold weather. Nitrate toxicity may be a problem only in recirculating systems due to constant water reuse.

Nitrates are the least toxic of inorganic nitrogen compounds. The effects on aquatic animals are similar to nitrite having to do with osmoregulation and oxygen transport, but the concentrations at which fish are affected are much higher. The safe values of NO_3-N for many fish and invertebrates lie between 1000 to 3000 mg/ litre (Monsees, 2018).

Phosphorus

Phosphorus is the second main nutrient in fish culture. Like nitrogen, phosphorus is recycled through a complex cycle. It is present in aquatic systems in many chemical forms, ranging from inorganic phosphate ions to organic molecules. The chemical balance among the various forms is a function of many variables including pH, concentration of metal ions such as calcium and aluminum, oxidation-reduction potential, extent of stirring bottom sediments and presence of pollution. The role of phosphorus is to build the parts of living plants and animals. It appears that an interaction between phosphorus in the water column and in the sediments helps to maintain a more constant phosphorus level in the water.

The amount of phosphorus used in fish culture is usually one fourth of the nitrogen, viz., Nitrogen: 4 kg N /ha per week and Phosphorus: 1 kg P / ha/ week.

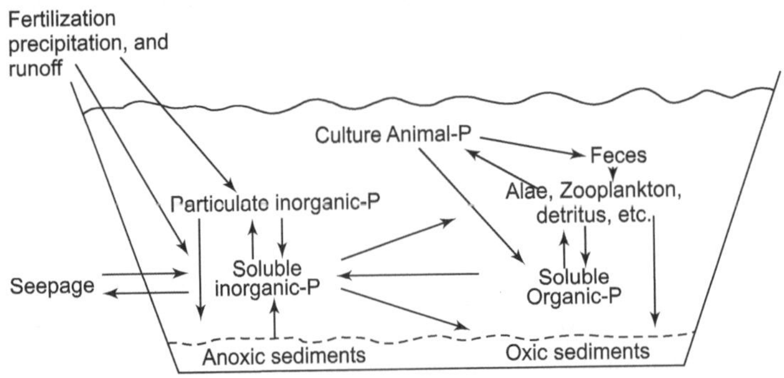

Fig. 9.5: The phosphorus cycle in a culture pond (Source- Knud-Hansen *et al.*, 1998).

Turbidity

Turbid water has many particles suspended in it. These may be phytoplankton or zooplankton or suspended solids (silt, mud or clay). Plankton is important food sources for fish and so are beneficial to fish growth. Suspended solids, however, are not good for fish culture for a number of reasons. They reduce the amount of light that can enter the water and so reduce the rates of photosynthesis and productivity. They damage fish gills, reduce visibility, can be very bad for zooplankton and also absorb nutrients added to ponds preventing phytoplankton from using them.

There are a number of ways of removing suspended solids from pond water:

- The most effective is to use organic fertilizers such as manures and compost. If added often enough, these will make suspended particles sink and so clear the water. At the same time, care must be taken not to cause an oxygen problem in the pond.
- Remove the cause by making sure the pond banks are covered with grass. If incoming water is very turbid, use a settling tank or pond to remove turbidity before using the water to fill the pond.
- Add positively charged ions (cations) to the water. The most effective compound for removing suspended solids is alum. This should be used at 20-30 mg/litre of pond water, but this concentration will destroy 10-15 mg/litre of alkalinity which is very bad for fish. This effect can be prevented by adding $Ca(OH)_2$ at the same time as the alum at 0.37mg/litre per 1 mg/litre of alum used.

Conclusion

There is a high potential for utilization of livestock manure in fish culture. There are also indirect benefits in terms of food security, economic gain as well as environmental protection. The biodigester is considered to be a key link in ecological agriculture in view of the many positive impacts at smallholder farmer level. These include biogas for cooking, saving of firewood and improved human health through less use of open fires, environmental improvement and, especially, the use of effluent from the biodigester as a source of nutrient inputs for a range of agricultural production systems. The balance of the evidence indicates beneficial effects on fish polyculture from the use as fertilizer of biodigester effluent rather than fresh manure, but the results are often confounded by associated effects of supplementary pelleted feed. There is a need for more information on the effects on fish growth of processing manure through biodigesters, especially the low cost plastic model, which is a relatively recent development.

REFERENCES

Boyd, C. E. (2015). Nitrogen. In *Water Quality* (pp. 223-241). Springer, Cham.

Boyd, C. E. (2017). General Relationship between Water Quality and Aquaculture Performance in Ponds. In *Fish Diseases* (pp. 147-166).

Cassidy, R. A. (2018). Water Temperature, Dissolved Oxygen and Turbidity Control in Reservoir Releases. In *Alternatives in Regulated River Management* (pp. 37-72). CRC Press.

Devi, P. A., Padmavathy, P., Aanand, S., & Aruljothi, K. (2017). Review on Water Quality Parameters in Freshwater Cage Fish Culture. *IJAR*, *3*(5), pp114-120.

Edwards, P. (1980). A Review of Recycling Organic Wastes into Fish, with Emphasis on the Tropics. Aquaculture, 21(3), pp261-279.

EL-SHEBLY, A. A., & Gad, H. A. M. (2017). Effect of Chronic Ammonia Exposure on Growth Performance, Serum Growth Hormone (GH) Levels and Gill Histology of Nile tilapia (Oreochromis niloticus). *Journal of Microbiology and Biotechnology Research*, *1*(4), pp. 183-197.

Haque, M. R., Islam, M. A., Rahman, M. M., Shirin, M. F., Wahab, M. A., & Azim, M. E. (2015). Effects of C/N ratio And Periphyton Substrates on Pond Ecology and Production Performance in Giant Freshwater Prawn *Macrobrachium rosenbergii* (De Man, 1879) and Tilapia *Oreochromis niloticus* (Linnaeus, 1758) Polyculture System. *Aquaculture Research*, *46*(5), pp. 1139-1155.

Jana, B. B. (1998). Sewage-fed Aquaculture: the Calcutta Model. Ecological Engineering, 11(1-4), pp73-85.

Jones, C. L., Taylor, R., Mogane, M., Mayo, M., & Power, S. (2016). The Underlying Mechanisms for Nitrogen and Phosphorus Removal in High Rate Algal Ponds Used to Treat Brewery Effluent; Harvesting Algae using Filter-feeding Fish; The Use of Brewery Effluent in Agricultural Crop Production; and Duckweed as Wastewater Treatment Solution, WRC Report No 2284/1/16, ISBN 978-1-0855-5.

Knud-Hansen, C. F. & Clair, D. (1998). Pond Fertilization: Ecological Approach and Practical Application (p. 112). Corvallis, Oregon: Pond Dynamics/Aquaculture Collaborative Research Support Program, Oregon State University.

Monsees, H. (2018). Overcoming Major Bottlenecks in Aquaponics-A Practical Approach.

Piedrahita, R. H., Boyd, C. E., Batterson, T. R., Szyper, J. P., & Diana, J. S. (2017). Water Quality in Ponds. In *Dynamics of Pond Aquaculture* (pp. 53-71). CRC Press.

Shyam, S. S., Safeena, P. K., & Athira, N. R. (2015). Does India Really Need to Export Fish: Reflections and Upshots? Agricultural Economics Research Review, 28, 117-125.

Stickney, R. R. (2017). Tilapia Feeding Habits and Environmental Tolerances. *Tilapia in Intensive Coculture*, pp. 25-35.

Tucker, C. S., Mischke, C. C., Brown, T. W., & Torrans, E. L. (2017). Water Quality and Plankton Communities in Hybrid Catfish (@& Channel Catfish, Ictalurus punctatus×B& Blue Catfish, Ictalurus furcatus) Ponds After Partial Fish Harvest. *Journal of the World Aquaculture Society*, *48*(1), pp46-56.

Verma, R. K., Saini, V. P., Dahiya, T., & Yadav, P. K. (2010). Fish Diseases & Health Management.

Weihrauch, D., Joseph, G., & Allen, P. (2018). Ammonia Excretion in Aquatic Invertebrates: New Insights and Questions. *Journal of Experimental Biology*, *221*(2), jeb169219.

Product Development and Waste Recycling Pages 102-111
Edited by: Pawan Kumar 'Bharti'
ISBN: 978-93-86841-94-0
Edition: 2019
Published by: Discovery Publishing House Pvt. Ltd., New Delhi (India)

10

Egyptian Experiments in Industrial Solid Waste Management

[1]Hebatalrahman A.

ABSTRACT

Solid Waste Management (SWM) is challenge affecting both environment and health. Waste management is not limited to the collection of waste and its disposal; it includes collection, transportation, sorting and recycling of waste. In this work the solid waste management methods, laws and logistics in the national and international scale are discussed. Assessment of solid waste management in Egypt will be evaluated. Some industrial experiments in industrial waste recycling will be mentioned, the experiments discussed in this topics include some patents registered in the field of recycling of industrial solid waste in Egypt such as method for recycling of thermoset plastics, Method and machine for slag treatment in metal industries and industrial unit for preparation and recycling of marble, granite and building material industries in composite material manufacturing.

the three experiments are evaluated as new methods have advantages on the economics of this industries beside their environmental impacts. The research end with list of recommendations about tools and methods to activation, implementation and application of Egyptian patents to solve the problems of waste management in general and industrial solid waste specially.

Key words: solid waste, building industries, recycling, environment, economics

Introduction

Risk assessment tools and methods are the main aspect to achieve green system, in green system waste minimization is a methodology used to achieve waste reduction primarily through reduction at source, but also including recycling and re-use of materials. Figure 10.1 shows the waste minimization procedure. Green system promotes multifunctional, connected green spaces.

The European Commission defines green system as a strategically planned network of natural and semi-natural areas with other environmental features

[1] Dr. Eng. Consultant in Materials Sciences & Materials Applications, Egypt* 13 Al-Zubair bin Elawam, Sadat land –Elmalek Elsaleh-Cairo–Egypt.

designed and managed to deliver a wide range of ecosystem services. It incorporates green spaces (or blue if aquatic ecosystems are concerned) and other physical features in terrestrial (including coastal) and marine areas. On land, GS is present in rural and urban settings. Green infrastructure can link and strengthen various ecosystems in urban and rural areas. It consists of spatially or functionally connected areas which maintain ecological coherence as an essential condition for healthy ecosystems.

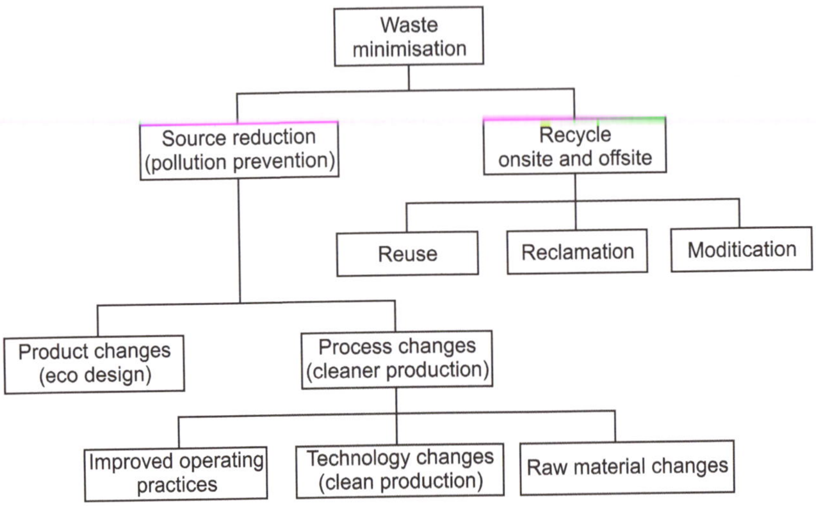

Fig. 10.1: The waste minimization procedure

Its added value however comes from broader investments in natural capital with a view to 'greening' existing system and strengthening the functionality of ecosystems for delivering goods and services as well as mitigating and adapting to climate change effects, and enhancing the quality of life (health, tourism, conserving historic and cultural heritage).

Under this call, NERC welcomes proposals that build on and use environmental data, expertise and skills to develop.

- decision support tools around the value of GS.
- models to allow demonstration of value of GS.
- innovative approaches that could assist in the development of new business models and processes underpinning GS.

Topics covered include the evolution of solid waste management; legislative trends and impacts figure 10.2 shows impacts of waste managements includes social , economics, environmental, technological and political impacts; sources, types, composition and properties of municipal solid wastes; sources, types and properties of hazardous wastes found in municipal solid waste; engineering principles of solid waste generation, collection, separation, storage, transport, processing and transformation both at the source and off-site; disposal of solid wastes and residual matter (landfills, landfill leachates and landfill gases); separation, transformation and recycling of waste materials, including biological conversion technologies; closure, restoration and rehabilitation of landfills; and solid waste management and planning issues.

In order that the integrated waste management be sustainable, all required aspects, such as financial, social, institutional, political, legal, and environmental that assesses the feasibility of the management should be addressed in a sustainable way. The different dimensions are interrelated and their linkages institutionally, legally and economically enable the overall function of the system.

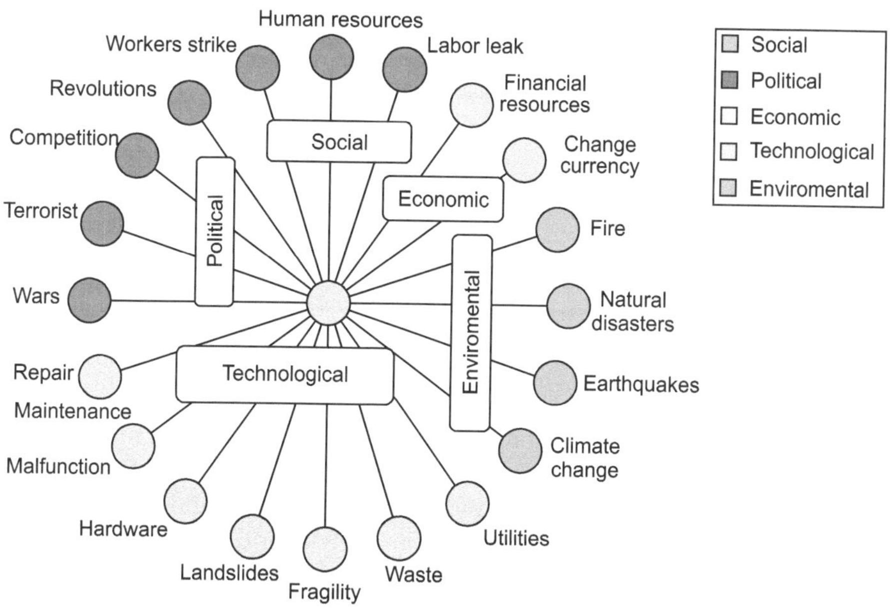

Fig. 10.2: The assessment of impacts of wastes

I. Risk and impact ranking of solid waste managements are define before the start seeking out risks. If you have an Ordinal risk process of ranking relative comparisons Low, Medium, High, then you risk process is seriously flawed this depends mainly on type of waste hazardous or non hazardous.

II. Deep uncertainties characterize the challenge as each major component in the information and decision-making chain from the frequency and intensity of a disruptive event The qualitative and quantities analysis challenges to deal with these interdependencies and uncertainties.

III. considering their primary decision goals and context mapping the range of modeling and assessment methods against different decision contexts, critical gaps in knowledge and tools are identified to support the decisions maker. figure 10.3 shows risk management processes in waste management of green system.

IV. Finally recycling change the risk into benefit, where the risks are kept, along with the information about the risk, and most importantly item is Handling processes or Risk Responses.

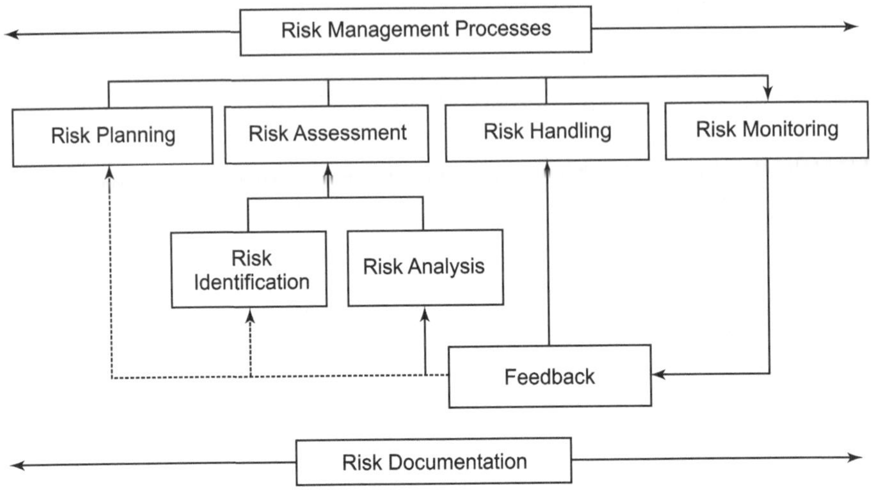

Fig. 10.3: Risk management processes in waste management of green system

Solid Wastes in Egypt

With approximately 85 million inhabitants, Egypt is the most densely populated country in the Middle East. In 2011, the volume of municipal solid waste amounted to around 21.1 million tones per year and it is forecast to rise by 3.4% each year due to population growth and changing patterns of consumption. Table 10.1 shows Typical composition of solid waste in Egypt according to EEAA (Egyptian Environmental Affairs Agency) program in 1990. The regulatory framework and the expansion of services and infrastructure cannot keep pace with these growth rates. Industrial wastes are expected to increase rapidly due to expected industrial development program in Egypt. Table 10.2 shows percentage of industrial wastes relative to other wastes. There are three experiments in development of new technologies to recycle of different types of industrial wastes in production of special building materials for special applications such as walls cover, raised floor tiles and insulated materials.

Table 10.1: Typical Composition of Solid Waste in Egypt

Type of waste	(%)
Organic waste	60
Paper	10
Plastic	12

Glass	3
Metals	2
Textiles	2
Other	11

Typical Composition of Solid Waste in Egyptian Cities
Source: EEAA, Action Plan for Sanitary Landfills in Egypt, 1998.

Table 10.2: Industrial Wastes Relative to Other Wastes

	Source 1*	Source 2**
Household	68	64.3
Street Sweepings and Green Refuse	12	12.3
Commercial	11	14.9
Industrial	5	2.3
Institutions (including Hospitals)	4	—
Educational	—	0.9
Hotels	—	0.7
Hospitals	—	0.09
Other	—	4.15

Sources of Municipal Solid Waste (Estimated as a Percent of Total Waste)
Source 1: Arab Republic of Egypt, National Environmental Action Plan, Cairo, 1992
Source 2: Project in Development and the Environment Comparing Health Risk in Cairo, V2:C 1994.

Experiments in Industrial Solid Waste Management

Separating, recovering, and reusing components of solid waste that may still have economic value is called recycling. creation of new composite material from industrial wastes can also be considered as recycling process, some patents registered in the field of recycling of industrial solid waste in Egypt such as method for recycling of thermoset plastics, method and machine for slag treatment in metal industries and industrial unit for preparation and recycling of marble and granite in building material industries and /or composite material manufacturing.

The Benefits of this Integrated Management Approach Including

- Conservation of natural resources,
- Reduced amount of waste to be recycled or transported to landfills or waste recycling facilities,
- Decreased air pollution and the production of greenhouse gases,
- Reduced toxicity of waste,
- Reduced costs of waste collection and disposal,
- development of new technologies depends on national technology,

- Transformation of waste into product which enhance economic of the industries.

(*a*) **Method for Recycling of Thermoset Plastics:** New method for the recycling of thermosetting plastics reinforced by different types of additives and fibers, which is non-recyclable by traditional methods. Temperature controller is installed to maintain the temperature of the mixture constant. The compound formed maintain in the elastic form. it shredded to the appropriate sizes. Material is cooled after deformation by air stream. The resulting material is combined with thermoplastics or metals materials and manufactured under certain conditions of temperature and pressure appropriate to the type of matrix.

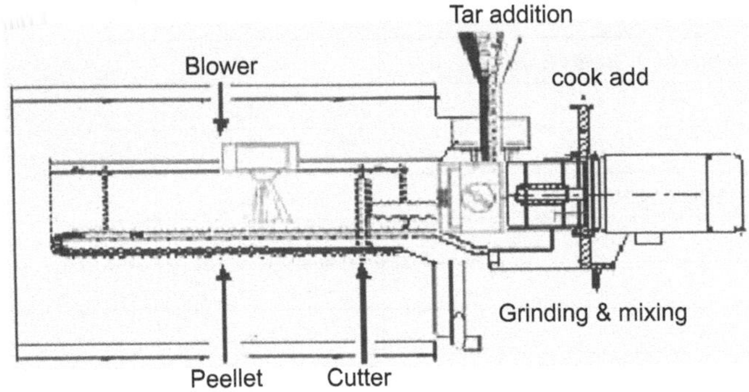

Fig. 10.4: Recycling of thermoset plastics machine (28)

(*b*) **Method and Machine for Slag Treatment:** The method and machine to treat slag of metal industries, the method based on improve the mechanical properties of the slag as well as prevent its interaction with water, improvement is done by bonding slag with binders in slag treatment machine. consists of mill for crushing and grinding of slag, mixer to achieve homogeneity, bunker to assemble the bonding materials that do not need grinding, tank to collect and heat mixture to become viscous and easy deformed in pipes and a bowl to collect the treated slag.

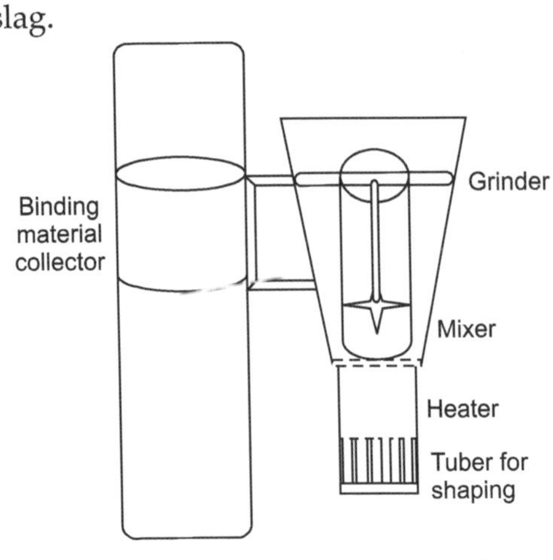

Fig. 10.5: Slag recycling machine(29)

(c) Recycling of Mining Wastes: Industrial unit for preparation and recycling of mining wastes (marble & granite) in building material industries for composite manufacturing.

Industrial unit for treatment of marble and granite wastes by physical methods, it treats both wet and dry wastes. After treatment, wastes are used as filler or reinforcement for composite materials industries. Metal Molds are used in manufacturing for good surface finish and dimension stability. The molds have heaters and gas cooling system. Heating and cooling rates depends on the properties required in the final products. Final products have different shapes, properties, dimensions, thicknesses, lengths and colors.

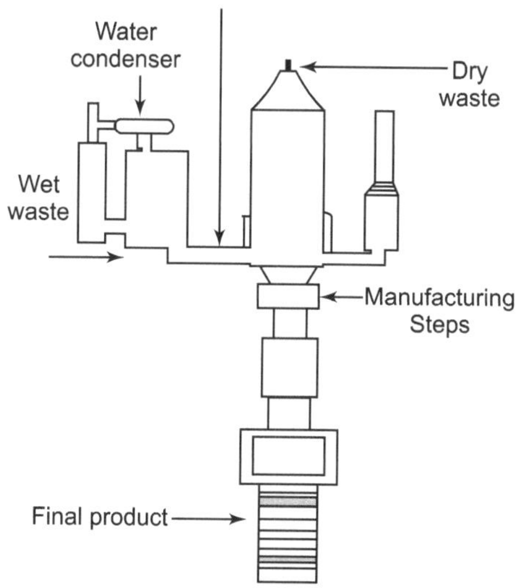

Fig. 10.6: Unit for marble and granite recycling

Fig. 10.7: Prototype of the marble and granite waste recycling unit

Environment has set up the Integrated Solid Waste Management Sector (ISWMS) as an interim solution under the authority of the ministry., the Egyptian Solid Waste Management Agency (ESWA). Together with existing actors, it will offer new waste management services, including policy and strategy development and implementation, support to and supervision of the governorates, and development and implementation of sustainable financing models.

Conclusions

1. Solid wastes are divided into five main categories municipal waste from urban, and rural areas; hazardous waste from hospitals; industrial non-hazardous, waste; industrial hazardous waste; and agricultural waste.
2. Recycling of industrial non-hazardous wastes play significant role in the economic of the industries.
3. The composition of municipal waste depends to a large extent on the affluence of the population contributing to the waste stream.
4. It is essential to know the composition of waste, both at the source and at disposal, to assess the most suitable option for disposal and recovery.
5. The feasibility of slid wastes is determined by a combination of the quantities of waste generated and the proportion of industrial waste, amongst other factors.
6. Recycling of solid waste in site improve the environmental of the industrial zones.
7. Despite international support, the institutions responsible for waste collection and disposal are not yet able to perform their complex tasks. The legal framework is inadequate, there is no strategic planning, and the allocation of responsibilities and tasks remains unclear. The sector is significantly underfinanced and there is an enormous need for sustainable investments and services.
8. Enabling management of the generated solid waste in an adequate approach will mitigate any adverse impacts to the environment, natural resources, and the public health.
9. Technology has provided better design for the consumable products with less material in size, weight and packaging. In addition same technology offered the possibility of waste re-using in modern applications.

Recommendations

1. Recycling of wastes must be considered as the main concept in risk assessment of wastes because the volume of municipal solid waste amounted to around 21.1 million tones per year and this figure is forecast to rise by 3.4% each year due to population growth and

changing patterns of consumption. The regulatory framework and the expansion of services and infrastructure cannot keep pace with these growth rates.

2. Government and non-governmental actors have the capacity to set up and sustainable operate an effective and cost-covering waste management system at national, governorate and local level.
3. Development of Arabian code and Egyptian code for solid waste management as risk assessment procedure.
4. Establishment of national and international companies integrated solid waste management (ISWM) contracts involve sorting, recycling and composting of wastes.
5. Make technical and economical feasibilities studies for all patents and scientific research related to waste recycling.

REFERENCES

A. Gawande, Better, A Surgeon's Notes on Performance, New York: Henry Holt, 2007.

B. E. White, Complex Adaptive Systems, IEEE International Systems Conference, Montreal, Canada, Apr. 2008.

Bjorklund A, Bjuggren C, Dalemo M, Sonesson U. System Boundaries in Waste Management Modelling—A Comparison of Different Approaches. In: Proceedings from the International workshop, 25–26 February 1998.

Cox, L.A. Jr., 'What's Wrong with Risk Matrices?', Risk Analysis, Vol. 28, No. 2, 2008.

Finnveden G. Life Cycle Assessment of Integrated Solid Waste Management Systems. In: Proceedings from the International Workshop, 25–26 February 1998, Goteborg, Sweden. AFR report 229, Stockholm, Sweden: AFR, Swedish EPA, 1998:261–75.

Goddard Space Flight Center, NASA, Risk Management Reporting, GSFC-STD-0002, 8 May 2009.

Hall, J., Le Masurier, J., Baker-Langman, E., Davis, J., and Taylor, C. (2004). "A Decision-support Methodology for Performance-based Asset Management." *Civil Engineering and Environmental Systems*, Online Publication Date: 1-Mar-2004.

Hebatalrahman, Egyptian Patent Office Patent no 1068/2015

Hebatalrahman, Egyptian Patent Office Patent no 25718/2012 registered 2008.

Hebatalrahman, Egyptian Patent Office Patent no 320/2011

http://ec.europa.eu/echo/files/about/COMM_PDF_SEC_2010_1626_F_staff_working_document_en.pdf.

http://www.al-monitor.com/pulse/originals/2013/11/egypt-suez-canal-uae-q

http://www.cabinetoffice.gov.uk/media/cabinetoffice/corp/assets/publications/reports/national_risk_register/national_risk_register.pdf.

http://www.cnbc.com/

http://www.planat.ch/ressources/planat_product_en_501.pdf.

http://www.unisdr.org/eng/library/lib-terminology-eng.htm.

Inside Risk: A Strategy for Sustainable Risk Mitigation, Editors:Claudio Margottini and Scira Menoni, September 2010, FP 6 Project.

International Organization for Standardization, Space Systems Risk Management, ISO 17666.

PLANAT (Nationale Plattform Naturgefahren): *Protection against Natural Hazards in Switzerland: Vision and Strategy*, 2005,

R. Stevens, Engineering Mega-Systems: The Challenge of Systems Engineering in the Information Age, Boca Raton, Fla.: Auerbach/Taylor & Francis, (2011), pp. 118–120.

Renni, E., Basco A., Busini, V., Cozzani, V., Krausmann, E., Rota, R. and Salzano,E., 2010: *Awareness and Mitigation of Natech Accidents: Toward a Methodology for Risk Assessment*, Chemical Engineering Transactions, Vol. 19, pp. 383-389.

Richard Pascale, Jerry Sternin, and Monique Sternin, The Power of Positive Deviance: How Unlikely Innovators Solve the World's Toughest Problems, Boston: Harvard Business Press, 2010.

Risk management Guide, Fifth Edition (version 2.0), June 2003, US Department of Defense, Defense Acquisition University.

Steinberg, J.L., Sengul, H. and Cruz, A.M., 2008: *Natech Risk and Management: An Assessment of the State of the Art*, Natural Hazards, Vol. 46, pp. 143-152.

Sundberg S, Nybrandt T, Silvertun A editors. System Engineering Models for Waste Management. Proceedings from the International Workshop, 25–26 February 1998, Goteborg, Sweden. AFR report 229, Stockholm, Sweden: AFR, Swedish EPA, 1998.

Udo de Haes HA, Editor. Towards a Methodology for Life Cycle Impact Assessment. Brussels: SETAC-Europe, 1996.

UN International Strategy for Disaster Reduction Sec, 15 January 2009,

United States Department of Defense, Risk Management Guide for DoD Acquisition, August 2006

William Seidman and Michael McCauley, Harvesting the Experts' "Secret Sauce" to Close the Performance Gap, Performance Improvement Journal, Jan. 2003, Vol. 42, no. 1, pp. 32–39.

www.drewry.co.uk/ciw

Product Development and Waste Recycling **Pages 112-142**
Edited by: Pawan Kumar 'Bharti'
ISBN: 978-93-86841-94-0
Edition: 2019
Published by: Discovery Publishing House Pvt. Ltd., New Delhi (India)

11

Role of Vermiwash in Agriculture

[1]A. Solaimalai, [2*]M.Jayakumar, [3]A. Rajkumar and [4]A. Palanisamy

Introduction

Presently use of chemical fertilizers is increasing in agriculture day by day which ultimately destroys the fertility of soil. Control the hazardous effect of chemical fertilizer can be reduce by the use of organic fertilizers. In this way, vermiwash may be used for better yielding of crops. Vermiwash protect the environment from various chemical fertilizers. Vermiwash is a liquid extract of organic waste material, which is collected after the passage of water through the different layers of earthworm culture units. Vermiwash is used as a liquid major nutritive and enzymatic element for promoting growth of all green plants.Vermiwash, the extracted body fluid of earthworms is also nutrient rich with components promoting good plant growth (Gorakh Nath and Keshar singh, 2009). Very few researches are available in favour of vermiwash and its influence on the growth and development of plants. Earthworm has an efficiency to consume all types of wastage *viz.,* that kitchen waste, temple waste, animal house waste, industrial waste, hospital waste and other organic wastes etc. Earthworms play a vital role in converting organic wastes to useful vemicompost. The dead worm's tissue discharges nitrogen in form of nitrates 25%, ammonia 45%, organic soluble compound 3% and other material 27% (Satchell, 1967). These materials improve the nutrient quality of vermiwash.

Vermi Wash

Recently, vermiwash production has drawn the attention of commercial vermiculturists. Vermiwash is a watery extract of organic compost, the wash of earthworms present in the medium and is honey brown in colour.

[1] Associate Professor (Agronomy), Department of Fruit Crops, Horticultural College & Research, TNAU, Periyakulam – 625 604, Tamil Nadu, India.

[2] Scientist, Regional Coffee Research Station, Thandikudi, Dindigul (Dt), Tamil Nadu, India.

[3] Assistant Professor (Horticulture), Krishna College of Agriculture & Technology, Sree Rangapuram, Usilampatti (TK), Madurai (Dt), Tamil Nadu, India.

[4] Assistant Professor (Horticulture), Krishna College of Agriculture & Technology, Sree Rangapuram, Usilampatti (TK), Madurai (Dt), Tamil Nadu, India.

Fig. 11.1: Earthworms

Principles

Worm worked in the soils have burrows formed by the earthworms. Bacteria richly inhabit these burrows also called as the drilospheres (Fig. 11.1). Water passing through these passages washes the nutrients from these burrows to the roots to be absorbed by the plants. This principle is applied in the preparation of vermiwash.

Properties of Vemiwash

Vermiwash is coelomic fluid extraction contains several enzyme, plant growth hormones like cytokinins, gibberlines and vitamins along with mocro and macro nutrients (Buckerfield *et al.*, 1999). In vermiwash nitrogen present in the form of mucus, nitrogenous excretory substances growth stimulating hormones and enzyme (Tripathi and Bhardwaj, 2004). Vermiwash bio-fertilizer was obtained from vermicomposting waste corn pulp blended with cow dung manure. The pH and electrical conductivity was higher in the vermicompost compared to the vermiwash. The nitrogen and potassium content were 57% and 79.6% higher in the vermicompost as compared to the vermiwash respectively. However, the phosphorous content was 84% higher in the vermiwash as compared to the vermicompost. The vermiwash was 89.1% and 97.6% richer in Ca and Mg as compared to the vermicompost (Table 11.1, 11.2 and 11.3).

Table 11.1: Chemical Composition of Vermiwash

Particulars	Content
pH	7 ± 0.03
EC	0.008 ± 0.001
Organic carbon	0.01 ± 0.001%
Nitrogen	0.01 ± 0.001%
Phosphorous	1.70%

Potassium	26 ppm
Sodium	8 ppm
Calcium	3 ppm
Copper	0.01ppm
Iron	0.06 ppm
Magnesium	160 ppm
Manganese	0.60
Zinc	0.02 ppm
Total heterotrophs (actinomycetes)	1.79×10^3 CFU/ml
Nitrosomonas	1.01×10^3 CFU/ml
Nitrobacter	1.12×10^3 CFU/ml
Total fungi	1.46×10^3 CFU/ml

(**Source:** http//www.erfindia.org/vermiwash.asp)

Furthermore, the vermiwash was 97.8% rich in sodium content compared to the vermicompost (Manyuchi *et al.*, 2013). It increases the disease resistant power of crop, (Yadav *et al.*, 2005). Varghese and Prabha (2014) suggested that vermiwash revealed potential application in sustainable development in agriculture biotechnology with respect to its origin, cost effectiveness, availability, reproducibility, reliability as well as bio pesticide and ecofriendly soil conditioner. Zambare *et al.*(2008) conclude that vermiwash contains various enzymescocktail of protease, amylase urease and phosphatase and alsoMicrobial study of vermiwash found that nitrogen fixingbacteria like *Azotobacter sp., Agrobacterium sp.*and*Rhizobium sp.* and some phosphate solubilizing bacteria.

Table 11.2: Nutrient Composition of Vermiwash

Particulars	Content
pH	6.4
Electrical conductivity(dS/m)	2.7
Nitrogen (%)	0.02
Phosphorus (%)	0.01
Potassium (%)	0.02
Calcium (%)	0.001
Mg(%)	0.001
S (%)	0.001
Cu(ppm)	0.13
Zn (ppm)	0.14
Fe (ppm)	0.15
Mn (ppm)	0.02

(Pradeepand Sharanappa, 2014)

Table 11.3: Chemical Composition of Vermiwash Produced by Different Methods

Parameters	Vermiwash (heat stress)	Vermiwash (cold stress)	Vermiwash (field)
pH	7.98	7.40	7.52
EC (dS m-1)	0.56	0.42	1.10
Organic carbon (%)	0.042	0.036	0.009
Total nitrogen (mg L^{-1})	55.0	52.0	61.02
Total phosphorus (mg L^{-1})	19.15	17.80	18.20
Total potassium (mg L^{-1})	46.24	45.20	55.20
Sodium (mg L^{-1})	119.40	110.80	120.10
Calcium (mg L^{-1})	181.08	175.25	178.60
Magnesium (mg L^{-1})	196.34	186.90	198.00
IAA (mg L^{-1})	16.08	15.05	15.02

(Amita Chattopadhyay, 2015).

Buckerfield *et al.* (1999) has reported that, it is coelomic fluid extraction contains several enzyme, plant growth hormones like cytokinins, gibberlines and vitamins along with mocro and macro nutrients. It increases the disease resistant power of crop, (Umamaheswari *et al.,* 2003; Phathak and Ram, 2004; Nath *et al.,* 2009a, 2009b).Rai and Bansiwal (2008) opined that vermiwash is a nutrient rich liquidproduced by earthworms, feeding on organic waste material and plants residues. Itis also nontoxic and ecofriendly, which arrests bacterial growth and forms as aprotective layer for their survival and growth. Vermiwash contains N, P, K, Ca andhormones such as auxin, cytokinine, some other secretions and many usefulmicrobes like heterotrophic bacteria, fungi etc. The quality of vermiwash producedby earthworms depends on the vermicompost that is used.Increase in the microbial activity in vermicompost and its extracts, could result in production of significant quantities of plant growth regulators such as IAA gibberellins and cytokinines by microorganism(Edwards and Fletcher,1998).

Methods of Preparationof Vermiwash

- Eco-science research foundation method
- Ismail's method
- Karunas method
- Economic technique
- KAU's method
- Using plastic drum (1000 liters) method
- Households device
- Kales method

- Earthworms body fluid method.

Most commonly and commercially followed methods are Eco-science research foundation method and Ismail's method. They are used for preparing vermiwash in large scale, which is simple, easy and economical for the farmers. Economic technique, simple method, is followed to prepare vermiwash in small quantity from vegetable waste and is used for kitchen garden for nutritional need.

Common Method-1

1. Select one sufficiently large container made of concrete or plastic bucket or earthen pot.
2. Drill a hole at the base of the container to fix a tab to it (Fig. 11.2).
3. A base layer of gravel or broken small pieces of bricks are placed to a height of 10-15 cm.
4. Above the gravel layer another layer of coarse sand of 1 -15 cm is put.
5. On the coarse sand layer place 40-45 cm pre-decomposed organic wastes and moistens the different layer by using water.
6. Introduce about 2000 Nos. of earthworms into the container. Fig. 11.2.

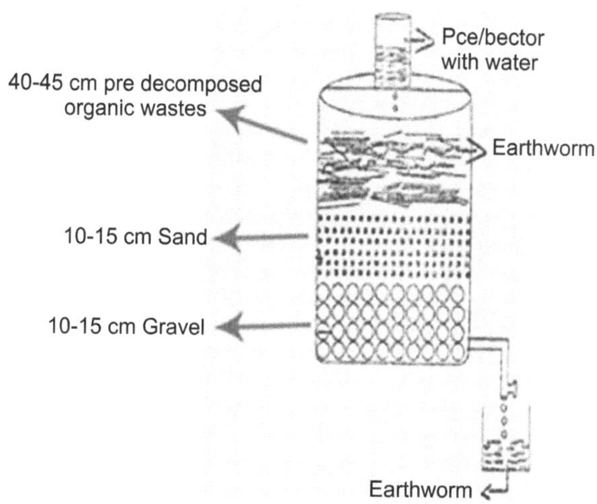

Fig. 11.2

Common method -1

7. After that, a layer of paddy straw having 6 cm thickness is given.
8. To get vermiwash continuously suspend a mud pot or a small bucket with some holes. Cotton wicks or bamboo sticks are place in the holes so that water can trickle down. Every day 4-5 litres of water is to be poured in the hanging pot.

9. After 10 days vermiwash starts forming in the container.
10. Keep another pot under stop cork to collect the vermin wash.
11. Everyday about 3-4 lits of vermiwash can be collected.

Common Method-2

Vermiwash units can be set up either in barrels or in buckets or even in small earthen pots. It is principle that is important (Fig. 11.3). The procedure explained here is for setting up of a 250 litres barrel. An empty barrel with one side open is taken. On the other side, a hole is made to accommodate the vertical limb of a 'T' jointed tube in a way that about half to one inch of the tube projects into the barrel. The one end of the horizontal limb is attached a tap. The other end is kept closed. T jointed tube if it gets clogged. The entire unit is set up on a short pedestal made of few bricks to facilitate easy collection of vermiwash. Keeping the tap open, a 25 cm layer of broken bricks of pebbles is placed. A 25 cm layer of coarse sand then follows the layer of bricks. Water is then made to flow through these layers to enable the setting up of the basic filter unit. On top of this layer is placed a 30 to 45 cm layer of loamy soil. It is moistened and into this area introduced about 50 numbers each of the surface (epigeic) and sub-surface (anecic) earth worms.

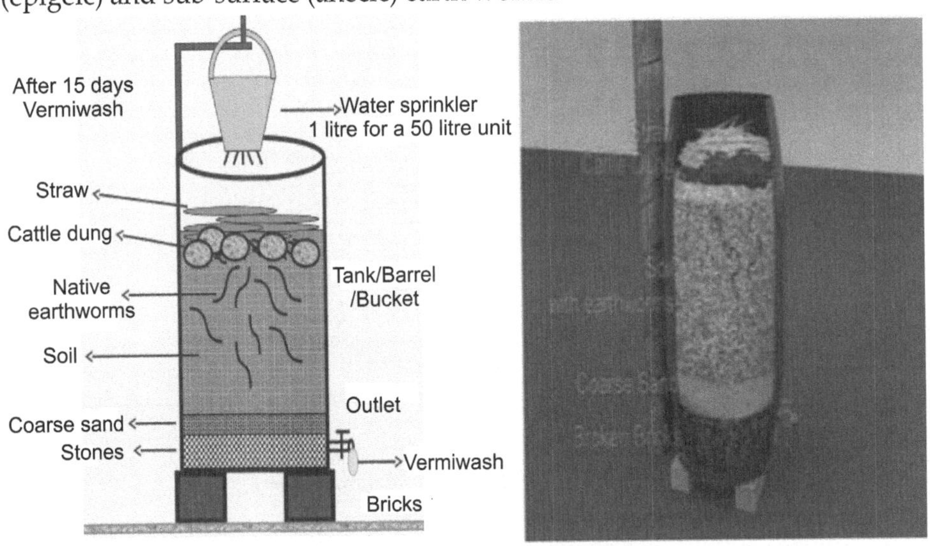

Fig. 11.3: Common method-2

Cattle dung pats and hay is placed on top of the soil layer and gently moistened. The tap is kept open for the next 15 days. Water is added every day to keep the unit moist. On the 16th day, the tap is closed and on top of the unit a metal container or mud pot perforated at the base as a sprinkler is suspended. About 5 liters of water (the volume of water taken in this container is one fifth of the size of the main container) is pured into this container and allowed to gradually sprinkle on the barrel overnight. This water percolates through the compost, the burrows of the earthworms and gets collected at the base. The tap of the unit is opened the next day morning and the vermiwash is collected. The tap is then closed and the suspended pot is refilled with 5 liters of water that evening to be collected again the following morning. Dung pats and hay may be replaced periodically based on need. The entire set up may be emptied and reset between 10 and 12 months of use.

Common Method–3 (Integrated Vermiwash Unit)

Vermiwash can also be prepared from vermicompost by allowing water to pass through vermicompost container and collecting it (Fig. 11.4). Verminwash unit may be established with vermicomposting beds for large scale production. The tap should be always kept open to collect the washings. The unit starts yielding good quality vermiwash after 10 days. The vermiwash should be stored in cool dry place. Water should be poured slowly. Do not mix undecomposed material while watering. Do not add any green material. Do not allow to compact the contents.

Fig. 11.4: Common method–3

Extraction of Vermiwash

Vermiwash extracted from vermiwash collecting device. The apparatus made from plastic or metals drum having capacity of 2 liter and a tap at the bottom the drum filled with broken breaks, about 10cm thickened which is followed by sand layer of 2-3 cm thickness lastly with filled with vermicompost with heavy population of earth worms simultaneously added fresh water in to drum and a container kept bellow the tap of drum. The watery extract of vermicompost, vermiwash drained out of drum. The colure of vermiwash ranges from yellowish to black. After 1 to 2 days the process of extraction has been completed. The different concentrations of collected vermiwash were used for foliar spray on crops.

Benefits of Vermiwash Unit

- It is a livelihood micro-enterprise for rural women.
- It helps less reliance on purchased inputs of nutrients leading to low cost of production.
- It increases soil productivity through improved soil quality.
- It helps for better quantity and quality of crops
- For landless labour provides additional source of income generation.
- It is a cost effective pollution abatement technology for industries.
- It creates no waste, no pollution, as they become valuable raw material for enhancing soil fertility.
- It boosts rural economy.
- It helps less wasteland formation.

Applications

1, The seedlings before transplanting are dipped in vermiwash solution which is diluted 5 times with water for 15 – 20 minutes and then transplanted.

2. Mix 1 litres of vermin wash with 7-10 litres of water and spray the solution in the leaf (upper and lower side) in the evening at the growing the crop.
3. Mix 1 litre of vermin wash with 1 litre of cow urine and then add 10 litres of water to the vermin urine solution and mixed thoroughly and keep it over night before spraying 50-60 litre of such solution and to be sprayed in one bigha of land to control various crop diseases.
4. Vermiwash is diluted 10 times with water and the soil is drenched with solution to prevent some of the soil borne pathogens.

Benefits of Vermiwash

- It is a liquid macro and micronutrients used as foliar spray.
- It contains sugars, phenols, amino acids, hormones and plant growth substances like IAA, GA_3, cytokinin and humic acids, etc.
- It contains beneficial microbes which help in plant growth.
- It helps to reduce many plant pests /diseases.
- It helps in initiating good flowering and produce good yield in some vegetable crops.
- It is a liquid fertilizer and reported that at 20 – 30% dilution inhibits the mycelial growth of pathogenic fungi.
- It acts as a biopesticide when diluted with 10% cow urine or neem extracts or garlic extract.

- It does not have any adverse effect on soil, plant and environment.
- It improves soil aeration, texture and tilth thereby reducing soil compaction.
- It improves water retention capacity of soil because of its high organic matter content.
- It promotes better root growth and nutrient absorption.
- It improves nutrient status of soil.
- It can also be added to compost pits to hasten the degradation process.
- It is a caulomic fluid extraction which has enzymes which stimulate the growth and yield of crops.

Effect of Vermiwash on Growth of Crop

Vermiwash is very good liquid manure and affect significantly on the growth and productivity of crop during foliar spray (Subasashri, 2003). Application of 100% RDF + vermiwash @100 litres/ ha was recorded significantly the highest plant height, number of primary branches, number of secondary branches, leaf area index and dry matter accumulation as compare to Other Treatments (Verma*et al.,* 2017). Manuring with vermicompost or in combination with foliar spray of vermiwash (5 or 10%) recorded higher number of pods plant-1 (12.7-15.8) as compared to that in untreated control (7.9 pods /plant) and positively influenced nodulation and plant growth, and significantly increased number of pods per plant, number of seeds per pod(Mahto and Yadav, 2005). Suthar *et al.,* (2005) reported that significant effect of vermiwash on the seed germination and development of legumes. Rao and Chandra (2005) studied that vermiwash is an effective liquid fertilizers initiation and lasting inflorescence of *Anthoriums*. Large amount of humic acid present in vermiwash which produced during vermicomposting and has been positive effect on the growth (Atiyeh *et al.,* 2002; Arancon *et al.,* 2003 and Ramamoorthy, 2004).

Tiwari and Singh (2016) reported that foliar applications of combinations of vermiwash obtained from animal dung and MSW with bio-pesticides neem (*Azadiracta indica*) oil, aquous extract of leaf, bark and vermiwash alone caused significant growth, start early flowering, enhance productivity of tomato crop. The highest growth of tomato (50.09 ± 1.29 cm) and maximum significant early flowering were observed after foliar application of mixture of vermiwash with neem oil in ratio of (2:1) whereas, the maximum significant early flowering period obtained after treatment of vermiwash of buffalo dung and MSW (2:1 ratio) with neem oil. Different combinations of vermiwash (buffalo dung) + gram bran with neem oil and aqueous extract of garlic is effective for increased the growth, early flowering and enhanced the productivity of gram up to three times over control (Nath and Singh, 2015).

Combination of vermiwash obtained from buffalo dung + vegetable wastes with neem oil is very effective combination for growth and productivity of Soybean. It can be also stated that the use of foliar spray of vermiwash obtained from vermicomposts of buffalo dung + agro / kitchen wastes have sufficient potency to increase the growth, flowering, productivity and reduced pest's infestation of crop (Nath and Singh, 2011). Use of vermiwash extracted from vermicomposts of different combination of animal agro and kitchen wastes, is one of the effective liquid bio fertilizer for growth and productivity of crops. The present study assesses that it has caused significant effect on the growth and productivity of paddy (*Oryza sativa*), maize (*Zea mays*) and millet (*Penisetum typhoides*) crops. The 10mg m^{-2} of vermiwash buffalo dung with straw shows significant growth (89.2 ± 2.7cm) and 30mg m^{-2} concentration of similar combination shows highly significant growth in paddy crops (102.6 ± 2.3 cm) after 75 days. The 10mg m^{-2} concentration of combination horse dung with gram bran caused significant growth (85.2 ± 4.3 cm) 50 days while at the same time 30 mg m^{-2} concentration of combination of straw with buffalo dung and horse dung caused highly significant growth in maize crops. The combinations of buffalo dung with gram bran and with straw; and combination of horse dung with gram bran and with straw have significant growth in millet crops.

All the concentrations of different combinations of animal agro and kitchen wastes have significant early start in flowering and enhance the productivity of crops (Nath and Singh, 2012). Vermiwash at a higher dilution is able to bring about increased germination rate and enhanced seedling growth in plants studied. The degree of response of the plants has varied and this could be attributed to the physiology of the plants under consideration and the concentration of vermiwash needs to be standardized to suit the plant to which it is applied (Anasri and Kumar, 2010). Nutrients and growth promoting substances present in the vermiwash showed its potentiality in seed germination and seedling vigour (Chattopadhyay, 2015). The vermiwash were found to significantly increase the growth parameters of the mulberry plant and enhance the nutritive level of the mulberry leaves. Such leaves fed to the silkworm larvae (*Bombex mori* L) showed a significant positive effect on larval growth in terms of larval and silk gland weights and cocoon characters including fresh wet cocoon weights, wet weights of de-flossed cocoons, dry weight of de-flossed cocoons, and shell ratio percent as compared with controls (Rawgol *et al.*, 2011).

Kumar *et al.*, (2013) observed that the application of vermiwash enhanced plant height and number of leaves (56.29 cm and 6.14 days at 45 days after bud emergence), spike length and rachis (90.68 cm and 47.07 cm), number of florets (15.08), vase-life (10.02 day) number of corms m^{-2} (28.66), weight of corms (50.68 g) and number of cormels /plant (56.66). Same treatment was also effective to reduce number of days taken to spike emergence (81.73 day). Nath and

Singh (2016) reported that the effect of vermiwash of different vermicomposts of animal agro and kitchen wastes observed on the growth, flowering periods and productivity of different *Rabi* crops viz. wheat, gram, pea and mustered. In case of wheat after 30 days of sowing the vermiwash of combination of goat dung with wheat and goat dung with vegetable wastes shows higher 26.20 ± 0.97 and 26.45 ± 0.53 cm growth respectively, whereas the maximum growth 65.00 ± 0.88 observed in conc. of 30 mg m^{-2} of combination of buffalo dung with rice bran. The significant productivity observed in combination of buffalo dung with rice bran i.e. 0.496 ± 0.01 kg m^{-2} which is followed by the treatment of 10 mg m^{-2} concentration buffalo dung with rice bran. The highest significant productivity recorded in goat dung with wheat bran i.e. 0.621 ± 0.06 kg m^{-2} conc. in 30 mg m^{-2}. Chauhan and Singh (2015) reported that the significance germination of okra seed in vermiwash with aqueous extract of neem bark (VW+NB) 97 ± 5.21% than other combinations and early germination was observed (11.48 ± 0.49 days). The maximum height of okra 42.42 ± 0.79 cm was observed in after 90 days by sprays of VW+NB. The combination of VW + NF was important for high productivity of okra. The maximum productivity of okra plant was observed 773.23 ± 20.64 g m^{-2} in treated with VW + NF.

Effect of Vermiwash on Yield Attribute and Yield

Adams (1986) reported that vermiwash application had a positive effect inbringing colour to tomato fruits, since nitrogen is the main component for synthesisof lycopene along with other micronutrients.Ismail (1995) reported that vermiwash was very effective for foliar application of nurseries, lawns and orchids.Ismail (1997) reported that vermiwash was very effective for foliarapplication of nurseries, lawns and orchids.Lozek and Gracova (1999) reported that vermisol application increased yield by 7.3 per cent and resulted indecrease in fruit nitrate content by 15 per cent. Thangavel *et al.* (2003) showed that both vermiwash and vermicast extractsincreased the growth and yield of paddy. Maximum plant height (68.5 cm), grainyield (6.7 t/ha) and straw yield (7.65 t/ha) were achieved with 100 per centvermiwash extract.

Karuna *et al.* (1999) revealed that foliar applied earthworm exudates showed better growth of cut flowers than other treatments. Karuna *et al.* (1999) revealed the effect of foliar applied earthworm exudates on the production of cut flowers (Crinkle Red Variety *ofAnthurium and reanum* Lind) and results were compared with treatment receiving foliar applied urea (0.05%). The best yield of quality flowers was obtained in the 50 % exudates treatments. Vermiwash is earthworm's body fluid which is a rich source of nutrients, enzymes and growth regulators like cytokinins, minerals, amino acids and vitamins. It was found to be an excellent spray material for improving growth and yield of the crop (Pathak and Ram, 2002).

Giraddi *et al.* (2003)observed significantly lower leaf curl of chilli applied with vermiwash (soil drench 30 DAT), foliar spray 60 and 75 DAT) and higher yields vis-à-vis untreated crop. However, it wasinferior to other organics like vermicompost, neem cake application to soil.Among the various yield attributes studied, yield and number of seeds per fruit were significantly influenced by various levels of vermiwash, but not fruit size. Maximum number ofseeds per fruit was produced under vermiwash 50% + full NPK applied plots. Higher fruityield of 18.35 t/ha was obtained in the treatment receiving 50% concentration of vermiwashand full dose of NPK (Ranijasmin *et al.*, 2003).

Sivasubramanian and Ganeshkumar (2004) reported that the vermiwash-spray enhanced the growth parameters *i.e.* plant height (75.08 cm), number oflaterals (18.17), number of leaves per plant (94.30) and leaf area (87.10 cm^2) overcontrol (67.73 cm,15.33, 84.83and 74.96 cm^2, respectively) in African Marigold inTamil Nadu in a pot culture experiment. Yield parameters like number of days toflowering (40.2 days), number of flowers per plant (28.3) and flower weight(168.30g) was increased due to foliar application of vermiwash. The mean numberof days taken to flower was distinctly low in vermiwash treatment. It wassuggested that extracts from earthworms offer a valuable resource which could beeffectively exploited for increasing the production of ornamentals like marigold.

Table 11.4: Effect of Different Organic Sources on Fruit Set, Fruit Yield and Fruit Firmness of Apricot

Treatments	Fruit set (%)	Fruit yield (kg/tree)	Firmness (kg/cm^)
A1 B1U1V1	50.23	24.35	5.68
A1 B1U1V2	50.38	24.35	5.77
A1 B1U2V1	50.36	24.40	5.79
A1 B1U2V2	50.44	24.47	5.99
A1 B2U1V1	50.52	24.43	6.11
A1 B2U1V2	50.59	24.35	6.16
A1 B2U2V1	50.67	24.46	6.22
A1 B2U2V2	50.77	24.37	6.37
A2 B1U1V1	57.14	25.84	6.60
A2 B1U1V2	57.22	25.92	6.65
A2 B1U2V1	57.28	26.00	6.70
A2 B1U2V2	57.39	25.94	6.74
A2 B2U1V1	57.49	26.25	6.77
A2 B2U1V2	57.55	26.40	6.80
A2B2U2V1	57.59	26.26	6.85
A2 B2U2V2	59.63	27.06	6.88

A3 B1U1V1	57.67	26.45	7.04
A3 B1U1V2	59.59	26.57	7.11
A3 B1U2V1	59.65	26.83	7.15
A3 B1U2V2	59.88	26.88	7.24
A3 B2U1V1	59.92	26.93	7.34
A3 B2U1V2	59.89	27.01	7.30
A3B2U2V1	59.94	26.92	7.39
A3 B2U2V2	59.99	26.95	7.40
Control	57.13	25.74	6.06
CD 5%	0.04	0.22	0.21

(Meera Devi, 2006).

A_1 : Vermicompost 30 kg /tree, A_2 : Vermicompost 40 kg /tree, A_3 : Vermicompost 50 kg /tree, B_1: Biofertilizer 40 g/ tree, B2: Biofertilizer 60 g/ tree, U_1: Cow urine 1:4 (Cow urine:water), U_2: Cow urine 1:8 (Cow urine:water), V_1: Vermiwash 1:4 (Venniwash:water), V_2: Vermiwash 1:8 (Venniwash:water), Control: Recommended doses of NPK + FYM

At Solan (Himachal Pradesh), vermicompost (50 kg/tree) + bio fertilizers (60 g/tree) + cow urine (1:8) + vermiwash (1:8) during the year 2005 and vermicompost (40 kg /tree) + bio fertilizers (60 g /tree) + cow urine (1:8) + vermiwash (1:8) during the year 2006 was found to be most effective in producing better growth, yield, quality of apricot cv. New Castle and increased leaf and available soil nutrient status (Table 4). However, increased physical and biological properties (organic carbon, water holding capacity, particle density, porosity, *Azotobacter sp., Pseudomonas sp., Bacillus sp.* and VAM spore population) of soil was observed with vermicompost (50 kg /tree) + biofertilizers (60 g /tree) + cow urine (1:8) + vermiwash (1:8) during both the years (Meera Devi, 2006).

Ansari (2008) carried out the investigation to study the effect of vermicompost and vermiwash in reclaimed sodic soils on the productivity of onion during 1998-2000 in Lucknow (India). The yield of onion was significantly higher in plots treated with vermiwash (1:10 v/v in water), whereas the average weight of onion bulbs was significantly greater in plots amended with vermicompost and vermiwash (1:5 v/v in water).Gorakh Nath and Keshav Singh (2009) reported that vermiwashsignificantly increased growth and productivity and decreased flowering period.Maximum significant growth was observed in 30 mg/m^2 concentration ofcombination of buffalo dung with rice bran 38.0 ± 1.3 cm. in case of okra, 30 mg m^{-2} concentration of combination of buffalo dung with gram bran (seed of*Cicer arientinum*) 215.5 ± 5.2 cm., in lobia crops and 30 mg/m^2 concentration ofbuffalo dung with gram bran 20.4 ± 1.4 cm. The significant early start of floweringand increase in productivity was found in all treated groups with respect to control.

Venkataramana *et al.* (2009) studied the influence of foliar sprays ofvermiwash (VW) and cow dung wash (CDW) on leaf yield and leaf attributingparameters in comparison to control in Mulberry. It was found that the leaf yield (72600 kg/ha/year) and yield attributing parameters such as plant height (199.50 cm), length of shoot (189 cm), number of branches (13.00/ plant),number of leaves (155/plant), weight of leaves (1.200 kg/plant), leaf moisturecontent (73 per cent) and leaf moisture retention capacity (85 per cent) weresignificantly higher in 200 ppm vermiwash, followed by 200 ppm cow dung wash, 150 and 100 ppm vermiwash and 150 and 100 ppm cow dung wash treatment in adescending order. Tharmaraj *et al.* (2010) reported that the vermi-product treated plantsexhibited faster and higher growth rate and productivity than the control plants. Itwas found that among the treated group, the growth rate was high in the mixture ofvermicompost and vermiwash treated plants, than the vermicompost andvermiwash un-treated plants in Black Gram. The maximum range of some plantparameters like number of leaves (33.1 ± 0.21), leaf length (4.1 ± 0.03 cm), height (9.5 ± 0.42 cm) and root length of plant (7.1 ± 0.10cm), were recorded in themixture of vermicompost and vermiwash.

Karuppaiah *et al.* (2011) studied the effect of foliar application of organicnutrients (Vermiwash, Panchakavya, Humic acid and Tender Coconut Water) ongrowth, flowering and flower quality of Dendrobium orchid cv. Sakura Pink. Theresults revealed that foliar spray of vermiwash 1 per cent at 4 days interval foundto be optimum for flower quality of *Dendrobium orchid*. Even thoughrecommended dose of chemical fertilizers recorded higher values in vegetativegrowth and flowering characters however, it was on par with the plants treatedwith vermiwash 1 per cent at 4 days interval.Rajan and Murugesan (2012) studied the influence of vermiwash (50, 75 and 100 per cent) on germination and growth of cow pea (*Vigna ungiculata)* andrice (*Oryza sativa)* grown for a period of 25 days and increased vigor index wasfound in rice exposed to different concentrations of vermiwash. Growth parameterswere higher in 75 and 100 per cent of vermiwash sprayed in cow pea and rice. Karuppasamy and Lourdu (2013) observed that foliar spray of vermiwashin mulberry increased the physical parameters like number of buds, number ofleaves and weight of leaves.When *H.sabdariffa* and *P. anrens* seeds were planted in the soil containing10 % vermiwash resulted in increased root and hypocotyls lengthof vegetable crops (Fathimaand Sekar, 2014).

Application of 100% RDF + vermiwash @100 litres/ ha was recorded significantly the highest pods /plant, grains /pod, test weight, grain and stalk yield of pigeon pea as compare to other treatments (Verma, 2016). Foliar spray of vermiwash (at 50 litres/ha) and water at 15, 35 and 50 days of crop age and the water spray was given to the remaining plots as per treatment. The foliar spray of vermiwash recorded higher number of branches (3.23) over water spray (2.96). The mean grain yield was significantly higher (10.42 q /ha) with vermiwash compared to water spray (9.68 q /ha) (Khairnar *et al.*, 2012). Effect of vermi products and found that combined uses of vermicompost + vermiwash (5 or 10%) gave higher fresh yield of vegetable pea /plant by approximately 70% over control (Mahto and Yadav, 2005). Nath and Singh (2009b) observed that different combination of vermiwash of animal and kitchen wastes have better growth and productivity of crops. The vermiwash is less expensive than chemical fertilizers, easily producible, eco-friendly and one of the best organic manure for foliar spray on the different crops.

Ansari and Kumar (2010) study revealed that combination of vermicompost and vermiwash combination [VW+VC] showed a significantly greater yield response of okra by 64.27% as compared with the control. Esakkiammal *et al.*, (2015) reported that the combination of vermicompost and vermiwash showed maximum positive effects on the growth and yield of lablab beans. Application of vermiwash increases growth, flowering and corm yield characters of gladiolus when they are applied along with recommended fertilizers doses (Kumar *et al.*, 2013). At Kittur (Karnataka), significantly higher mean annual fresh leaf yield of 5.79 kg per plant was obtained by foliar spray of vermiwash at 50% dilution compared to 5.05 kg in control. Among nutritional treatments, the recommended dose of fertilizer (RDF) + farm yard manure (FYM) with vermiwash foliar spray at 50% dilution, recorded higher annual fresh leaf yield (8.00 kg/plant) followed by FYM + RDF without foliar spray of vermiwash (6.95 kg/plant) and FYM along with vermiwash (6.60 kg/plant), compared to control (2.92 kg/plant). Foliar spray of vermiwash at monthly intervals also recorded slightly higher essential oil content in fresh leaves (0.44%), compared to control (0.42%) in curry leafcrop Cv. Suvasini (Hegde*et al.*, 2012).

At Bengaluru (Karnataka), application of enriched bio digested liquid manure (EBDLM) at 125 kg N equivalent (eq.)/ha + 3 sprays of panchagavya (3%) or vermiwash recorded significantly higher plant height (87.0 cm), branches/plant (32.9), leaf-area index (2.00), leaf-area duration (51.9 days), total dry-matter production/plant (105.7 g), dry fruit yield (0.90 t/ha), fruits/plant (39.0), 100fruit weight (135.1 g), fruit length (14.4 cm), ascorbic acid (137.3 mg/100 g) capsaicin content (0.64%), total extractable colour (280.8 ASTA units), oleoresin content of chilli (*Capsicum annuum* L.) (15.4%), gross return (1,51,668), net returns (96,281), benefit: cost (2.74) ratio, and significantly higher soil organic carbon (0.63%), available nitrogen (377.9 kg/ha), phosphorus (87.3 kg/ha), potassium (206.7 kg/ha), bacteria (37.0×10^6 cfu/g soil), fungi (23.2×10^3 cfu/g soil) and Actinomycetes (13.2×10^3 cfu/g soil) population as compared to the controlduring the rainy (kharif) season in sandy clay loam soils (Gopakkali Pradeep and Sharanappa, 2014).

Plants treated with vermiwash had the taller plants, longer pods, number of pods per plant, number of lateral branches and number of pods, but the higher plant dry weight and longer internodes were from plants treated with vermicompost leachate @ 7 t/ha. Vermiwash combined with vermicompost leachate negatively affected vegetative characteristics and yield. With leaching, the negative effects of vermicompost related to high electrical conductivity decreased and continuous application of this material may be possible. Vermicompost leachate and vermiwash can be used as fertilizer for sustainable French dwarf bean (*Phaseolus vulgaris* L.) cultivation(Ayyobi *et al.,* 2014). Meghvansi *et al.* (2014) reported that in okra, foliar spray of 20% vermiwash exhibited the larger increase in marketable weight among all the treatments. The plants of Naga chilli receiving foliar spray of 20% vermiwash registered a 27.47% increase in shoot height and 11.93% increase in chlorophyll content (SPAD) as compared with control. In regards to yield attributes of the Naga chilli, foliar spray of 20% vermiwash resulted in a 23.07% increase in number of seeds per fruit and 43.47% increase in average fruit weight in comparison with control.

Table 11.5: Yield Parameters and Bulb Yield as Influenced by Various Organic Sources of Nutrients

Treatment	Fresh weight of bulb (cm)	Neck diameter (cm)	Bulb diameter (cm)	Bulb length (cm)	Bulb yield (t/ ha)
BDLM at 75 kg N eq./ha	93.0	0.84	3.63	3.75	20.9
BDLM at 75 kg N eq./ha + 3 sprays of vermiwash 3%	94.6	0.87	3.67	3.82	22.1
BDLM at 75 kg N eq./ha + 3 sprays of panchagavya 3%	95.0	0.89	3.69	3.83	22.6
BDLM at 100 kg N eq./ha	125.8	1.19	5.15	4.78	34.1
BDLM at 100 kg N eq./ha + 3 sprays of vermiwash 3%	126.3	1.20	5.17	4.80	34.8
BDLM at 100 kg N eq./ha + 3 sprays of panchagavya 3%	126.9	1.22	5.20	4.82	35.3
EBDLM at 75 kg N eq./ha	109.6	1.03	4.38	4.28	27.6
EBDLM at 75 kg N eq./ha + 3 sprays of vermiwash 3%	111.0	1.04	4.40	4.28	28.5
EBDLM at 75 kg N eq./ha + 3 sprays of panchagavya 3%	111.2	1.06	4.43	4.33	28.9
EBDLM at 100 kg N eq./ha	141.4	1.35	5.92	5.27	40.3
EBDLM at 100 kg N eq./ha + 3 sprays of vermiwash 3%	142.8	1.38	5.97	5.30	41.8
EBDLM at 100 kg N eq./ha + 3 sprays of panchagavya 3%	143.7	1.42	6.02	5.36	42.8
RDF (30 t FYM + 125:50:75 kg NPK/ha)	139.0	1.36	5.92	5.27	35.9
CD 5 %	14.7	0.12	0.68	0.43	7.0

(Pradeepand Sharanappa, 2014)

At Bengaluru, (Karnataka), application of enriched biodigested liquid manure (EBDLM) at 100 kg N equivalent/ha + 3 sprays of panchagavya 3% recorded higher fresh weight of bulb (143.7 g), bulb yield (42.8 tonnes/ha), neck diameter (1.42 cm), bulb diameter (6.02 cm), bulb length (5.36 cm) and bulb size index (32.26 cm^2/bulbwhich was followed by application of EBDLM at 100 kg N equivalent/ha + 3 sprays of vermiwash3% (Table 5)(Pradeepand Sharanappa, 2014).

Tiwari and Singh (2015) reported that the foliar application of aqueous mixture of combination of vemiwash with neem oil, leaf and bark have increased the brinjal plant growth, early flowering, increased productivity. At Gorakhpur (Uttar Pradesh), vermiwash of vermicompost of goat dung with vegetable wastes 10 mg/m^2 shows significant growth in wheat which is followed by goat dung with wheat bran after 30 days of showing. After 50 days the combination of buffalo dung with vegetable wastes show significant growth in case of wheat crops. The combination of buffalo dung with gram bran gives highly significant growth of gram plant. The combination of horse dung with gram bran has maximum growth in mustard and pea plants. The foliar spray of all the different concentration of vermiwash has significant decreasing in flowering period of all the Rabi crops (wheat, gram, pea and mustard). The maximum significant productivity observed in crops treated with different concentration of vermiwash (10, 20 and 30 mg/m^2 using foliar spray)with respect to control (Gorakh and Keshav Singh,2016). Organic formulations could be a potent source to improve crop productivity and quality and additionally control of pest and diseases. This could additionally make a possibility elective to fertigation which is becoming common in most of the crops (Verma *et al.*, 2017).

Table 11.6: Effect of Vermiwash and Vermicompost on Okra

Treatments	Plant height (cm)	Leaves/ plant	Stem girth (cm)	Marketable yield	Fats (%)	Protein (%)
Control	31.67	9	2.23	24.69	0.52	3.41
Cattle dung	36.00	10	2.50	31.63	1.78	6.37
Urea	44.33	14	3.77	75.43	2.68	5.73
Vermiwash	42.33	11	2.47	30.36	3.00	6.35
Vermicompost	39.33	12	3.17	59.04	3.15	6.82
Vermiwash + Vermicompost	45.83	13	3.10	69.11	3.52	7.15
CD 5 %	12.48	3.8	1.26	4.29	NS	NS

(Ansari and Kumar, 2010)

Kale (1998) reported that vermiwash as foliar spray was effective in increasing the growth and yield response of anthurium. Hatti *et al.* (2010)

reported that the seedling of *Vigna munga, Vigna radiate, Sesamum indicum,* resulted in increases of growth of parameters lie the root length, shoot length, number of twigs and leaves and total biomass of the plant after spraying the vermiwash of *Perionyx excavates.* Similarly, Muscolo *et al.* (1999) also found an auxin-likeeffect of earthworm-worked humic substances on cell growth and nitrogen metabolism in carrot. The beneficial effect of vermiwash was observed on okro by Ansari and Kumar (2010)(Table 11.6).

Table 11.7: Effect of Vermiwash on Spikes Yield, Corm Diameter, Corm Weight, Cormels Weight and Corms Yield of Gladiolus

Treatments	Spikes yield (Nos /ha)	Corm diameter (cm)	Corm weight / plant(g)	Cormels weight / plant (g)	Cormels / plant-	Corms yield (Nos / ha)
Vermiwash @ 5%	149829	6.00	56.82	16.41	30.59	149829
Vermiwash @ 10 %	149149	6.03	57.34	16.83	30.75	149149
Control	138095	5.06	42.79	12.85	24.63	138095
CD 5 %	3613	0.19	3.47	1.56	2.77	3613

(Tamrakar, 2016)

At Raipur (Chhattisgarh), both the levels (5 and 10 %) of vermiwash resulted significantly earlier 50 per cent emergence of corms, increased emergence of plants, plant height, length and number of leaf at 30 and 60 DAP and width of leaf at 60 DAP; earlier 50 per cent initiation, first and 50 per cent colour break, 50 per cent flowering; increased length of spikes and rachis, durability of a spike and flowering duration, diameter of basal floret and number of spikes hectare, beside this increasing the diameter of corm, weight and number of corm and cormels per plant as well as yield of gladiolus var. Candyman in comparison to control (water spray) (Table 11.7) (Tamrakar, 2016).

Table 11.8: Effect of Vermiwash Spray on Yield Parameters and Yield of Radish

Treatments	Single radish weight (g)	Total yield (t/ha)	Marketable yield (t/ha)
water + vermiwash (1:1)	84.40	56.26	42.20
water + vermiwash (1:2)	86.06	57.37	43.03
water + vermiwash (1:3)	88.68	59.11	44.34
water + vermiwash (1:4)	90.90	60.59	45.45
Control	80.06	53.37	40.03
CD 5 %	6.50	4.33	3.25

(Jadhav *et al.*, 2015)

At Nare (Maharashtra), yield obtained with 100 % RDF as fertigation and vermiwash foliar twice times spray 1:4 at 15 and 30 days after sowing seeds was significantly higher than all other treatments in growth and yield attributes such as root diameter (5.53 cm), length (25.90 cm), weight (90.90 g), yield/plot (18.18 kg), yield/ha (60.59 t/ha) and marketable yield (45.45 t/ha) of radish cv. Local variety (Table 8). Thus, it can be concluded that foliar spray of vermiwash (1:4) effective than control(Jadhav *et al.,* 2015).

Table 11.9: Effect of Vermiwash on Seedlings, Germination and Vigour of Green Gram

Treatments	Root length (cm)	Shoot length (cm)	Seedling height (cm)	Germi-nation (%)	Vigour-index
Control (water only)	3.0 ± 0.2	5.0± 0.3	8.0 ± 0.5	65 ± 5	520
Heat stress vermiwash: water (1:1)	3.0 ± 0.3	5.0 ± 0.3	8.0 ± 0.6	80 ±6	640
Heat stress vermiwash: water (1:5)	4.0 ± 0.4	4.0 ± 0.3	8.0 ± 0.7	80 ± 5	640
Cold stress vermiwash: water (1:1)	4.0 ± 0.2	4.5 ± 0.3	8.5 ± 0.5	70 ± 5	595
Cold stress vermiwash: water (1:5)	6.5 ± 0.8	10.0 ± 0.7	16.5 ± 1.5	100	1650
Vermiwash produced normally: water (1:1)	4.0 ± 0.6	6.0 ± 0.6	10.0 ± 1.2	80 ± 5	800
Vermiwash produced normally: water (1:5)	5.5 ± 0.9	6.0 ± 0.5	11.5 ± 1.4	95 ± 5	1092
Undiluted heat stress vermiwash	2.5 ± 0.2	3.0 ± 0.3	5.5 ± 0.5	85 ± 5	467
Undiluted cold stress vermiwash	2.0 ± 0.2	3.5 ± 0.2	5.5 ± 0.4	90 ± 5	495
Undiluted normally produced vermiwash	2.0 ± 0.1	3.0 ± 0.2	5.0 ± 0.3	90 ± 4	450

(Amita Chattopadhyay, 2015). (mean ± SD)

At Bhubaneswar (Odisha), vermiwash produced by cold stress diluted at the ratio of 1:5 showed 100% germination of mung seed followed by 1:5 ratio vermiwash produced naturally that resulted 95% of seed germination (Table 11.9). Undiluted vermiwash produced naturally and by cold stress showed 90% of germination ofmung seed than the undiluted vermiwash produced by heatstress. Cold stress produced vermiwash diluted with 1:5 ratio showed a vigour index of 1650 followed by naturally produced 1:5 ratio diluted vermiwash which showed a vigour index of 1092. However, the undiluted naturally produced vermiwashshowed the lowest vigour index of 450 (Amita Chattopadhyay, 2015).

Prabhu (2006) reported that vermiwash improved the germination percentage of the seeds andseedling vigour of seeds such as cowpea and paddy crops. This vermiwash contains enzymes, secretions of earthworms which would stimulate the growth and yield of crops and even develop resistance in crops receiving this spray (Shield 1982; Anand *et al.* 1995). The effect of vermiwash spray significantly increased dry chilli yield (George *et al.* 2007).

At Kermanshah (Iran), using vermicompost extracts (vermiwash with 80% sheep manure + 20% wheat straw and vermiwash with potato, lettuce, sheep manure- wheat straw) was responsive to the nutritional needs of tomato plant. These treatments acted better than control treatment (soil cultivation). Overall, it was found that the superiority of vermitea extracts over vermiwash extracts. Also the mixed treatment extracts functioned better than animal manure extracts (compost tea with 80% sheep manure + 20% wheat straw and compost tea with potato, lettuce, sheep manure) with respect to having needed rich elements and inserting significant effects on the morphological traits of tomato plant (Allahyari*et al.,* 2014).

At Gwalior (M.P), when vermiwash was sprayed on thetomato plants, it showed a significant growth of plants i.e. length of shoot as well as number of leaves per plant. Vermiwash when mixed with vermicompost increased the shoot length to 19.61±0.18 cm as compared to control 17.92±0.21 cm. when vermiwash was directly sprayed on the plants of tomato the length of shoot was recorded to be 19.72±0.30 cm which was higher as compared to control group 17.92±0.21 cm (Hemant*et al.,* 2013).

At Kudlu (Kerala), coconut leaf vermiwash (CLV) was produced fromactively vermicomposting coconut leaf litter + cowdung substrate (10: 1 w/w basis) by *Eudrilus* sp. Itsignificantly increased the seedling vigour index of cowpea and paddy at 1: 10 and 1: 15 dilutions inlaboratory trials (Table 11.10). Field trials carried out in red sandyloam soil (Arenic Paleustults) resulted in increase of 36% fresh biomass weight of cowpea with application of CLV at 1: 10 dilution. In maize, increase in cobyield by 5–10% and in bhendi (okra) 22–33% increasein fruit yield were recorded at 1 : 5 dilutions of CLV (Murali *et al.,* 2010).

Table 11.10: Effect of Coconut Leaf Vermiwash on Cob Yield and Fresh Biomass of Maize (Results are Values of 50 Plants Per Treatment)

Treatment	Cob yield (% change)	Cob weight (kg) (% change)	Fresh biomass (kg) (% change)
Control	42	3.1	9.07
CLV (1 : 5)	44 (+5%)	5.1 (+64%)	11.33 (+30%)
CLV (1 : 10)	45 (+7%)	4.4 (+42%)	9.87 (+9%)
CLV (1: 20)	46 (+10%)	4.8 (+29%)	9.24 (+2%)

(Murali*et al.,* 2010). CLV: coconut leaf vermiwash

Similarly, vermicompost leachate has also beenreported to be suitable as formulation for liquid fertilizer (Gutirréz-Miceli *et al.,* 2008) and other agricultural uses (Tejada *et al.,* 2008). Zaller (2006) had reportedthat foliar applications of vermicompost leachate improvedcertain quality parameters of tomatoes besides suppressing*Phytophthora* disease.Samadhiya *et al.* (2013) observed that both growth and development of tomato increased with the application of vermiwash andvermicast extracts.

At Malad (Mharashtra), yield obtained with 100% RDF as fertigation andvermiwash foliar thrice times spray of 2% at 15, 30 and 45 DAS had significantly higher plant height (84.10 cm), root length (18.37 cm), number of branches (6.80), total number of pods (34.48/plant), straw weight (0.85 kg/ plot), seed weight (1161 kg /ha) and straw weight (2833 kg / ha), respectively (Table 11.11). This treatment had maximum harvest index (29.03%), net maximum realization (₹ 39, 620.80 /ha) and cost benefit ratio (1:3.17) out all other treatments than control (Jadhav *et al.,* 2014).

Table 11.11: Effect of Different Levels of Vermiwash Spray on Yield of Fenugeek

Treatments	Seed yield (kg/ha)	Straw yield (kg/ha)
Control	841.33	2296.00
Spraying vermiwash 0.5 %	946.67	2468.00
Spraying vermiwash 1.0 %	1024.00	2602.67
Spraying vermiwash 1.5 %	1093.33	2736.00
Spraying vermiwash 2.0 %	1161.33	2833.73
CD 5 %	67.47	116

(Jadhav *et al.,* 2014).

Foliar application was made 200 l/ha with knapsack sprayer in the evening hours thrice at 15, 30 and 45 days after sowing.

Effect of Vermiwash on Quality of Grain

Maheshwari *et al.* (2004) compared the effect of foliar organic fertilizers and vermiwash at 1:3 and 1:5 (vermiwash : water ratio) on the quality of chilli and highest ascorbic acid content was observed in treatment combination of vermiwash at 1:5 with basal and top fertilizer dressing. Saha *et al.* (2005) reported that application of different organic fertilizers in the form of vermicompost and vermiwash was effective and comparable to the inorganic fertilizers in increasing the gel moisture, gel ash and aloin content. The organic *Aloea vera*thus produced is expected to be a better marketable product.

Table 11.12: Quality Parameters of Onion as Influenced by Various Organic Sources of Nutrients

Treatment	Ascorbic acid (mg/100 g)	TSS (%)	Reducing sugar (%)	Non-reducing sugar (%)	Total Sugar (%)
BDLM at 75 kg N eq./ha	20.3	10.5	3.15	7.51	10.66
BDLM at 75 kg N eq./ha + 3 sprays of vermiwash (3%)	21.0	10.6	3.24	7.58	10.82
BDLM at 75 kg N eq./ha + 3 sprays of panchagavya (3%)	21.7	10.7	3.28	7.66	10.95
BDLM at 100 kg N eq./ha	24.1	12.5	3.46	8.07	11.53
BDLM at 100 kg N eq./ha + 3 sprays of vermiwash (3%)	24.5	12.6	3.57	8.12	11.69
BDLM at 100 kg N eq./ha + 3 sprays of panchagavya (3%)	24.9	13.5	3.66	8.84	12.51
EBDLM at 75 kg N eq./ha	22.8	11.0	3.30	7.90	11.20
EBDLM at 75 kg N eq./ha + 3 sprays of vermiwash (3%)	23.2	11.1	3.34	7.94	11.28
EBDLM at 75 kg N eq./ha + 3 sprays of panchagavya (3%)	23.6	11.1	3.36	7.99	11.35
EBDLM at 100 kg N eq./ha	25.1	13.9	3.77	8.90	12.67
EBDLM at 100 kg N eq./ha + 3 sprays of vermiwash (3%)	25.4	14.2	3.81	8.96	12.78
EBDLM at 100 kg N eq./ha + 3 sprays of panchagavya (3%)	26.1	14.4	3.98	9.05	13.03
RDF (30 t FYM + 125:50:75 kg NPK/ha)	23.9	13.4	3.61	8.27	12.05
CD 5 %	1.9	1.7	0.39	0.91	1.00

(Pradeepand Sharanappa, 2014)

At Bengaluru, (Karnataka), application of enriched bio digested liquid manure (EBDLM) at 100 kg N equivalent/ha + 3 sprays of panchagavya (3%) recorded higher quality parameters viz., ascorbic acid (26.1 mg/100 g), total soluble solid (14.4%), reducing sugar (3.98%), non-reducing sugar (9.05%), total sugar (13.03%) which was comparable with application of EBDLM at

100 kg N equivalent/ha + 3 sprays of vermiwash 3% which was followed by application of EBDLM at 100 kg N equivalent/ha + 3 sprays of vermiwash 3% (Table 11.12) (Pradeep and Sharanappa, 2014).

The application of 100% RDF+vermiwash @100 litres/ ha was recorded highest protein yield as comparable to other treatments (Verma, 2016). Use of biological inputs and organic materials to improve the quality of crops and increase production without extension of cultivated lands is a significant issue in hydroponics (soilless culture) culture. The factors included two cultivars of tomato, and four nutrient solution (manure vermiwash, mixed vermiwash, manure compost tea, mixed compost tea), with soil bed as control. The results showed that the effect of nutrient solutions and interaction effect between variety and the nutrient solution were significant for all traits except for root dry weight. The results of qualitative traits analysis of extracts showed that the effect of nutrient solutions for the elements of phosphorus and potassium was not significant but for the other elements there were significant difference at the 1%level of probability (Allahyari *et al.*, 2014). Ansari and Kumar (2010) reported that combination of vermicompost and vermiwash [VW+VC] recorded greater percentage of fats and protein content in okra as compare to control. Edwards *et al.* (2004) have been reported that vermiwash influence the fruit quality. Organic formulations have potential to enhance the quality of crop (Verma *et al.*, 2017).

Effect of Vermiwash on Insect-pest

Combined uses of vermicompost + vermiwash (5 or 10%) gave better performance with lower pest infestation in vegetable pea by 24.26% over control (Mahto and Yadav, 2005). Organic formulations have to capacity to reduce pest and diseases infestation (Verma *et al.*, 2016). Foliar applications of combinations of vermiwash obtained from animal dung and MSW with bio-pesticides neem (*Azadiracta indica*) oil, aquous extract of leaf, bark and vermiwash alone caused significant reduction ($P > 0.05$) in pest infestation of tomato crop (Tiwari and Singh, 2016). Vermiwash (buffalo dung) + gram bran with neem oil and aqueous extract of garlic is effective for the control of pod borer infestation on gram plant (Nath and Singh, 2015). Gopalakrishnan *et al.* (2015) conducted an experiment on washings of vermicompost (called biowash or vermiwash) prepared from foliage of Jatropha (*Jatropha curcas*), Annona (*Annona squamosa*) and Parthenium (*Parthenium hysterophorus*) and evaluated against fungal pathogens viz. *Fusarium oxysporum* f. sp. ciceri (FOC; causes wilt in chickpea), *Sclerotium rolfsii* (causes collar rot in chickpea) and *Macrophomina phaseolina* (causes charcoal rot in sorghum). Crude biowash of the botanicals were partitioned against ethyl acetate and the resultant organic and aqueous fractions were tested against the fungi. Vermiwash acts as pesticide, disease curative and crop tonic and increase the yield of lab lab beans (Esakkiammal *et al.*, 2015).

Table 11.13: Influenced by Organics and Vermiwash Sprays on Number of Fruits, Dry Chilli Yield and Parasitoid Population

	Fruits (Nos/ plant)	Dry chilli yield (q/ha)	Coccinellids (Nos/plant) at 100 DAT	Chrysopids (Nos/ plant) at 100 DAT
VC 2.5 + VW (1:1)	73.11b	2.98ab	0.52 (0.994)a	0.51 (0.991)a
VC 2.5 + VW (1:2)	57.11cd	2.61bcd	0.45 (0.959)ab	0.45 (0.965)ab
VC 2.5 + VW (1:4)	46.59e	2.54bcd	0.37 (0.921)bc	0.44 (0.957)abc
NC 0.5 + VW (1:1)	66.32bc	2.96bc	0.50 (0.985)a	0.49 (0.983)a
NC 0.5 + VW (1:2)	48.42de	2.52bcd	0.45 (0.965)ab	0.43 (0.951)abc
NC 0.5 + VW (1:4)	40.30e	2.20cd	0.35 (0.912)bc	0.34 (0.921)bcd
VC 1.25 + NC 0.25 + VW (1:1)	66.14bc	2.93bc	0.44 (0.961)ab	0.39 (0.946)abc
VC 1.25 + NC 0.25 + VW (1:2)	44.05e	2.27cd	0.43 (0.955)ab	0.34 (0.907) bcd
VC 1.25 + NC 0.25 + VW (1:4)	39.48e	2.15d	0.31 (0.896)cd	0.33 (0.903)cd
RPP	88.02a	3.90a	0.21 (0.855) d	0.25 (0.871)d
CD 5%	10.01	0.72	0.54	0.05

Soumya George, 2006).
VC – Vermicompost, NC – Neem cake, RPP – Recommended package of practices, VW – Vermiwash, Figures in parenthesis are Öx + 0.5 transformed values.

At Dharwad (Karnataka), vermiwash foliar spray at 1:1 dilution proved better than 1:2 and 1:4 dilutions (Table 13). Vermicompost @ 2.5 t/ha at planting, vermiwash 1:1 seedling dip and foliar spray was mosteffective which registered significantly lower population of thrips, mites and leaf curl index,comparable to standard check (Table 11.9). This treatment also promoted higher plant height, number ofbranches, number of fruits per plant and yield (2.98 q/ha) of chilli (cv. Byadagi) being on par with check (3.90 q/ha) (Soumya George, 2006).

Mishra *et al.,* (2015) concluded that the vermiwash with bio-pesticide is the better option of the chemical fertilizer and pesticides for the management of *Leptocoryza varicornis* as well as productivity of rice crop. Since vermiwash is mild bio pesticides and plant allelochemicals in their combination shows synergistic effect reduce the *Leptocoryza varicornis* population which ultimately enhances the productivity. Mishra *et al.,* (2014) concluded that the vermiwash with bio-pesticide is the better option for the growth, productivity as well as management of *Lucinodes orbanalis* infestation on brinjal crop. The foliar spray of vermiwash provides necessary nutrients to the growing plant for elongation, early flowering and fruiting phase. The bio-pesticide are more effective against larvae and caterpillar of fruit and shoot borer without contamination of fruits, so it is the best alternative of chemical fertilizers and pesticides for management of *Lucinodesorbanalis* population and enhancement of the productivity of fruit yield.

Effect of Vermiwash on Soil Property

Organic formulations could be a potent source to move forward soil fertility (Verma *et al.*, 2017). Combination of vermicompost and vermiwash [VW+VC] recorded a significant influence on the biochemical characteristics of the soil with marked improvement in soil micronutrients and better qualitative improvement in the physical and chemical properties of the soil (Ansari and Kumar, 2010) . Tharmaraj *et al.* (2011) reported that soil treated with mixture of vermicompost and vermiwash had significantly improved soil physico-chemical properties comparison to unamended soil.

Role of Vermiwash in Sustainable of Crop Production

Vermiwash revealed potential application in sustainable development in agriculture biotechnology with respect to its origin, cost effectiveness, easily availability, time saving, reproducibility, reliability and eco-friendliness (Zambare *et al.*, 2008). It can be used as a potent bio-fertilizer to improve the germination and seedling survival rates in crop plants growing on nutrition depleted soils thus paving the way for sustainable agriculture using organic farming practices (Fathima and Sekar 2014). It could be utilized effectively for sustainable plant production at low input basis green farming (Edwards *et al.*, 2004). It recorded significant growth and productivity in the black gram (Sobha *et al.*, 2003). Weerasinghe *et al.*, (2006) have suggested that vermiwash is a natural growth supplements for tea, coconut and horticultural crops.

Conclusion

The effect of vermiwash was observed on the plants and it was found that the results obtained were almost similar to the results of vermicompost. The vermiwash proves to be an effective fertilizer which contributes the growth, yield of plants when sprayed directly as well as mixed with a definite ratio of fertilizer or manure. It was also observed that the plants treated with vermiwash were reduced insect-pest population. Experiment shows that vermiwash along with vermicompost can be used as a substituent of commercial fertilizers available in market however the effect of other parameters has to be analyzed.

REFERENCES

Adams, P. (1986). Mineral Nutrition. In The Tomato Crop, Artherton, J.G. and Rudish, J (Ed) Chapman and Hall Ltd., pp. 281-324.

Allahyari, S., S. J. Honarmand, M. Khoramivafa and H. Zolnorian (2014). Effect of Vermicompost Extracts (Compost Tea and Vermiwash) on the Vegetative Growth of Tomato (Lycopersicon Esculentum Mill) under Hydroponic Conditions. *International Journal of Biosciences,* 4 (11): 171-181.

Allahyari, S., S.J. Honarmand, M. Khoramivafa and H.Zolnorian(2014). Effect of Vermicompost Extracts (Compost Tea and Vermiwash) on the Vegetative Growth of

Tomato (*Lycopersicon esculentum* Mill) Under Hydroponic Conditions. *International Journal of Biosciences,* 4(11):171-181.

Amita Chattopadhyay (2015). Effect of Vermiwash of Eisenia Foetida Produced by Different Methods on Seed Germination of Green Mung, *Vigna radiate. International J. Recycl. Org. Waste Agric.,* 4:233–237.

Anand, J.A., M.D.P. Wilson and R.D. Kale (1995). Effect of Vermiwash on Seed Germination and Seedling Growth. *J. Soil Biol. Ecol.,* 15:90–95.

Ansari, A.A. (2008). Effect of Vermicompost and Vermiwash on the Productivity of Spinach (*Spinacia oleracea*), Onion (*Allium cepa* L.) and Potato (*Solanum tuberosum*). *World Journal of Agricultural Sciences* 4(5): 554-557.

Ansari, A.A. and S. Kumar (2010). Effect of Vermiwash and Vermicompost on Soil Parameters and Productivity of Okra (*Abelmoschus esculentus*) in Guyana. *African Journal of Agricultural Research,* 5 (14): 1794 - 1798.

Arancon, N.Q., S.Lee, C.A. Edwards and R.M.Atiyeh (2003). Effects of Humic Acids Derived from Cattle Food and Paper Waste Vermicomposts on the Growth of Green House Plant. *Pedobiologia,* 46: 17-19.

Atiyeh, R.M., N.Q. Arancon, C.A. Edwards and J.D. Metzger (2002). The Influence of Humic Acid Derived from Earthworms Processed Organic Wastes on the Plant Growth. *Biores. Technol.,* 13: 84-147.

Ayyobi, H., E. Hassanpour, S. Alaqemand, S. Fathi, J. A. Olfati and G. Peyvast (2014). Vermicompost Leachate and Vermiwash Enhance French Dwarf Bean Yield. *International Journal of Vegetable Science,* 20 (1): 21-27.

Buckerfield, J.C, T,Flavel, K.E, Lee and K.A.Webster (1999).Vermicompost Soil and Liquid form as Plant Growth Promoter. *Pedobiologia,* 42:753-759.

Chauhan, H.K., and K. Singh (2015).Potancy of Vermiwash with Neem Plant Parts on the Infestation of Eariasvittella (fabricius) and Productivity of Okra (*Abelmoschus esculentus*) (L.) Moench. *Asian Journal of Research in Pharmaceutical Science,* 5(1):36-40.

Edwards, C.A. and K.E. Fletcher (1998). The Use of Earthworm in Breakdown and Management of Organic Wastes. In: Edwards, C.A. (eds.) Earthworm Ecology. CRC Press Boca Raton, FI. pp. 329-354.

Edwards, C.A., J. Domínguez and N.Q. Arancon (2004). The Influence of Vermicomposts on Plant Growth and Pest Incidence. In, S.H Shakir and W.Z.A. Mikhaïl, (Eds. Soil Zoology for Sustainable Development in the 21st century, P: 397-420.

Esakkiammal, B., L. Lakshmibai and S.Sornalatha (2015). Studies on the Combined Effect of Vermicompost and Vermiwash Prepared from Organic Wastes by Earthworms on the Growth and Yield Parameters of Dolichous Lab lab. *Asian J. Pharmaceutical Sci. Technol.,* 5(4):246-252.

Fathima, M. and M.Sekar (2014). Studies on Growth Promoting Effects of Vermiwash on the Germination of Vegetable crops. *Int. J. Curr. Microbiol. App. Sci.,* 3(6):564-570.

George, S., R.S. Giraddi and R.H. Patil (2007). Utility of Vermiwash for the Management of Thrips and Mites on Chilli (*Capsicum annuum* L.) Amended with Soil Organics. *Karnataka J. Agric. Sci.,*20:657–659.

Giraddi, R.S., M.S. Smitha and B.B. Channappagoudar (2003). Organic Amendments for the Management of Chilli (cv. Byadagi kaddi) Insect Pests and their Influence on Crop Vigour. *Proceedings of National Seminar on Perspective Inspices, Medicinal and Aromatic plants,* ICAR Complex, Goa, 27-29 November 2003, pp. 361-365.

Gopakkali Pradeep and Sharanappa (2014). Effect of Organic Production Techniques on the Growth, Yield, Quality and Economics of Chilli (*Capsicum annuum*) and Soil Quality in Dry Zone of Karnataka. *Indian Journal of Agronomy*, 59 (1): 151-156.

Gopalakrishnan, S., I.G.K. Kannan, G. Alekhya and P.Soumya George (2015).Role of vermicompost, Vermiwash and other Organics in the Management of thrips and mites in chilli. M.Sc (Ag) Thesis, Department of Agricultural Entomology, College of Agriculture, University of Agricultural Sciences, Dharwad-580005, Karnataka.

Gorakh Nath, S.and D.K. Keshav Singh (2009). Utilization of Vermiwash Potential on Certain Summer Vegetable Crops. *Journal of Central European Agriculture*, 10(4): 24 – 27.

Gorakh Nath, S. and D.K. Keshav Singh (2009). Chemical Analysis of Vermicompost/ Vermiwash of Different Combination of Animal, Agro and Kitchen Wastes. *Aus. J. Bas. & Appl. Sci.*, 3(4):3672-3676.

Gorakh, Nath, S. and D.K. Keshav Singh (2016). Vermiwash: A potent liquid biofertilizer. *Research Journal of Science and Technology*, 8 (1): 24-32.

Gutirréz-Miceli, F. A., R.C. García-Gómez, R.R. Rosales, M. Abud-Archila, O.L.M. Angela, M.J.G. Cruz and L. Dendooven (2008), Formulation of Liquid Fertilizer for Sorghum (*Sorghumbicolor* (L.) Moench) using Vermicompost Leachate. *Bioresour. Technol.*, 99: 6174–6180.

Hatti S.S., R.L. Londonkar, S.B. Patil A.K. Gangawane and C.S. Patil (2010). Effect of Perionyx Excavatus Vermiwash on the Growth of Plants. *Journal of Crop Science*, 1 (1): 1- 5.

Hegde, N.K., R. Siddappa and S.I. Hanamashetti (2012). Response of Curry Leaf (*Murraya koenigii* spreng) 'Suvasini' for Foliar Spray of Vermiwash and Nutritional Treatments. *Acta Hortic.*, 933: 279-284.

Hemant, S., P. Dandotiya, J. Chaturvedi and O.P. Agrawal (2013).Effect of Vermiwash on the Growth and Development of Leaves and Stem of Tomato plants.*International Journal of Current Research*,5 (10): 3020 – 3023.

Ismail, S.A. (1995). Vermicompost and Vermiwash. In *Proceedings of National Workshop on Tropical Organic Farming*.UPASI Kottayam. Sept. 1995.

Ismail, S.A. (1997). Vermicology: The Biology of Earthworms. Orient Longman Ltd., Chennai, India.

Jadhav, P.B., A. Kireeti, D.J. Patel, S.S. Dekhane, N.B. Patil and S.J. Patil (2015). Utilization of Vermiwash Spray on Growth and Yield of Radish cv. Local Variety. *Intern. J. Forestry & Crop Improv.*, 6 (1) : 36-40.

Jadhav, P.B., N.B. Patil, S.N. Saravaiya, S.S. Dekhane, G.S. Tekale, N.B. Harad, K.P. Jadhav and D. J. Patel (2014). Effect of Different Level of Vermiwash Spray on Growth and Yield of Fenugeek cv. Local.*International Journal of Development Research*, 4 (8): 1547-1549.

Kale, R.D. (1998). Earthworms. Natures Gift for Utilization of Organic Wastes. In Earth Worms Ecology. Edwards, C.A (Ed.) CRC Press LLC. BOCCA. Raton, Florida. pp. 355- 376.

Karuna, K., C.R. Patil, P. Narayanswamy and R.D. Kale (1999). Stimulatory Effect of Earthworm Body Fluid (vermiwash) on Crinkle Red Variety *of Anthurium and reanum* Lind. *Crop Research (Hisar)*,17(2): 253-257.

Karuppaiah, P., S.R. Kumar and R. Sendhilnathan (2011). Studies on Effect Offoliar Application of Organic Nutrients on the Growth, Flowering and Flower Quality of Dendrobium Orchid's cv. Sakura Pink. *Advances in Plant Sciences*, 24(2): 609-612.

Karuppasamy, K. and I. Lourdu (2013). Effect of Vermiwash on the Growth of Mulberry Cuttings.*World Journal of Agricultural Sciences*, 9(1): 69-72.

Soumya George (2006). Role of Vermicompost, Vermiwash and Otherorganics in the Management of Thrips and Mites in Chilli. M.Sc (Ag) Thesis, Department of Agricultural Entomology, College of Agriculture, University of Agricultural Sciences, Dharwad-580005, Karnataka.

Subasashri, M. (2003). Vermiwash Collection and Its Pesticidal Properties. The Hindu, June, 17:1-2.

Suthar, S., R.R. Choyal , S.Singh and Sudesh (2005). Stimulatory Effect of Earthworm Body Fluid on Seed Germination and Seedlings Growth of Two Legumes. *J. Phytol. Res.*,1 (2); 219-222.

Tamrakar, S.K. (2016). Effect of Plant Growth Regulators, Vermiwash and Cow Urine on Vegetative Growth, Flowering, Corm Production and Vaselife of Gladiolus var. Candyman.Ph. D. Thesis, Department of Horticulture, College of Agriculture, Indira Gandhi Krishi Vishwavidyalaya, Raipur, Chhattisgarh.

Tejada, M., J.L. GonzalezM.T. Hernandez and L. Garcia (2008), Agricultural Use of Leachates Obtained from Two Different vermin Composting Processes. *Bioresour. Technol.*, 99: 6228–6232.

Thangavel, P., R. Balagurunathan, J. Divakaran and J.Prabakaran (2003). Effect ofvermiwash and Vermicast Extract on Soil Nutrients, Growth and Yield of Paddy. *Adv. Plant Sci*,16: 187–190.

Tharmaraj, K., P. Ganesh, K. Kolanjinathan, R. Suresh Kumar and A. Anandan (2011). Influence of Vermicompost and Vermiwash on Physico Chemical Properties of Rice Cultivated Soil. *Current Botany*, 2(3):18-21.

Tharmaraj, K.P., Ganesh, K. Kolanjinathan, R. Kumar, Suresh and A. Anandan (2010). Influence of Vermicompost and Vermiwash on Physico Chemical Properties of Black Gram Cultivated Soil. *International Journal of Recent Scientific Research*, 3: 77-83.

Tiwari, K.S. and K.Singh (2015). Potency of Combination of Liquid Biofertilizer with Biopesticide on Productivity of Brinjal and Infestation of Leucinodes Orbonalis (Pyraustidae: Lepidoptera). *Int. J Pure App. Biosci.*, 3(5):62-72.

Tiwari, K.S. and K. Singh (2016). Combined Effect of Liquid Biofertilizer with Biopesticide on Yield of Tomato (*Solanum lycopersicum* l.) and Infestation of *Helicoverpa armigera* (hubner). *J. Bio. Innov.*, 5(1):144-163.

Tripathi, G. and P. Bharadwaj (2004). Comparative Studies on Biomass Production, Life Cycles and Composting Effiency of *Eisenia foetida* (Savigny) and *Lampito mauritii* (Kingberg). *Biores. Technol.*, 92:275-278.

Umamaheswari, S., S. Viveka and G.S. Vijaylakshmi (2003). Indigenous Vermiwash Collecting Device. The Hindu, Jul. 17, p. 1-2.

Varghese, S.M. and M.L. Prabha (2014).Biochemical Characterization of Vermiwash and Its Effect on Growth of Capsicum Frutescens. *Malaya Journal of Biosciences*, 1(2):86-91.

Venkataramana, P., B. Murthy, R. Narasimha, J.V. Krishna and C.K. Kamble (2009). Efficacy of Foliar Sprays of Vermi Wash and Cow Dung Wash on Biochemical and Yield Attributes and Yield of Mulberry (*Morus alba*L.).*Karnataka J. Agric. Sci.*, 22(4): 921-923.

Verma, S. (2016). Bio-efficacy of Organic Formulations Along with Fertilizers on Growth, Yield and Quality of Pigeonpea [*Cajanus cajan*(L.) Millsp]. Ph.D Thesis, Institute of Agricultural Sciences, Banaras Hindu University, Varanasi, Uttar Pradesh.

Verma, S., A. Singh, S.S. Pradhan, R.K. Singh and J.P. Singh (2017). Bio-efficacy of Organic Formulations on Crop Production-A Review.*Int. J. Curr. Microbiol. App. Sci.*, 6(5):648-665.

Weersinghe, K.L.K., K.M. Mohotti, C.N. Herath, A. Sanarajeewa, V. Liyangunawardena, H.M.G.S.B. Hitinayake (2006). Biological and Chemical Properties of Vermiwash a Natural Plant Growth Suppliment for Tea, Coconut and Horticulture Crops 12 September Forestry and Environment Symposium, University of Jayewardenepura, Sri Lanka. p. 45.

Yadav, A.K., K. Kumar, S. Singh and M.Sharma (2005). Vermiwash-A Liquid Bio-fertilizer, Uttar Pradesh, *J. of Zoology*, 25(1):97-99.

Zaller, J.G.(2006), Foliar Spray of Vermicompost Extracts: Effects on Fruit Quality and Indications of Late-blight Suppression on Field Grown Tomatoes. *Biol. Agric. Hortic.*, 24: 165–180.

Zambare, V.P, M.V. Padul, A.A. Yadav and T.B. Shete (2008). Vermiwash: Biochemical and Microbiological Approach as Ecofriendly Soil Conditioner. *ARPN Journal of Agricultural and Biological Science*, 3 (4): 1 - 5.

Product Development and Waste Recycling **Pages 143-160**
Edited by: Pawan Kumar 'Bharti'
ISBN: 978-93-86841-94-0
Edition: 2019
Published by: Discovery Publishing House Pvt. Ltd., New Delhi (India)

12

Bioremediation-Application of Biotechnology in Waste Management

[1]Sanjana Ghosh, [2]Chiranjib Bhattacharjee, [3]Ranjana Das

ABSTRACT

The growth of manufacturing industries and agricultural sectors has outburst the occurrence of a wide range of 'xenobiotic' compounds to the environment. Excessive foot print of hazardous waste has lead to paucity of clean potable water and deterioration of soil quality, thereby limiting the agricultural developments. Maintenance of the quality life to fit the demands of society, newer developments in different sectors have led unfavorable environment condition with improper control and management. Economically and environmentally friendly approach of toxin removal has become crucial to maintain quality life. In this context, bioremediation of contaminated industrial sites has become a promising field of environmental biotechnology and bioremediation has experienced a remarkable development. The control and optimization of bioremediation processes is a complex art involving large operational factors including existence of a microbial population capable of degrading the pollutants, the availability of contaminants to the microbial population and the environment factors (type of soil, temperature, pH, the presence of oxygen or other electron acceptors, and nutrients). In principle, the bioremediation technique has some short of deficiencies and is limited for chlorinated organic and high aromatic hydrocarbons hence are difficult to clean-up in bioremediation exercise. Bioremediation techniques are typically more economical than conventional technologies with less or negligible possibilities of toxin production with reduced exposure risks for clean-up personnel and transportation allied accidents.

Introduction

The quality of life depends inextricably to quality of the environment. The natural resources are going to be depleted due to improper utilization planning and management and also become contaminated due to lack of awareness regarding waste disposal. The problem prevailing worldwide and number

[1,3]Chemical Engineering Department. Jadavpur University. 188, Raja S.C. Mullick Road, Kolkata-700032. India

of contaminants are also increasing with increasing industrial developments (Cairney 1993, Vidali 2001).

Improper industrial practices have resulted in large scale environmental contamination and pollution. The risk to human and environmental health is rising and there is evidence that this cocktail of pollutants is a contributor to the global epidemic of cancer, and other degenerative diseases. These pollutants belong to two main classes: inorganic and organic. Recent challenge to industries is to development of innovative and cost effective solutions to decontaminate polluted environments, to make environment safe for human habitation and consumption, to protect life supporting ecosystems (Prasad 2011). The conventional techniques of remediation involve digging up of contaminated soil and removing it for land filling, or to cap and contain the contaminated areas of a site. The conventional method simply moves the contamination elsewhere and may create significant risks in the excavation, handling, and transport of hazardous material. Additionally, it is becoming very difficult and expensive to locate new landfill sites for the final disposal of the material. The 'cap and contain' method is only an interim solution since the contamination remains on site, requiring monitoring and maintenance of the isolation barriers long into the future, with all the associated costs and potential liability.

An ecofriendly approach to completely destroy the pollutants with least possible formation of transformed products and to transform them to innocuous substances is 'bioremediation'. Some technologies that have been used are high-temperature incineration and various types of chemical decomposition (like, base-catalyzed dechlorination, UV oxidation). They can be very effective at reducing levels of a range of contaminants, but have several drawbacks, like technological complexity, the cost for small-scale application, and the lack of public acceptance, especially for incineration that may increase the exposure to contaminants for both the workers at the site and nearby residents

The principles, techniques, advantages, and disadvantages of bioremediation are not completely known to the site owners, regulators and waste management persons. In this text an effort has been made to present a straight forward and pragmatic view of the processes involved in bioremediation, the pros and cons of the technique, and the critical issues involved with the implementation of the technique. Some tests make an exhaustive examination of the literature of bioremediation of organic (King *et al.* 1997, National Research Council 1993, Norris *et al.* 1993, Vidali 2001) and inorganic pollutants (Hinchee *et al.* 1995, Vidali 2001), and another test takes a look at pertinent field application case histories (Flathman *et al.* 1993, Vidali 2001). Several research groups have presented detail information about the prospect of bioremediation process. These techniques operate through the principles of 'biogeochemical cycling'. If the processes transpire in the same place of pollution occurrence, then it is termed *'in-situ'* bioremediation. In contrast, deliberate relocation of the contaminated material (soil and water) to a different place to accelerate biocatalysis is referred to as *'ex-situ'* bioremediation. Bioremediation has been successfully applied for cleaning up of soil, sediments, groundwater and surface water, ecosystem restoration. It has been unambiguously illustrated in several research publications, about the efficiency of bioremediation in removing large variety of 'xenobiotics' (antioxidants, pesticides, antibiotic drugs, hydrocarbons and food additives). Bioremediation is generally considered to include natural attenuation (little or no human action), bio-stimulation or bio-augmentation, the deliberate addition of natural or engineered micro-organisms to accelerate the desired catalytic capabilities. Hence, 'bioremediation', 'phytoremediation' and 'rhizoremediation' contribute significantly to the fate of hazardous waste and can be used to remove these unwanted compounds from the biosphere (Ma *et al.* 2011, Schroeder and Schwitzguebel 2004, Prasad 2011). The complexity of bioremediation process, limitations and scope in the contemporary science are presented in Figure 1 (adopted from Prasad 2011). Transgenic plants engineered for the transformation of explosives and metabolic pathway engineering for degradation of xenobiotics are in progress (Abhilash *et al.* 2009, Van Aken, 2009, Prasad 2011). Herbicide phytoremediation using transgenics is one of the most successful examples. Plant physiology, agronomy, microbiology, hydrogeology, and engineering are combined to select the proper plant and conditions for a specific site. The specific mechanisms that are emphasized in an application depend on the mobility, solubility, degradability, and bioavailability of the contaminants of concern. Phytoremediation involves the use of certain plants to cleanup soil and water contaminated with inorganics and/or organics. The use and transformation of over thousands of individual compounds whose current locations are largely unknown have resulted in the establishment of new fields of research, which have one thing in common: they link ecological, physiological, and chemical/analytical lines. This complex system of interactions and interrelations requires in intensified efforts to provide integrated information on the status and development of environmental quality.

The bioremediation process can be determined by measuring changes in total pollutant concentrations by several analytical techniques (chromatographic and spectroscopic techniques etc). Attempts are also being made to use biosensors, especially microbial whole-cell biosensors, to monitor the rate of pollutant elimination. Bioremediation processes can also be assayed through a multifaceted approach like, natural attenuation, sensing environmental pollution, metabolic pathway engineering, applying phyto and microbial diversity to problematic sites, plant-endophyte partnerships and systems biology (Prasad et al 2010). Bioindicators and biomonitors have proven to be excellent tools in many of these cases and could provide information which cannot be derived from technical measurements alone (Markert *et al.* 2003, Prasad 2008, Prasad 2011).

Biotechnology and systems biology approaches are also implicated in bioremediation and are gaining considerable importance in promotion of bioremediation (De Lorenzo 2008, Van Aken 2009, Prasad 2011). It is strongly believed that there are three dimensions for the effectiveness of vital bioremediation process, i.e., chemical landscape (nutrients-to-be, electron donors/acceptors and stressors), abiotic landscape and catabolic landscape of which only the catabolic landscape is 'genuinely' biological. The chemical landscape has a dynamic interplay with the biological interventions on the abiotic background of the site at stake. This includes humidity, conductivity, temperature, matrix conditions, redox status, etc. (De Lorenzo 2008, Prasad 2011).

Materials and Methods

Bioremediation is a process whereby organic wastes are biologically degraded under controlled conditions to an innocuous state, or up to a concentration level as prescribed and established by regulatory authorities (Mueller 1996). It is the use of living organisms principally 'microorganisms' for degradation of environmental contaminants into less toxic forms. Research has demonstrated that there are very few environments where microbes have not been able to survive and adapt. Microbes are able to utilize a near infinite combination of electron donors and electron acceptors to drive their metabolism. In addition to these redox (oxidation / reduction) reactions, they have also developed a myriad of other strategies enabling them to detoxify their environment. Bioremediation applies these principles to select a suitable combination of microbial community activity, electron donor, acceptor, contaminant concentrations and other physical and practical parameters to remediate a targeted pollutant. Bioremediation strategies are often more beneficial than conventional strategies as, it can be implemented *in situ*. Innovative *in situ* technologies permit biological treatment of contaminated water by means of reactive molecules produced by microbes. This provides a simpler, less intrusive, and cheaper method than conventional 'pump and treat' systems that often employ hazardous chemicals that create and additional environmental risk (Heerden *et al.* 2009).

Microbial Populations for Bioremediation

Microorganisms can be isolated from almost any environmental conditions. Microbes can adapt and grow at subzero temperatures, as well as extreme heat, desert conditions, in water, with an excess of oxygen and in anaerobic conditions, with the presence of hazardous compounds or on any waste stream. The main requirements are an energy source and a carbon source (Vidali 2001, Kumar *et al.* 2011). Because of the adaptability of microbes and other biological systems, these can be used to remediate environmental hazards. Natural organisms, either indigenous or extraneous (introduced), are the key factors used for bioremediation (Prescott *et al.* 2002, Kumar *et al.* 2011). The type of microorganisms utilized for remediation depends on chemical nature of pollutants and are to be selected carefully as they only survive within a limited range of chemical contaminants (Prescott *et al.* 2002, Dubey 2004, Kumar *et al.* 2011). A novel work was patented for a biological remediation agent in 1974, being a strain of *Pseudomonas putida* (Prescott *et al.* 2002, Kumar *et al.* 2011) that was able to degrade petroleum. In 1991, about 70 microbial genera were reported to degrade petroleum compounds and almost an equal number has been added to the list in the successive two decades (Glazer and Nikaido 2007, Kumar *et al.* 2011). In bioremediation, fundamental biological activities are exploited to degrade or transform contaminants of concern. The biological activity to be exploited depends on the specific contaminants of concern and the media where the contamination is located.

Types of Microbes in Bioremediation

Microbes used in bioremediation process broadly classified in different categories like, aerobic, anaerobic, Ligninolytic fungi and Methylotrophs. The aerobic microbes prefer aerobic environments for degradation pathway. These microbes gain energy and carbon for building cell materials from these biochemical reactions (EPA 2006). Examples of aerobic bacteria recognized for their degradative abilities are reported to belong in the class of *Pseudomonas, Alcaligenes, Sphingomonas, Rhodococcus,* and *Mycobacterium*. These microbes have often been reported to degrade pesticides and hydrocarbons, both alkanes and polyaromatic compounds. Many of these bacterial strains use the contaminant as the sole source of carbon and energy (Kumar *et al.* 2011). Anaerobic microbial metabolism involves microbial reactions in absence of oxygen and includes many processes including fermentation, methanogenesis, reductive dechlorination, sulfate-reducing activities and denitrification. In anaerobic metabolism, nitrate, sulfate, carbon dioxide, oxidized metals, or organic compounds may replace oxygen as the electron acceptor. For example, in anaerobic reductive dechlorination, chlorinated solvents may serve as the electron acceptor (EPA 2006). Anaerobic bacteria are usually used for bioremediation of polychlorinated biphenyls (PCBs) in river sediments, dechlorination of the solvent trichloroethylene (TCE) and chloroform (Kumar *et al.* 2011). Another class embraces Ligninolytic fungi such as the white rot fungus *Phanaerochaete chrysosporium* have the ability to degrade an extremely diverse range of persistent or toxic environmental pollutants. Methylotrophs are also an important class of aerobic bacteria that grow utilizing methane for carbon and energy utilize broad substrate range and is active against a wide range of compounds, including the chlorinated aliphatic trichloroethylene and 1, 2 dichloroethane (EPA 2006). Table 12.3 illustrates the microorganisms having biodegradation potential of xenobiotics (Kumar *et al.* 2011).

In case of *cometabolism,* microbes do not gain energy or carbon from degrading a contaminant. Instead, the contaminant is degraded via a side reaction. Technologies based on cometabolism are more difficult to use since the microbes do not benefit from the desired reactions. Cometabolic bioventing is an example of cometabolism. In this technology, microbes may be fed propane, and they degrade trichloroethylene (TCE) or less chlorinated ethenes as well (Kumar *et al.* 2011).

Constrains of Bioremediation

The most important principle of bioremediation is that microorganisms (mainly bacteria or fungi) can be used to destroy hazardous contaminants or transform them to less harmful products. Thus, bioremediation of contaminants is an application of the microbial metabolic activity. Microorganisms, through their enzymatic pathways, act as biocatalysts and facilitate the progress of biochemical reactions that degrade the targeted contaminants. As a result, bioremediation techniques are only applicable in environments that can sustain life. The microorganisms act against the contaminants only when they have access to a variety of materials-compounds to help them generate energy and nutrients to build more cells. The proper combination of metabolic characteristics for microorganisms and physicochemical properties of the targeted contaminants specify whether the possibility of bioremediation. Basically it depends on the environmental conditions of the site of interaction. Specific constrains should therefore be fulfilled for a successful bioremediation attempt. These constrains encompass the microbial, chemical and environmental characteristics of the targeted site (Hatzikioseyian 2010). This category includes (i) Microbial constrains, a consortia of naturally existing species or genetically engineered microorganisms responsible for an efficient bioremediation process (Neilson *et al.* 2008, Aislabie *et al.* 2008, Hatzikioseyian 2010). (ii) Chemical constrains, refer to the physical state and chemical structure of the contaminant for better possibility of efficient contact between the microorganism and the contaminant and to improve bioavailability (Naidu 2008; Neilson *et al.* 2008, Beek 2001). (iii) Growth environmental constrains, incorporate some crucial factors like, temperature, pH of treatment medium, moisture content and water activity, redox potential, mass transfer characteristics, site hydrogeologic characteristics. Table 1 and Table 2 illustrate the various factors of bioremediation. Moisture is a very important variable in bioremediation which affects the bioavailability of contaminants, toxicity level of contaminants, microorganisms' growth characteristics. The redox potential of the soil is directly related to the concentration of O_2 in the gas and liquid phases which restrict aerobic reactions and may promote anaerobic processes such as denitrification, sulfate reduction, and fermentation. Mass transport characteristics modulate the rates of liquids or gases movement through soil and infiltration rate (Sara 2003, Lehr 2004, Hillel 1998, Reddi 2000, Fitts 2002). Site hydrogeologic factors includes mainly aquifer type along with hydraulic conductivity, hydrogeologic gradient, permeability, recharge capability, depth to groundwater, moisture content/field capacity, thickness of the saturated zone, homogeneity, depth to contamination, extent of contamination, and plume stability (Suthersan *et al.* 1999, Sara 2003, Lehr 2004, Hillel 1998, Reddi 2000, Fitts 2002). Environmental constrains also include presence of nutrients, oxygen air, hydrogen peroxide, metal ions toxic compounds, biogeochemical parameters and presence of electron acceptors like nitrate (NO_3^-), nitrite (NO_2^-), nitrous oxide (N_2O).

Types of Bioremediation

The field of bioremediation can be divided into several broad categories. For example, bioremediation technologies may be applied to *'in situ'* or *'ex situ'* media (EPA 2006).

'In situ' biodegradation involves supplying oxygen and nutrients by circulating aqueous solutions through contaminated soils to stimulate naturally occurring bacteria to degrade organic contaminants. It can be used for soil and groundwater. Generally, this technique includes conditions such as the infiltration of water containing nutrients and oxygen or other electron acceptors for groundwater treatment (Vidali 2001). *'In situ'* bioremediation of groundwater has become one of the most widely used technologies for contaminated site treatment because of its relatively low cost, adaptability to site-specific conditions, and efficacy when properly implemented (Stroo 2010). The three primary approaches to full-scale implementation for *'in situ'* bioremediation are classified as active, semi-passive, and passive treatment, distinguished by the need for active groundwater recirculation during operations (Stroo and Ward 2009, EPA December 2013). Biological treatment of domestic wastewater has been in use since the mid-1800s, and land treatment has been used for several decades to treat oil and other petroleum wastes by aerobic biodegradation (Loehr 1979, EPA December 2013). *In situ* Bioremediation may be classified into two categories, namely (*i*) intrinsic *in situ* bioremediation and (*ii*) engineered *in situ* bioremediation. Intrinsic bioremediation relies on natural processes to degrade contaminants without altering current conditions or adding amendments. Intrinsic bioremediation depends on indigenous microflora to degrade contaminants without any amendments (EPA, 2000). Intrinsic bioremediation may play a role in monitored attenuation (MNA) sites, which is a broader term defined by the National Research Council (NRC) and EPA as "biodegradation, dispersion, dilution, sorption, volatilization, radioactive decay, and chemical or biological stabilization, transformation or destruction of contaminants" (NRC 2000, EPA

1999). Enhanced bioremediation can be applied to ground water, and aquatic sediments. Additives such as oxygen (or other electron acceptors), nutrients, biodegradable carbonaceous substrates, bulking agents, and/or moisture are added to enhance the activity of naturally occurring or indigenous microbial populations (FRTR 2003, EPA 2006). Engineered bioremediation relies on accelerating the desired biodegradation reactions by encouraging the growth of more organisms, as well as by optimizing the environment in which the organisms must carry out the detoxification reactions (Hatzikioseyian 2010). Enhanced *in situ* bioremediation further can be subdivided into (*i*) Bioventing applicable for hydrocarbons or contaminants under surface (Vidali 2001), employ low air flow rate and minimize volatilization and release of contaminants to the atmosphere; (*ii*) Biosparging involves the injection of air under pressure below the water table to increase groundwater oxygen concentrations and enhance the rate of biological degradation of contaminants by naturally occurring bacteria; Figure 12.2 (adopted from EPA 2006) illustrates a 'biosparging' system used with soil vapor extraction, (*iii*) Biostimulation embraces modification of the environment by adding nutrients to stimulate the rate of biological degradation of contaminants by indigenous microorganisms (Hatzikioseyian 2010); (*iv*) Bioaugmentation represents the soil amendment with non-indigenous allochthonous microorganisms or cultivated indigenous species or engineered microbes via inoculation, or use of bio-products, like enzymes to enhance the rate of biodegradation for specific pollutants (Aislabie *et al.* 2008, Hatzikioseyian 2010); (*v*) Bioslurping technology involves application of vacuum-enhanced dewatering technologies for the remediation of hydrocarbon-contaminated sites (FRTR 2003). Figure 12.3 (adopted from EPA 2006) illustrates bioslurping technology.

'Ex Situ' Bioremediation processes involve the removal of the contaminated media to a treatment area (EPA 2006). In the case of ex-situ techniques, soil and groundwater are removed from their original locations for treatment. *Ex-situ* techniques include land farming, irrigation, compost piles, engineered biopiles, and ex-situ slurry techniques (Blackburn *et al.* 1993, Hatzikioseyian 2010). Figure 4 (adopted from EPA 2006) illustrates Biopiling system. *Ex situ* bioremediation technologies can most easily be classified by the physical state of the medium to which they are typically applied.

Phytoremediation

Phytoremediation uses plants to remove, transfer, stabilize, or destroy contaminants through biological, chemical, and physical processes that are influenced by plants and their roots (i.e., rhizosphere) that include degradation, extraction through accumulation in plant roots/shoots/leaves, metabolism of contaminants, and immobilization of contaminants at the interface of roots and soil (EPA 2004a).

Rhizofiltration is a type of phytoremediation, which refers to the approach of using hydroponically cultivated plant roots to remediate contaminated water through absorption, concentration, and precipitation of pollutants. It also filters through water and dirt. The contaminated water is either collected from a waste site or brought to the plants, or the plants are planted in the contaminated area, where the roots then take up the water and the contaminants dissolved in it. Many plant species naturally uptake heavy metals and excess nutrients for a variety of reasons: sequestration, drought resistance, disposal by leaf abscission, interference with other plants, and defense against pathogens and herbivores (Boyd *et al.* 1998).

Rhizofiltration may be applicable to the treatment of surface water and groundwater, industrial and residential effluents, downwashes from power lines, storm waters, acid mine drainage, agricultural runoffs, diluted sludges, and radionuclide-contaminated solutions. Plants suitable for rhizofiltration applications can efficiently remove toxic metals from a solution using rapid-growth root systems. Various terrestrial plant species have been found to effectively remove toxic metals such as Cu^{2+}, Cd^{2+}, Cr^{6+}, Ni^{2+}, Pb^{2+}, and Zn^{2+} from aqueous solutions (Dushenkov *et al.* 1995). It was also reported to efficiently remove low level radioactive contaminants from liquid streams (EPA 1998). A system to achieve this can consist of a "feeder layer" of soil suspended above a contaminated stream through which plants grow, extending the bulk of their roots into the water. The feeder layer allows the plants to receive fertilizer without contaminating the stream, while simultaneously removing heavy metals from the water (Raskin *et al.* 1997).

Rhizofiltration is cost-effective for large volumes of water having low concentrations of contaminants that are subjected to stringent standards (Miller 1996). The removal of radionuclides from water using sunflowers was estimated to cost between $2 and $6 per thousand gallons of water treated, including waste disposal and capital costs (Cooney 1996).

Monitored Natural Attenuation

Natural attenuation, often called as intrinsic remediation, intrinsic bioremediation, bioattenuation or monitored natural attenuation (MNA), consists of unassisted and unenhanced physical, chemical, and biological processes (e.g. biodegradation, abiotic transformations, mechanical dispersion, dilution, evaporation, volatilization and adsorption) that act to limit the migration and reduce the mass, toxicity, mobility, volume, or concentration of contaminants in soil, sediment, or groundwater (Alvarez 2006, Filler *et al.* 2008, Lehr 2004, Hatzikioseyian 2010). Natural attenuation, as an in-situ technology, is very important because it is often technically infeasible to clean a contaminated site to regulatory cleanup levels for a variety of conditions including the presence of low-permeability soils, the inability to remove all the contaminants from the individual soil particles etc.

While natural attenuation may not be a suitable remedy for all contaminated sites, it does offer the potential advantages of in-situ technologies:

(*i*) Generates less secondary wastes, reduced risk of human exposure during treatment, reduced potential for cross-media transfer of contamination.

(*ii*) Operates in-situ with minimal site disturbance.

(*iii*) Can be used in conjunction with other remediation technologies.

(*iv*) Reduced need for on-site structures associated with cleanup.

(*v*) Potentially reduces overall remediation costs (Hatzikioseyian 2010).

Biotransformation of Metals, Metalloids and Radionuclides

The toxicity and mobility of the elements depend primarily on their speciation, which is significantly influenced by soil pH, redox conditions, and surface chemistry. All these environmental factors can be optimized by manipulating microbial activities to reduce the risk posed by heavy metals in aquifer environments. Microorganisms cannot convert metals to different elements. However, they can modify the microenvironment around the microbial cell and can catalyze oxidation, reduction, methylation and de-alkylation reactions that affect the solubility and mobility of many metals. In addition, the microbial cell offers a large number of possible physico-chemical mechanisms of interaction like complexation, coordination, chelation, ion exchange, adsorption, microprecipitation with soluble metal, radionuclide and metalloid species resulting in immobilization of them (Singh *et al.* 2007, Violante *et al.* 2008, Gad 1993, Remoudaki *et al.* 2007, Gad 2004, Ehrlich 2001, White *et al.* 1993, Hatzikioseyian 2010).

Advantages and Disadvantages of Bioremediation

Several advantages of bioremediation process comprises

1. Bioremediation being a natural process perceived by the public as an acceptable waste treatment process for contaminated material such as soil.
2. Microbes from natural origin able to degrade the contaminants when the contaminant is degraded, the biodegradative population declines. The residues for the treatment are usually harmless products and include carbon dioxide, water, and cell biomass.
3. Bioremediation by principal is useful for the destruction of a wide variety of contaminants. Many compounds that are legally considered to be hazardous can be transformed to harmless products. This eliminates the chance of legal responsibility associated with treatment and disposal of contaminated material.
4. Instead of transferring contaminants from one environmental medium to another, this process involves complete destruction of targeted pollutants.

5. Bioremediation processes are often implemented on site, without causing any major disruption of normal activities. This also eliminates the need to transport quantities of waste off site and the potential threats to human health and the environment that can arise during transportation.
6. Bioremediation process assembles are less expensive than other technologies those are used for hazardous waste clean-up (Vidali, 2001).

Limitations of bioremediation process encompasses

(*i*) Specific action against contaminants hence, not all compounds are susceptible to degradation. Important site factors required for success include the presence of metabolically capable microbial populations, suitable environmental growth conditions, and appropriate levels of nutrients and contaminants.

(*ii*) Possibilities of more persistent or toxic product formation.

(*iii*) Difficulties to extrapolate from bench and pilot-scale studies to full-scale field operations.

(*iv*) Requires extensive researches to develop and engineer bioremediation technologies appropriate for sites with complex mixtures of contaminants.

(*v*) Prolonged time of treatment than other treatment options, such as excavation and incineration.

(*vi*) Uncertainty always leftovers regarding acceptable performance criteria for bioremediation. There is no accepted definition of "clean", evaluating performance of bioremediation is difficult, and there are no acceptable endpoints for bioremediation treatments (Vidali, 2001).

Results and Discussion

Bioremediation provides a technique for cleaning up pollution by enhancing the natural biodegradation processes (Kumar *et al.* 2011). It is a multidisciplinary technology and successful application requires deep understanding of all the relevant scientific fields and attenuation processes (Hatzikioseyian 2010). By developing an understanding of microbial communities and their response to the natural environment and pollutants and keeping in mind the environmental factors responsible for rendering degradation of pollutants, cost effective bioremediation techniques have been developed. Although the methodologies employed are not technically complex, considerable experience and expertise may be required to design and implement a successful bioremediation program, due to the need to thoroughly assess a site for suitability and to optimize conditions to achieve a satisfactory result (Vidali 2001). This technology offers an efficient and cost effective way to treat contaminated ground water and soil. Advantages of this process are generally overshadowing the allied disadvantages, which is evident by increasing number of research publications and sites endeavor this technology in practice (Kumar *et al.* 2011). Hence, bioremediation is a process of paving a way to greener pastures and a cleaner environment.

Table 12.1: Showing Factors of Bioremediation (Sharma 2012)

Factors	Conditions required
Microorganisms	Aerobic / Anaerobic
Natural biological processes of microorganism	Catabolism / Anabolism
Environmental factors	Temperature, pH, oxygen content, electron acceptor/donor
Nutrients	Carbon , nitrogen ,oxygen etc
Soil Moisture	25-28% of water holding capacity
Type of soil	Low clay or silt content

Table 12.2: Showing Environmental Conditions (Vidali 2001).

Environmental Factor	Optimum conditions	Condition required for microbialActivity
Available soil moisture	25-85% water holding capacity	25-28% of water holding capacity
Oxygen	>0.2 mg/L DO, >10% air-filled pore space foraerobic degradation	Aerobic, minimum air-filled porespace of 10%
Redox potential	Eh > 50 mill volts	
Nutrients	C:N:P= 120:10:1 molar ratio	N and P for microbial growth
pH	6.5-8.0	5.5 to 8.5
Temperature	20-30 °C	15-45°C
Contaminents	Hydrocarbon 5-10% of dry weight of soil	Not too toxic
Heavy metals	700 ppm	Total content 2000 ppm

Table 12.3: Microorganisms having Biodegradation Potential for Xenobiotics (Kumar *et al.* 2011).

Organism	Toxic chemicals	Reference
Pseudomonas spp	Benzene, anthracene, hydrocarbons, PCBs	Kapley *et al.* 1999, Cybulski *et al.* 2003, Lal and Khanna, 1996, Kumar *et al.* 2011
Alcaligenes spp	Halogenated hydrocarbons, linear alkylbenzene sulfonates, polycyclic aromatics, PCBs	Kumar *et al.* 2011

Arthrobacter spp	Benzene, hydrocarbons, pentachlorophenol, phenoxyacetate, polycyclic aromatic	Jogdand 1995, Kumar *et al.* 2011
Bacillus spp	Aromatics, long chain alkanes, phenol, cresol, Halogenated hydrocarbons, phenoxyacetates	Cybulski *et al.* 2003, Kumar *et al.* 2011
Corynebacterium spp	Aromatics	Jogdand 1995, Kumar *et al.* 2011
Flavobacterium spp	Aromatics	Jogdand 1995, Kumar *et al.* 2011
Azotobacter spp	Naphthalene, biphenyl aromatics, branched hydrocarbons, benzene, cycloparaffins	Jogdand 1995, Kumar *et al.* 2011
Rhodococcus spp	Hydrocarbons Aromatics	Dean Ross *et al.* 2002, Kumar *et al.* 2011
Mycobacterium spp	Aromatics	Sunggyu 1995, Park *et al.* 1998, Kumar *et al.* 2011
Methosinus spp	Phenoxyacetate, halogenated hydrocarbon diazinon	Jogdand 1995, Ijah 1998, Kumar *et al.* 2011
Methanogens	PCBs, formaldehyde	Jogdand 1995, Ijah 1998, Kumar *et al.* 2011
Xanthomonas spp	PCBs, polycyclic aromatics, biphenyls	Jogdand 1995, Kumar *et al.* 2011

Scope	Limitations
• Metallocimes, metabolomics, Proteomics, Genomics	• Database for contaminated sites
• Cell, genome, operon and pathway engineering	• Database for applicable biodiversity
• Site, habitat, niche, community and population	• risks of remediation
	• Recovery and reuse economics

Future Prospects

Bioremediation is still an emerging technology and its full potential is yet to be realized thoroughly. As the rules for conventional ground water and soil cleanup methodologies are getting more and more stringent, research for alternative cleanup technologies is escalating. Bioremediation is a potential alternative to conventional cleanup methods as it is easier to execute and comparatively less costly. Bioremediation poses a unique technological challenge as it incorporates a combination of the intricacies of microbial processes; and the physical challenges involving both microorganisms and contaminants make bioremediation difficult to understand as an appropriate cleanup strategy. Microorganisms are capable of performing a wide range of detoxification processes but the full prospective of bioremediation to treat contaminants cannot be realized as long as its use and mechanism is in mist. Extensive research exploration and industrial adaptation of the technologies would surely eliminate the controversies related to this highly multidisciplinary technology.

Fig. 12.1: Scope and limitation of bioremediation application (Prasad, 2011)

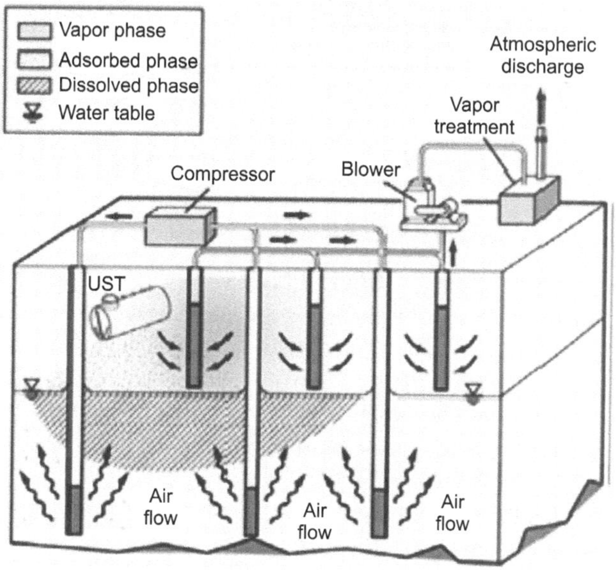

Fig. 12.2: A biosparging system used with soil vapour extraction (EPA 2006

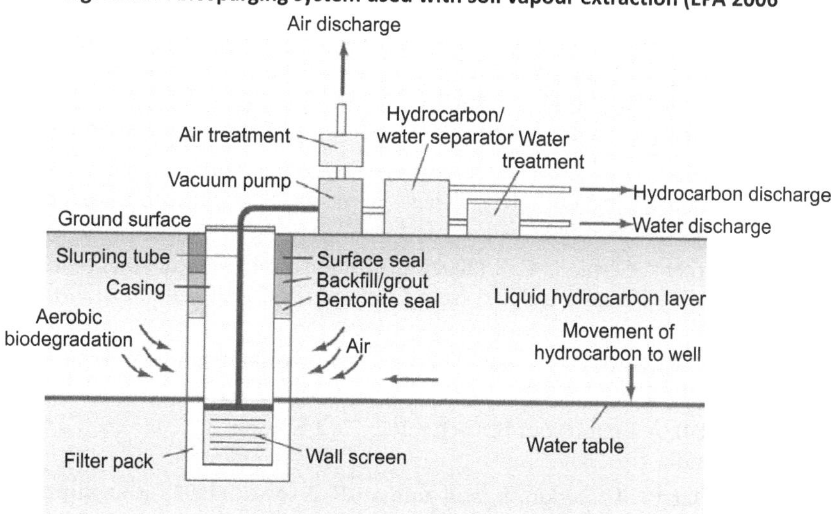

Fig. 12.3: Bioslurping technology (EPA 2006).

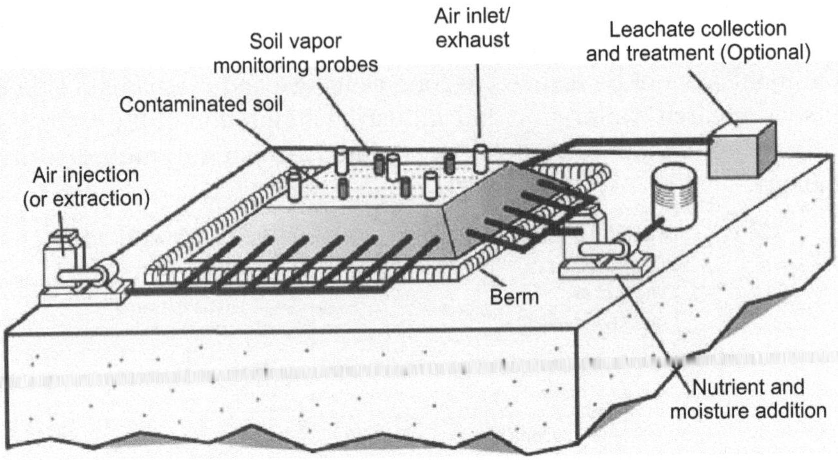

Fig. 12.4: A typical biopile system (EPA 2006)

REFERENCES

Abhilash, P. C., Jamil, S. and Singh, N. (2009): Transgenic Plants for Enhanced Biodegradation and Phytoremediation of Organic Xenobiotics, *Biotechnology Advances*, 27: 474.

Aislabie, J., and Foght, J. (2008): Bioremediation of Petroleum Hydrocarbons in Cold Regions, Filler, D.M., Snape, I., and Barnes, D.L. (Eds.), *Cambridge University Press.*

Alvarez, P. J. J., and Illman, W.A. (2006): Bioremediation and Natural Attenuation: Process Fundamentals and Mathematical Models, *John Wiley & Sons.*

Beek, B. (2001): The Handbook of Environmental Chemistry, Biodegradation and Persistence, *Springer-Verlag Berlin Heidelberg.*

Blackburn, J. W., and Hafker, W. R. (1993): The Impact of Biochemistry, Bioavailability and Bioactivity on the Selection of Bioremediation Techniques, *Trends in Biotechnology*, 11: 328.

Boyd, R. S. (1998): Plants That Hyperaccumulate Heavy Metals, *Ed. R. R. Brooks. Willingford, U.K.: CAB International.* pp. 181.

Cooney, C. M. (1996): Sunflowers Remove Radionuclides from Water in Ongoing Phytoremediation Field Tests, *Environmental Science and Technology*, 30: 194.

Cybulski Z., Dzuirla E., Kaczorek E., Olszanowski A. (2003): The Influence of Emulsifiers on Hydrocarbon Biodegradation by *Pseudomonadacea* and *Bacillacea* Strains, *Spill Science and Technology Bulletin* 8: 503.

Dean Ross D., Moody J., Cerniglia C. E. (2002): Utilization of Mixtures of Polycyclic Aromatic Hydrocarbons by Bacteria Isolated from Contaminated Sediment, *FEMS Microbiology Ecology*, 41: 17.

De Lorenzo, V. (2008): Systems Biology Approaches to Bioremediation, *Current Opinion in Biotechnology*, 19: 579.

Dubey, R. C., (2004): A Textbook of Biotechnology, 3rd Edition, *S. Chand and Company Ltd.* New Delhi, India, pp. 365.

Dushenkov, V., Harry, M., Raskin, I., and Kumar, P. B. A. N. (1995): Rhizofiltration: The Use of Plants to Remove Heavy Metals from Aqueous Streams, *Environmental Science Technology*, 30: 1239.

Ehrlich, H. L. (2009): Geomicrobiology, *CRC Press* pp: 89.

EPA (2000): Engineered Approaches to In Situ Bioremediation of Chlorinated Solvents: Fundamentals and Field Applications, EPA-542-R-00-008.

EPA (2006): Engineering Issue, In Situ and Ex Situ Biodegradation Technologies for Remediation of Contaminated Sites, US EPA.

EPA 2004(a): Treatment Technologies for Site Cleanup: Annual Status Report, Eleventh Edition, EPA-542-R-03-009, US EPA.

EPA (December 2013): Introduction to In Situ Bioremediation of Groundwater. EPA 542-R-13-018, US EPA.

Filler, D. M., Snape, I., and Barnes, D. L. (Eds.) (2008): Bioremediation of Petroleum Hydrocarbons in Cold Regions, *Cambridge University Press.*

Fitts, C. R. 2002, Groundwater: The Big Picture, Groundwater Science, *Academic Press.*

Flathman, P. E., Jerger, D. and Exner, J. E. (1993): Bioremediation: Field Experience, *Lewis,* Boca Raton, FL

FRTR. Remediation Technologies Screening Matrix and Reference Guide, Version 4.0. November 2003.

Gadd, G. M. (1993): Microbial Formation and Transformation of Organometallic and Organometalloid Compounds, *FEMS Microbiology Review,* 11: 297.

Gadd, G. M. (2004): Microbial Influence on Metal Mobility and Application for Bioremediation, *Geoderma,* 122, 109.

Glazer, A. N., Nikaido, H., (2007): Microbial Biotechnology: Fundamentals of Applied Microbiology, 2nd Edition, *Cambridge University Press,* Cambridge, New York, pp. 510.

Hatzikioseyian, Artin (2010): Principles of Bioremediation Processes, Trends in Bioremediation and Phytoremediation, *Research Signpost,* pp. 2354.

Heerden, E. V., Williams, P., Ojo, E., Kuloyo, K. and Posthumus, R. (2009): Bioremediation, Small Solutions to Big Problems. University of the Free State.

Hillel, D. (1998): Environmental Soil Physics: Fundamentals, Applications and Environmental Considerations, *Academic Press,* 0123485258.

Hinchee, R. E., Means, J. L., Burrisl, D. R. (1995): Bioremediation of Inorganics. *Battelle Press,* Columbus, OH.

Ijah U. J. J. (1998): Studies on Relative Capabilities of Bacterial and Yeast Isolates from Tropical Soil in Degrading Crude Oil, *Waste Management,* 18: 293.

Jogdand S. N. (1995): Environmental Biotechnology, 1st Edition, *Himalaya Publishing House,* Bombay, India, pp. 104-120.

Kapley A., Purohit H. J., Chhatre S., Shanker R., Chakrabarti T. (1999): Osmotolerance and Hydrocarbon Degradation by a Genetically Engineered Microbial Consortium, *Bioresource Technology,* 67: 241.

King, R. B., Long, G. M., Sheldon, J. K. (1997): Practical Environmental Bioremediation: The Field Guide, 2nd ed., *Lewis, Boca Raton,* FL.

Kumar, A., Bisht, B. S, Joshi, V. D., Dhewa, T. (2011): Review on Bioremediation of Polluted Environment: A management tool, *International Journal of Environmental Sciences,* 1(6): 1079.

Lal B., Khanna S. (1996): Degradation of Crude Oil by *Acinetobacter Calcoaceticus* and *Alcaligenes odoran, Journal of Applied Bacteriology,* 81: 355.

Lehr, J. H. (2004): Wiley's Remediation Technologies Handbook. Major Contaminant Chemicals and Chemical Groups, *John Wiley & Sons, Inc.*

Loehr, R. L., Jewell, W. L., Novak, J. D., Clarkson, W. W., Friedman, G. S. (1979): Land Application of Wastes, *Van Nostrand Reinhold Co.*, New York, NY.

Ma Y., Prasad M. N. V., Rajkumar M. and Freitas H. (2011): Plant Growth Promoting Rhizobacteria and Endophytes Accelerate Phytoremediation of Metalliferous Soils, *Biotechnology Advances* 29, 248-258.

Markert, B., Breure, A., Zechmeister, H. (eds.) (2003): Bioindicators and Biomonitors-Principles, Concepts and Applications, *Elsevier*, Amsterdam, New York, Tokyo.

Miller, R. (1996): Phytoremediation, Technology Overview Report, *Ground-Water Remediatoin Technologies Analysis Center*. PA, pp. 26.

Mueller, J. G., Cerniglia, C. E. Pritchard, P. H. (1996): Bioremediation of Environments Contaminated by Polycyclic Aromatic Hydrocarbons. In Bioremediation: Principles and Applications, pp. 125–194, *Cambridge University Press*, Cambridge.

Naidu, R. (Ed.) (2008): Chemical Bioavailability in Terrestrial Environments, *Elsevier Science*, 32.

National Research Council. (1993): In Situ Bioremediation: When Does It Work? *National Academy Press*, Washington, DC.

Neilson, A. H., Allard, A. S. (2008): Environmental Degradation and Transformation of Organic Chemicals, *CRC Press*.

Norris, R. D., Hinchee, R. E., Brown, R., McCarty, P. L., Semprini, L., Wilson, J. T., Kampbell, D. H., Reinhard, M., Bouwer, E. J., Borden, P. C., Vogel, T. M., Thomas, J. M. and Ward, C. H. (1993): Handbook of Bioremediation, *Lewis, Boca Raton*, FL.

Park A. J., Cha D. K., Holsen T. M., (1998): Enhancing solubilization of Sparingly Soluble Organic Compounds by Biosurfactants Produced by Nocardia Erythropolis, *Water Environment Research*, 70: 351.

Prasad, M. N. V. (2011): A State-of-the-Art Report on Bioremediation, Its Applications to Contaminated sites in India, Ministry of Environment & Forests, Govt. of India

Prasad, M. N. V. (ed) (2008): Trace elements as Contaminants and Nutrients: Consequences in Ecosystems and Human Health, *John Wiley and Sons Inc.* New York. pp. 777.

Prasad, M. N. V., Freitas, H., Fraenzle, S., Wuenschmann, S., Markert, B. (2010): Knowledge Explosion in Phytotechnologies for Environmental Solutions, *Environmental Pollution*, 158, 18.

Prescott, L. M., Harley, J. P., Klein, D. A., (2002): Microbiology, 5th Edition, *McGrawHill*, New York, pp. 1014.

Raskin, Ilya, Smith, Robert, D. Salt, David E. (1997): Phytoremediation of Metals: Using Plants to Remove Pollutants from the Environment, *Current Opinion in Biotechnology*, 8(2): 221.

Reddi, L. N., Inyang, H. I. (2000): Geoenvironmental Engineering: Principles and Application, *Marcel Dekker, Inc.*

Remoudaki, E., Hatzikioseyian, A., Tsezos, M. (2007): Metabolically Mediated Metal Immobilization Processes for Bioremediation, *Proceedings of Balkan Mineral Processing*, Delfi, Greece.

Sara, M. N. (2003): Site Assessment and Remediation Handbook, *Lewis Publishers*, CRC Press.

Schroeder, P. and Schwitzguebel, J. P. (2004): New Cost Action Launched: Phytotechnologies to Promote Sustainable Land Use and Improve Food Safety, *Journal of Soils and Sediments* 4 (3), 205.

Sharma S. (2012): Bioremediation: Features, Strategies and Applications, *Asian Journal of Pharmacy and Life Sciences*, 2(2): 202.

Singh, S. N., and Tripathi, R. D. (2007): Environmental Bioremediation Technologies, Springer-Verlag Berlin Heidelberg.

Stroo, H. and Ward, C. H. (eds.). (2009): In Situ Bioremediation of Perchlorate in Groundwater. SERDP/ESTCP Remediation Technology Monograph Series, *Springer Science & Business Media, LLC.* New York, NY. pp. 243.

Stroo, H. F. (2010): Bioremediation of Chlorinated Solvent Plumes, Stroo, H.F. and C.H. Ward (eds). In Situ Remediation of Chlorinated Solvent Plumes. SERDP/ESTCP Remediation Technology Monograph Series, *Springer Science & Business Media, LLC.* New York, NY. pp. 725.

Suthersan, S. S. (1999): Remediation Engineering Design Concepts, *CRC Press Lewis Publishers.*

Van Aken, B. (2009): Transgenic Plants for Enhanced Phytoremediation of Toxic Explosives, *Current Opinion in Biotechnology*, 20: 231.

Vidali, M. (2001): Bioremediation An overview, *Pure and Applied Chemistry*, 73(7): 1163.

Violante, A., Huang, P. M., and Gadd, G. M. (2008): Biophysico-chemical Processes of Heavy Metals and Metalloids in Soil Environments, *John Wiley & Sons.*

White, C., Gadd, G. M. (1993): Microbial Treatment of Metal Pollution—A Working Biotechnology, *Trends in Biotechnology*, 11: 353.

Product Development and Waste Recycling **Pages 161-186**
Edited by: Pawan Kumar 'Bharti'
ISBN: 978-93-86841-94-0
Edition: 2019
Published by: Discovery Publishing House Pvt. Ltd., New Delhi (India)

13

Use of Vermicompost in Crop Production

[1]A. Solaimalai, [2*]M. Jayakumar, [3]A. Rajkumar and [4]A. Palanisamy

Introduction

In India, nearly 7000 million tonnes of organic materials such as farm wastes, kitchen waste, dairy and industry waste are produced every year, which has a large potential for production of organic manures, be it be composting or vermicomposting Use of organic manures to meet the nutrient requirements of crop would be an inevitable practice in the years to come for sustainable agriculture since, organic manures generally improve the soil physical, chemical and biological properties along with conserving the moisture holding capacity of soil and thus resulting in enhanced crop productivity along with maintaining the quality of crop produce (Premsekhar and Rajashree, 2009). Use of vermicompost for horticulture in large scale can solve the problem for disposal of organic wastes and also resolvs the deficiency of organic matter in such soils (Alam *et al.,* 2007a). Although organic manures contain plant nutrients in small quantities as compared to the chemical fertilizers, the presence of growth promoting factors like enzymes and hormones, along with plant nutrients make them essential for improvement of soil fertility and productivity (Szczeck, 1999). Sustainability in agriculture refers to the capacity to remain productive while maintaining the soil fertility and increasing biodiversity. Manure and biologically active preparations of animal and plant origin are most commonly used for sustainable production (Premsekhar and Rajashree, 2009). Among such preparations, vermicompost has been recognized as having considerable potential for soil amendments.

1 Associate Professor (Agronomy), Department of Fruit Crops, Horticultural College & Research, TNAU, Periyakulam – 625 604, Tamil Nadu, India.

2 Scientist, Regional Coffee Research Station, Thandikudi, Dindigul (Dt), Tamil Nadu, India.

3 Assistant Professor (Horticulture), Krishna College of Agriculture & Technology, Sree Rangapuram, Usilampatti (TK), Madurai (Dt), Tamil Nadu, India.

4 Assistant Professor (Horticulture), Krishna College of Agriculture & Technology, Sree Rangapuram, Usilampatti (TK), Madurai (Dt), Tamil Nadu, India.

Nutrient Content of Vermicompost

Vermicompost is a finely divided manure peat like material with high porosity, aeration, drainage and water holding capacity and microbial activity and is stabilized by interaction between earthworms and microgranisms in a non-thermophilic process (Edwards and Burrows, 1988). Vermicomposts are products of organic matter degradation through interactions between earthworms and microorganisms (Arancon *et al.,* 2005). Vermicompost is made up primarily of carbon (C), hydrogen (H) and oxygen (O), and contains nutrients like as NO_3, PO_4, Ca, K, Mg, S and micronutrients which exhibit similar effects on plant growth and yield as inorganic fertilizers when applied to soil (Table 1 and 2) (Orozco *et al.,* 1996; Singh *et al.,* 2008). Similarly, vermicompost contains a high proportion of humic substances (humic acids, fulvic acids and humin) which provide numerous sites for chemical reaction; microbial components known to enhance plant growth and disease suppression through the activities of bacteria (*Bacillus*), yeast (*Sporobolomyces* and *Cryptococcus*) and fungi (*Trichoderma*), as well as chemical antagonists such as phenols and amino acids (Theunissen, 2010).

Plant nutrients play a significant role in cell division and differentiation, growth, photosynthetic rate, water-use efficiency, leaf expansion, axillary bud growth, shoot canopy, photosynthetic surface area, carbohydrate utilization and protein synthesis. The effect of humic substances is more prominent in stimulating root respiration, formation and growth. This result in increased efficiency of the rooting system which in turn improves upper growth including the shoots, leaves, flowers and fruit (Atiyeh *et al.,* 2002). Vermicompost acts as both plant growth promoter and plant growth protector. It protects plants against various pests and diseases either by suppressing or repelling them or by inducing biological resistance in plants to fight them or by killing them through pesticidal action (Sinha *et al.,* 2010a).

Table 13.1: NPK Value of Vermicompost Compared with Conventional Cattle Dung Compost

Nutrients	Cattle dung compost	Vermicompost
Nitrogen (%)	0.4-1.0	2.5-3.0
Phosphorus (%)	0.4-0.8	1.8-2.9
Potassium (%)	0.8-1.2	1.4-2.0
Agarwal (1999)		

Table 13.2: Nutritive Values of Conventional Composting and Vermicomposting Systems

Parameter	Conventional Composting (%)	Vermicomposing (%)
Total Carbon (%)	9.34	13.5
Total Nitrogen (%)	1.05	1.33
Available Phosphorus (%)	0.32	0.47
Iron (mg/100 g)	587.87	746.2
Zinc (mg/100 g)	12.7	16.19
Manganese (mg/100 g)	35.25	53.86
Copper (mg/100 g)	4.42	5.16
Magnesium (mg/100 g)	689.32	832.48

Jadia and Fulekar (2008)

Vermicompost contains plant growth regulators and other plant growth influencing materials produced by microorganisms (Tomati *et al.*, 1990) including humates (Atiyeh *et al.*, 2002). Krishnamoorthy and Vajrabhiah (1986) reported the production of cytokinins and auxins in organic wastes that were processed by earthworms. Vermicompost also contains large amounts of humic substances (Masciandaro *et al.*, 1997) and some of the effects of these substances on plant growth have been shown to be very similar to the effects of soil-applied with plant growth regulators or hormones (Muscolo *et al.*, 1999).

Vermicomposts are rich in microbial population and diversity, particularly fungi, bacteria and actinomycetes (Edwards and Burrows, 1998). Yasir *et al.*, (2009) reported that the antifungal activity of vermicompost is due to the presence of chitinolytic bacterial communities. Plant growth-promoting bacteria directly stimulate growth by nitrogen fixation (Han *et al.*, 2005), solubilization of nutrients (Rodriguez and Fraga, 1999), production of growth hormones, (Correa *et al.*, 2004) and indirectly by antagonizing pathogenic fungi by production of siderophores, chitinase, glucanase, antibiotics and fluorescent pigments (Han *et al.*, 2005).

Annual application of adequate amounts of vermicompost led to significant increase in soil enzyme activities such as urease, phosphomonoesterase, phosphodiesterase and arylsulphatase (Albiach *et al.*, 2000). Vermicomposts have large particulate surface area that provides many microsites for microbial activity and for the strong retention of nutrients (Shi-Wei and Fu-Zhen, 1991).

Vermicompost contains enzymes like amylase, lipase, cellulase and chitinase, which continue to break down organic matter in the soil (to release the nutrients and make it available to the plant roots) even after they have been excreted (Chaoui *et al.*, 2003). They also increase the level of important soil enzymes like dehydrogenase, acid and alkaline phosphatases and urease.

Urease play a key role in N-cycle as it hydrolyses urea and phosphatase to convert soil phosphorus into bio-available form for plants (Sinha *et al.,* 2010b).

Application of Vermicompost in Agriculture

Cereal Crops

In paddy, vermicompost @ 5 t /ha along with recommended dose of NPK recorded significantly higher yield of rice as compared to application of only N, P_2O_5 and K_2O (Vasanthi and Kumarswamy, 1996). Vermicompost influenced the growth and productivity of rice significantly (Edwards and Burrows, 1998; Rakshit *et al.,* 2008). Vermicompost application and vermiwash spraying increased plant growth and yield of rice (Tharmaraj *et al.,* 2011). At Siruguppa (Karnataka), Murali and Setty (2000) reported that application of vermicompost at 5 t/ha resulted in significantly higher yield (4889 kg/ha) compared to no vermicompost application in scented rice. In rain fed lowland rice, Singh *et al* (2005) indicated that the effective substitution of the recommended N dose of rice could be done up to 33% by vermicompost. Combined application inorganic and organic source had better buildup of soil organic C and available N, P and K after crop harvest. Barik *et al* (2006) showed that reduction of 50% recommended dose of fertilizer along with vermicompost @ 10 t/ha significantly influenced the growth and yield attributes of kharif rice which recorded higher grain and straw yield. Higher gross return was recorded from 50 % recommended dose of fertilizer with vermicompost at 10 t/ha which was significantly higher than the FYM treated plots. Pontillas *et al.* (2009) found that a significant favorable effect on the growth, yield and return on investment in rice production was observed when vermicompost was supplemented with inorganic in low land rice. Hossaen *et al* (2011) recorded maximum number of effective tiller, grain per panicle, test weight, longer panicle size, higher grain and straw yield of boro paddy with 70 % NPKS fertilizer along with poultry manure at 2.4 t /ha which is at par with 70% NPKS + vermicompost at 3 t /ha. Balamurugan and Sudhakar (2012) concluded that cultivation of rice with SRI method along with application of pressmud based vermicompost @ 3.0 t /ha will be a promising combination which resulted in higher yields and economic returns.

Table 13.3. Yield and Harvest Index of Aman Paddy

Treatments	Grain yield (t/ha)	Straw yield (t /ha)	Biological yield (t /ha)	Harvest index (%)
100 % NPK	5.02c	6.28c	11.30c	44.43ab
NPK + Vermicompost 2.5 t/ha	5.40ab	6.61b	12.01b	44.96a
75% NPK + Vermicompost 2.5 t/ha	5.32b	6.48bc	11.80b	45.08a
50 % NPK + Vermicompost 2.5 t/ha	4.32e	5.68e	10.00e	43.20b

100 %NPK+ Vermicompost 2.5 t/ha+ PSB @ 7.5 kg/ ha +*Azotobacter@* 7.5 kg/ha	5.56a	7.00a	12.56a	44.28ab
75% NPK + Vermicompost 2.5 t/ha + PSB @ 7.5 kg /ha + *Azotobacter@* 7.5 kg/ha	5.42ab	6.93a	12.35a	43.87ab
50 % NPK + Vermicompost 2.5 t/ha + PSB @ 7.5 kg/ha +*Azotobacter@* 7.5 kg/ha	4.68d	6.02d	10.70d	43.75ab
CD 5 %	0.20	0.23	0.28	1.45

(Tapan Kumar Garai, 2013). NPK: 80:40:40 kg /ha

At Burdwan (West Bengal), vermicompost alone or with bio-fertilizer unable to supplement 50% of the recommended dose of NPK fertilizer to get comparable yield of both *aman* rice (Table 13.3). But, biofertilizer at this level of NPK fertilizer significantly increases the rice yield. In *aman* season, on an average vermicompost alone increased 5.6 % grain yield whereas vermicompost along with biofertilizer increased grain yield by 10.23 % (Tapan Kumar Garai, 2013).

Increase in crop yield of wheat, soil nutrient status and nutrients uptake has been reported due to application of vermicompost (Roberts *et al.,* 2007). Rather and Sharma (2009) recorded significantly higher grain and straw yield of wheat along with maximum nutrient uptake by the crop was recorded with combined use vermicompost, Azotobacter and zinc along with 100% recommended fertilizer which remained at par with those recorded with 75% recommended fertilizer dose plus Zn, Vermicompost and Azotobacter.

Table 13.4: Effect of Vermicomposted Mustard Straw on Grain and Straw Yield of Barley

Treatment	Grain yield (q/ ha)	Straw yield (q/ ha)	B:C ratio
100 % NPK (80:40:0) (Control)	41.34	61.68	--
100 % NPK + 10 t FYM ha-1	41.34	76.11	2.28
75 % NPK + 5 t V.C ha-1	48.09	74.59	2.32
50 % NPK + 7.5 t V.C ha-1	48.97	77.98	2.00
CD 5 %	3.50	3.85	-

(Lal *et al.,* 2008)

At Durgapura (Rajasthan), application of 75% recommended dose of fertilizer (NPK) + 5 tonnes vermicomposted mustard straw /ha gave significantly higher grain and straw yield (48.09 and 74.59 q /ha) as compared to recommended dose of NPK (80:40:0 kg/ha) without organic manure *i.e.* 41.34 and 61.68 q /ha, respectively and found at par with 100 % recommended dose of NPK + 10 t FYM /ha and 50% recommended dose of NPK + 7.5 ton vermicomposted mustard straw/ ha (Table 13.4) (Lal *et al.*, 2008).

At Bijapur (Karnataka), addition of vermicompost @ 20 t/ha could be a substitute for recommended mineral N rate. The addition of vermicompost @ 10 t/ha in combination with 50% of recommended dose of NPK saved 50% of the mineral N requirement of sorghum during rabi (Mastiholi and Itnal, 1997). Similarly, a positive response was obtained with the application of vermicompost to sorghum (*Sorghum bicolor*) (Patil and Sheelavantar, 2000).

Application of 50 per cent RDF with 0.5 t/ha vermicompost recorded significantly higher maize yield than recommended dose of chemical fertilizer alone (CRIDA, 2003). Significantly higher grain yield of maize (67.47q /ha) was obtained with the application of vermicompost @ 2 t/ha and was on par with the grain yield of maize with the application of FYM @ 10 t/ha (65.22 q/ha) (Jayaprakash *et al.*, 2003). Vermicompost application increased plant growth and enhanced yield of maize (Kalantari *et al.*, 2011; Brito *et al.*, 2009). Guerrero (2010) reported that yields of corn fertilized with vermicompost at 5 t/ha was comparable with those for corn fertilized with 100% chemical fertilizers. Sirisha (2002) reported higher dry matter yields of maize (130.16 q/ ha) were recorded in vermicompost treated plots followed by poultry manure, FYM, Glyricidia and rice straw while the lowest was observed in control (64.35 q/ha). Reddy and Reddy (1999) observed that the DTPA extractable cationic micronutrients (Fe, Cu, Mn and Zn) were significantly increased with the integrated use of manures and fertilizers (25, 50, 75 and 100% of recommended N). Micronutrient availability was higher in treatments with vermicompost (VC) closely followed by poultry manure (PM), biogas slurry and FYM in maize – soybean cropping systems.

Table 13.5: Maize Grain Yield and Stover Yield as Influenced by Integrated Nutrient Management Involving Incorporation of Vermicomposts in Soil

Treatments	Yield (kg /ha)			Uptake of phosphorus (kg /ha)		
	Dry matter at 60 DAS	Grain	Stover	N	P	K
Control	3145	1862	4332	49.69	9.43	50.63
75 % RDFN (90 kg /ha)	3769	2734	5249	88.57	12.06	61.81
75% RDFN+ FYM (10 t/ha)	4358	3587	6052	104.15	14.81	72.34
100% RDFN (120 kg ha-1)	7096	5692	8241	195.14	32.64	124.88
100 % RDFN + FYM (10 t/ ha)	7524	5869	8516	210.67	36.11	133.92
75 % RDFN + VM with rice straw (2.5t/ha)	5037	5132	7623	123.40	18.63	85.12
75 % RDFN + VM with *Glyricidia sp* (2.5 t/ha)	6942	5601	8073	185.35	31.23	121.48

75% RDFN + VM with cow dung (2.5 t/ha)	6482	5562	8056	170.47	28.52	112.78
75 % RDFN + VM with *Parthenium* (2.5 t/ha)	5862	5375	7792	150.65	24.62	100.82
75% RDFN + VM with *Lantana camera* (2.5 t/ha)	5579	5229	7873	141.14	22.31	95.40
CD 5%	541	165	144	30.04	3.00	16.57

(Shailaja, 2005)

At Hyderabad (Telungana), dry matter, grain and stover yields, nutrient uptake by maize crop under vermicomposts treated plots were significantly more than in control (Table 13.5) (Shailaja, 2005).

Marjan *et al.* (2013) concluded that effect of mycorrhiza and Azotobacter in presence of vermicompost was greater in terms of yield grain of common millet.

Pulse Crops

Parthasarathi *et al* (2008) observed that vermicompost application increased yield and quality (protein and sugar content in seed) of black gram was enhanced in soils, particularly clay loam soil.

Combined application of FYM @ 5 t/ha and vermicompost at 3 t/ha was significantly superior and recorded higher grain yield of pigeonpea and finger millet over no fertilizer but they were on par with the treatment receiving 50% RDF (Gholve *et al.*, 2005).

The application of vermicompost gave higher germination (93%) of mung bean (*Vigna radiata*) compared with bio digested slurry (84%). Further, the growth and yield of mung bean was also significantly higher with vermicompost application (Karmegam *et al.*, 1999).

Lopes *et al.* (1996) reported that an increase in levels of vermicompost up to 10 t/ha significantly increased nodulation and dry matter yield of cowpea over rest of treatments. Likewise, in another pot culture experiment, the fresh and dry matter yields of cowpea (Vigna unguiculata) were higher when soil was amended with vermicompost than with biodigested slurry (Karmegam and Daniel, 2000). Rajan and Mahalakshmi (2007) reported that the number of leaves produced in cowpea seedlings were higher in treatment containing 75% vermicompost. Netwal (2003) conducted a field experiment at Jobner during *kharif* season of 2001 and reported that application of vermicompost of 5 t/ha, significantly increased the pods per plant, seeds per pod, harvest index and seed and straw yield of cowpea over control 5 t FYM and 2.5 t vermicompost/ha.

Application of vermicompost @ 3 t/ha produced significantly higher seed yield of chickpea over control and was on par with that of vermicompost applied @ 2 t/ha(CRIDA, 2003). Similar results made by Jat and Ahlwat (2004) in chickpea with application of vermicompost @ 3 t/ha produced significantly higher dry matter, (19.78 g per plant), LAI (1.57), number of pods per plant (27.38), seed yield (2.35 t/ ha) and straw yield (3.81 t/ ha).

The yield of pea (Pisum sativum) was also higher with the application of vermicompost (10 t/ha) along with recommended N, P and K than with these fertilizers alone (Reddy *et al.*, 1998).

Manivannan *et al.* (2009) studied that the increased growth and yield of the bean, (*Phaseolus vulgaris*) influences the physical conditions of the soil and supported better aeration to the plant roots, absorption of water, induction of N, P and K exchange there by resulting better growth of the plants. Soil application of vermicompost increased growth and yield of common bean (*Phaseolus vulgaris*) (Ansari and Jaikishun, 2011).

Oil Seed Crops

In soybean increase in dry matter accumulation in the plant by 40-70 per cent was observed with application of vermicompost as compared to without application of vermicompost (Luishuxin *et al.*, 1991). Further 50% RDF + vermicompost was significantly superior in increasing the seed yield of soybean over RDF alone and 50% RDF alone to soybean in soybean – cotton cropping system (Babalad, 1999).

At Junagadh (Gujarat), application of vermicompost @ 3 t/ha in groundnut crop during *Kharif* found higher yield (2144 kg/ha), gross return (Rs. 80888/ha) and B:C ratio (6.16) as compared to application of only of recommended dose of fertilizers (1858 kg/ha) (Table 13.6) (Chavda and Singh, 2015).

Table 6. Performance of Vermicompost on *kharif* Groundnut Crop

Treatments	Pod yield (kg/ha)	Gross return (Rs./ha)	Net return (Rs./ha)
Recommended dose of fertilizers	1858	69546	57476
vermicompost @ 3 t/ha	2144	80888	67756

(Chavda and Singh, 2015)

A positive response was obtained with the application of vermicompost to sunflower (Helianthus annuus) (Devi and Agarwal, 1998). At Hisar (Haryana), Devi - Dayal *et al.*, (1998) found that the hybrid sunflower cv. *Badhshah gave* higher yield with the combination of organic manures @ 10 t/ha + 80 kg N/ha + 40kg P_2O_5 /ha. Among the organic manures, vermicompost showed superiority at the level of 10 t/ha in respect of yield of sunflower on sandy loam soil during the spring season.

Commercial Crops

Application of RDF + vermicompost produced significantly higher kapas yield of cotton over RDF alone to cotton crop in soybean – cotton cropping system

(Babalad, 1999). Badole and More (2000) observed that combined application of neem seed cake @ 2 t/ha + *Azospirillum* + PSM recorded higher dry matter yield (2587 kg /ha) and seed cotton yield (1415.85 kg/ha) over control but was on par with pressmud @ 25 t/ha, neem seed cake @ 2 t/ha, vermicompost @ 5 t/ha + *Azospirillum* + PSM and gliricidia @ 10 t/ha+ *Azospirillum* + PSM respectively. Soil application of organically bound micronutrient mixture (100 kg/ha) recorded significantly higher number of bolls per plant (36), boll weight (6.1g) and kapas yield (17.9 q/ha) over control (Murthy *et al.*, 2000). On deep black soil at Rahuri, application of vermicompost @ 10 t /ha recorded significantly higher seed cotton yield (14.75 q/ha) over control (Raut and Mehetre, 2008). Similarly, on sandy loam at KVK, Sirsa, noticed that 50 % RDN through fertilizer + 50 % through vermicompost recorded higher yield and quality parameters like fibre length, fibre finess and fibre manturity ratio over control (Jat and Ahlwat, 2004). The organic nutrient management with vermicompost equivalent to 100% RDN produced on par yield and yield components with RDF + FYM which recorded higher mean boll weight, seed cotton yield (1230 kg/ha), bundle strength (40.27 g) and fibre length (29.79 mm) over other treatments (Shivalingayya, 2010).

At Junagadh (Gujarat), application of vermicompost @ 5 t/ha in cotton crop produced higher yield. (3500 kg/ ha), gross return (₹ 172375/ha) and BC ratio (4.66) as compared to application of recommended dose of fertilizers (3044 kg/ ha) during *Kharif* season (Table 13.7) (Chavda and Singh, 2015).

Table 13.7: Effect of Vermicompost on Yield and Economics of Cotton Crop

Treatments	Kapas yield (kg/ha)	Gross return (Rs./ha)	Net return (Rs./ha)
Recommended dose of fertilizers	3044	151006	117572
vermicompost @ 3 t/ha	3500	172375	135395

(Chavda and Singh, 2015)

In saline soil, Jambhekar and Bhiday (1992) observed that height and girth of internode of sugarcane increased by 5% each with the addition of vermicompost @ 10 t/ha over control. Similarly, percentage of Jaggery to sugarcane juice was 17 and 13% more with vermicompost and recommended fertilizer application than that of control, respectively. The addition of vermicompost reduced the electrical conductivity by 36 and 50% over original and chemical fertilized soil, respectively, while the application of recommended fertilizer increased the electrical conductivity by 26% to original soil.

Table 13.8: Effect of Different Organic Manures on Millable Canes, Cane Yield and Sugar Yield of Sugarcane Plant–Ratoon System

Treatments	Millable canes/ ha		Canes yield (t/ha)		Sugar yield(t/ha)	
	Plant	Ratoon	Plant	Ratoon	Plant	Ratoon
RDF	88,166	81,423	87.42	80.22	11.06	9.79
FYM (25 t/ ha) + RDF	95,338	84,390	94.18	86.12	12.92	10.62
PMC (12 t/ ha) + RDF	92,926	85,122	90.12	84.88	11.67	10.36
VC (2.5t/ ha) + RDF	94,458	86,450	93.88	85.94	12.59	10.60
NADEP	92,336	84,130	91.58	82.12	12.20	10.14
CD 5%	2010	1918	4.52	3.59	1.52	1.26

At Anakapalle (Andhra Pradesh), Farm Yard Manure + RDF registered higher cane yield (94.18 t/ha) and sugar yield (12.92 t/ha) than application of entire 'N' through RDF alone (cane yield: 87.42 t/ha and sugar yield: 11.06 t/ha) but was found at par with vermicompost + RDF (cane yield 93.88 t/ha; sugar yield: 12.59 t/ha) (Table 13.8) (Rama Lakshmi *et al.*, 2011).

Application of Vermicompost in Horticulture

Fruit Crops

Vermicompost application along with other organic manures increased plant growth and enhanced yield of banana (Athani *et al.*, 2009; Athani *et al.*, 1999).

Vermicompost application suppressed infection of insect pests, repel crop pests and induce biological resistance in plants against pests and diseases due the presence of antibiotics and actinomycetes in strawberry (Arancon *et al.*, 2006; Munroe, 2007). Arancon *et al.* (2004) reported significant increase in leaf area, number of flowers, shoot weights and total marketable fruits in strawberry the application of vermicomposts prepared from different wastes (food and paper wastes). Application of vermicompost enhanced plant growth and yield in strawberry (Singh *et al.*, 2008; Arancon *et al.*, 2004). Gupta and Tripathi (2012) found that the combined application of Azotobacter at 7 kg/ ha + vermicompost at 30 t/ha significantly increased height of plant (19.45 and 17.65 cm, respectively), number of leaves (63.60 and 59.60, respectively), number of crowns (7.28 and 6.27, respectively), number of runners (5.34 and 4.32, respectively) per plant, whereas maximum number of flowers (67.48 and 64.51, respectively) and fruits set (39.21 and 36.19, respectively) per plant with increased duration of harvesting (71.04 and 69.02 days, respectively) and minimum number of days taken to produce first flower (56.15 and 54.15 days, respectively) and fruit set (6.44 and 5.94 days, respectively) with significantly more yield (324.38 and 320.39 g/plant, respectively) were also observed in

Azotobacter at 6 kg/ha + vermicompost at 30 t/ha applied plants of strawberry cv. Chandler.

Vegetable Crops

Hashemimajol *et al.* (2004) revealed that vermicompost produced from raw dairy manure (RDM) along with some other compost (sewage sludge + rice hull) gave greater shoot and root dairy matters (DM) of tomatoes than the control (soil + sand) in tomato. Abduli *et al.* (2012) found that growth of tomato plants significantly rise by increasing ration of vermicompost combined with soil. Samawat *et al.* (2001) reported that vermicompost had a significant effect on root and fruit weight of tomatoes. In 100 per cent vermicompost treatment, fruit weight and shoot and root weight were three, five and nine times more than the control, respectively. Arancon *et al.* (2003) reported significant increase in leaf area, number of flowers, shoot weights and total marketable fruits in pepper by the application of vermicomposts prepared from different wastes (food and paper wastes). Application of vermicompost increased plant growth and enhanced yield in tomato (Azarmi *et al.*, 2008; Lazcano *et al.*, 2009; Chanda *et al.*, 2011; Mogle and Chamle, 2011). Arancon *et al* (2002) found significantly higher growth and yields of field tomatoes with vermicomposts as compared to chemical fertilizer alone. Rasool *et al.* (2008) recorded higher growth and yield of tomato with vermicompost at 15 t /ha. Vermicompost with rate of 15 t /ha increased EC of fruit juice and percentage of fruit dry matter up to 30 and 24 %, respectively. The content of K, P, Fe and Zn in the plant tissue increased 55, 73, 32 and 36 % compared to untreated plots respectively. At Dharwar, Patil *et al.*, (1998) noted the higher yield of tomato (18.66 t/ha) and net income (Rs. 28970 /ha) under the combined application of 100% NPK (100:75:100 kg NPK /ha) with vermicompost @ 2t/ha. Vermicompost @ 4t/ha with 50 % NPK produced yield of 18.10 t/ha and net income of Rs. 27,490/ha.

Vermicompost application increased plant growth and enhanced yield of brinjal (Guerrero and Guerrero 2006; Premsekhar and Rajashree, 2009)

Mishra *et al.*, (2009) studied the effect of source of nutrients (Organic and inorganic and biofertilizers on growth yield and economic of okra cv. VRO-6 the present experiment was conducted at Indian Institute of Vegetable Research, Varanasi during summer season of 2006-07 and 2007-08. The results revealed significant improvement in all the growth and yield parameters over recommended dose of N, P, K. The maximum length of fruit, diameter of fruit, fresh weight of fruit, dry weight of fruit and yield was recorded with application of vermicompost @ 2-5 t/ha + NPK (120:60:60 kg/ha) + PSB + *Azotobacter* over rest of the treatments. Vanmathi and Selvakumari (2012) reported that the application of vermicompost increased the vegetative growth and yield of *Hibiscus esculentus*. Usha Kumari *et al.* (1999) reported that 12 t/ha vermicompost + full dose of recommend fertilizer (50: 80: 25 kg NPK /ha) produced higher yield and vermicompost as an organic source significantly reduced the cost of okra production. Ramdhan (2004) conducted an experiment on cauliflower and found that application of 7.5 t ha^{-1} vermicompost increased the volume of curd significantly. The highest number of fruits per plant (6.8) in case of okra was obtained with 4 t per ha of compost, split applied twice at planting and five weeks after planting. Similarly, Chander *et al.* (2005) recorded higher yield of okra in the treatment comprising 100% recommended NPK + vermicompost @ 10, 11.10 and 11.63 t /ha. Bairwa *et al.* (2009) reported that okra produced higher number of fruits (18.36), fruit yield (182.50 g /plant and 135.18 q /ha), fruit weight (17.65 g), length of fruits (12.26 cm) and thickness of fruits (1.898 cm) with the application of neem cake 6 q /ha + vermicompost 10 q /ha + *Azotobacter* + PSB + 60% recommended dose of NPK through inorganic fertilizers. Sharma *et al.* (2009) reported that higher yield of okra was recorded in the treatment comprising 100% recommended NPK + vermicompost @10 t /ha. Sharma *et al.* (2010) recorded that application of 5 t vermicompost / ha recorded significantly higher values of yield attributes, fruit yield (69.2/ ha) and protein content (18.0%) as well as B:C ratio (2.11) with net returns of Rupees 35614/ ha in okra crop.

Table 13.9: Effect of Bio-organics on Growth Parameters, Yield Attributes, Yield and Quality of Okra

Bio-organics	Plant height (cm)	Braches / plant	Leaf area (cm^2)	Fruits/ plant	Fruits Yield (q/ha)	Fruit quality (%)		
						Nitro-gen	Protein	Crude fiber
Control	95.43	2.10	985	19.55	105.61	0.191	1.19	1.36
Azotobacter	104.82	2.39	1110	22.51	128.56	0.233	1.46	1.33
Vermicompost @ 5 t/ha	111.32	2.63	1210	24.32	146.93	0.274	1.71	1.30
Vermicompost (5 t/ha) + *Azotobacter*	116.82	2.81	1265	25.98	164.23	0.314	1.96	1.27
CD 5 %	5.09	0.14	68	1.58	3.19	0.011	0.08	NS

(Yadav, 2014)

At Jobner (Rajasthan), application of vermicompost @ 5 t /ha + *Azotobacter* significantly increased the above growth yield and quality parameters as compared to rest of treatments. Higher net return (₹ 147867 /ha) and B: C ratio (1:3.0) were recorded in vermicompost @ 5 t /ha + *Azotobacter* (Table 9) (Yadav, 2014).

Yadav and Yadav (2010) conducted an experiment on okra and observed that the integrated application of 75 per cent RDF with vermicompost @ 6.5 t/ha gave significantly higher marketable fruit yield (86.40 g/ha), which was at par with the treatments namely 50 per cent RDF with vermicompost @ 6.5 t/ha and 75 per cent RDF + Neem cake @ 3.5 t/ha. Gupta *et al.* (2011) found that biofertilizer and vermicompost showed positive effect in improving quality and quantity of the okra crop and the best results were obtained in the plot with combination of chemical fertilizers, biofertilizer and vermicompost. The maximum root length, shoot length, dry weight of plant, number of fruits and total fruits production was found to be 13.20 cm, 37.56 cm, 12.64 and 4864 kg/ha respectively in case of combination of chemical fertilizers, biofertilizer and vermicompost. At Jabalpur (Chhattisgarh), vermicompost @ 5 t/ha + vermiwash 5 sprays at 10 days interval after 30 DAS showed maximum plant height (128.09 cm), nodes per plant (40.80), internodal length (8.03 cm), days taken to 50% flowering (46 days) and nodes to first flowering (8.20) in okra var. Kashi Pragati. Number of fruits per plant (21.36), fruit length (13.31 cm), fruit girth (17.01 mm), fruit weight (14.33 g), fruiting span (48.66 days), fruit yield per plant (134.48 g) and yield per hectare (74.62 q) were observed maximum by the application of vermicompost @ 5 t/ha + vermiwash 5 sprays at 10 days interval after 30 DAS. However, the maximum C:B ratio of 1:1.94 was obtained by application of recommended dose of NPK + vermiwash as soil application + foliar spray of vermiwash 3 sprays at 10 days interval after 30 DAS followed by the treatment vermicompost @ 5 t/ha + vermiwash 5 sprays at 10 days interval after 30 DAS.

Sreenivas *et al.* (2000b) worked with ridge gourd cv. Pusa Nasdar found that the increased rates of vermicompost increased fruit yield. The vermicompost @ 10 t/ha + 50:25:50 kg NPK /ha increased the fruit volume, fruit weight, fruit yield per vine in ridge gourd.

Chander *et al.* (2005) recorded maximum yield (14.67 t /ha) of onion was observed in plots receiving 100 % recommended NPK + 25 t vermicompost / ha. Sharma *et al.* (2009) reported that maximum yield of onion was observed in plant receiving 100 % recommended NPK + 25 t vermicompost /ha.

Rajan and Mahalakshmi (2007) reported that the leaf area, tuber length, and wet weight of radish were higher in 100 per cent vermicompost applied plots.

Vermicompost application increased plant growth and enhanced yield of red amaranth (Alam *et al.*, 2007b). Uma and Malathi (2009) found that growth, survival rate was better with vermicompost as compare to chemical fertilizer in Amaranthus species.

Amending soils with vermicompost can increase the growth and yield of coriander (Vadiraj *et al.*, 1998).

In potato, Patil *et al.* (1995) found that application of vermicompost @ 4 t /ha + 50% RDF recorded significantly higher yield (34 t/ha) and number of leaves per plant compared to recommended dose of fertilizer alone. Vermicompost application increased plant growth and enhanced yield of potato (Ansari 2008). In Level Barind Tract (Bangladesh) soils, application of 100 % inorganic fertilizers with 5-10 t/ha of vermicompost was suitable for higher production of potato and economically profitable (Alam *et al.,* 2007a). At Jorhat (Assam), Mrinal *et al.,* (1998) reported that an application of 75 % recommended dose of NPK along with 2.5 t/ha vermicompost produced the higher tuber yield of potato (14.1 t/ha).

Species Crops

Surindra Suthar (2009) observed that the maximum range of some plant parameters *i.e.* root length, shoot length, leaf length, fresh weight, number of cloves in garlic were in the treatment using 15 t/ha vermicompost + 50% NPK and with applied vermicomposted FYM showed a comparatively better result of plant production than composted manure. Arguello *et al.,* (2006) observed that vermicompost application caused early bulbing (18 to 20 days) in garlic (*Allium sativum*) and increased scorodose accumulation which is directly related to harvest index, resulting in greater yield besides bulb quality.

Arancon *et al.* (2002) found significantly higher growth and yields of peppers with vermicomposts as compared to chemical fertilizer alone. Arancon *et al.* (2005) reported significant increase in leaf area, number of flowers, shoot weights and total marketable fruits in pepper by the application of vermicomposts prepared from different wastes (food and paper wastes).

Significantly higher plant height, number of fruits per plant, number of branches and yield was recorded with the application of 20 t /ha of vermicompost over control in chilli (Jagvir singh *et al.,* 1997). Vitakar *et al.* (2007) reported that treatment with 50 per cent N through vermicompost and 50 per cent N through neem cake produced the maximum plant height, number of primary branches, number of fruits per plant, fruit weight, fruit length, fruit diameter and total yield compared to recommended dose of fertilizers in chilli crop. Kondappa *et al.* (2009) studied the effect of integrated nutrient management on growth, yield and economics of chilli cv. Byadgi Dabbi and concluded that use of integrated application of vermicompost with fertilizers remained beneficial. There was a positive and significant effect of compost (vermicompost or coirpith compost) along with organic booster, cow dung urine slurry or inorganic fertilizer on green fruit chilli yield and yield attributes over recommended dose of NPK. Though coir pith compost @ 2.5 t /ha + organic booster @ 1 liter per m^2 recorded highest green chilli yield, it was on par with vermicompost @ 5 t/ ha + organic booster at 1 liter per m^2 (Hangarge *et al.,* 2002).

Other Crops

Nethra *et al,* (1999) reported that the fresh weight of flowers of Chrysanthemum chinensis increased with the application of different levels of vermicompost. Also, the number of flowers per plant (26), flower diameter (6 cm) and yield

(0.5 t /ha) were maximum with the application of 10 t/ha of vermicompost along with 50% of recommended dose of NPK fertilizer. However, the vase life of flowers (11 days) was high with the combined application of vermicompost at 15 t /ha and 50% of recommended dose of NPK fertilizer.

Application of vermicompost increased plant growth, leaf area index and flower yield of salvia, china aster (Balaji, 1994). Vermicompost application increased plant growth and enhanced yield of ornamental and flowering plant 'Dream Neon Rose' (Chamani *et al.*, 2008). Amending soils with vermicompost increased the growth and yield of water cress (*Lepidium sativum*) (Masciandaro *et al.*, 1997).

Singh *et al.* (1998) reported that oat var. Kept produced the higher fresh and dry forage yield when 75% NPK was supplemented with vermicompost @ 10 t/ha. In vertisol of Jabalpur showed that the application of vermicompost @10 t/ha alone produced higher fodder yield of oat (411.2 q/ha) over FYM (357.8 q/ha) and was found at par to 50% NPK alone (Anonymous, 1998).

At Akola, Murarkar *et al.* (1998) noticed that application of full dose of NPK fertilizer (300:120:120 kg NPK/ha) with vermicompost @ 6 t/ha and half dose of FYM (10 cart load/ha) was significantly better than control which increased the number of branches, plant height, number of leaves per plant and leaf yield per plant in mulbery crop. Chakraborty *et al.* (2008) reported that the application of vermicompost rendered better performance in respect of all round growth of mulberry plants in the lateritic soil of South West Bengal.

Vermicompost application increased plant growth and enhanced yield of *Jatropa curcas* (Kumara *et al.*, 2009).

Potting Medium

According to Atiyeh *et al.*, (2002) vermicompost has the potential for improving plant growth when added to greenhouse container media or soil and also it increases germination, growth and yield of various vegetables and ornamental plants significantly and consistently. Application of vermicompost increased plant growth in potting medium (Warman and AngLopez, 2010).

Nutrient Uptake

The earthworms are the agents of turning, fragmentation and aeration. It also increase N_2 fixation by both nodular and free living N_2 fixing bacteria and thus enhance plant growth. Vermicompost has been proved as cheapest source of nitrogen and other essential elements for better nodulation and yield particularly in legumes. Such plants can meet their N needs through both biological nitrogen fixation (symbiosis) and native nitrogen in the soil (Ranganathan and Parthasarathi, 2000). Sreenivas *et al.*, (2000a) studied the integrated effect of application of fertilizer and vermicompost on soil available nitrogen (N) and uptake of ridge gourd (Luffa acutangula). Soil available N increased significantly with increasing levels of vermicompost and highest N uptake was obtained at 50% of the recommended fertilizer rate plus 10 t /ha vermicompost. Similarly, the uptake of N, phosphorus (P), potassium (K) and magnesium (Mg) by rice (Oryza sativa) plant was highest when fertilizer was applied in combination with vermicompost (Jadhav *et al.*, 1997). Similarly, Sailaja kumari and Ushakumari (2002) studied the effect of enriched vermicompost with rock phosphate on the yield and uptake of nutrients by cowpea and revealed that enriched vermicompost showed its superiority over other treatments for uptake of major nutrients like N, P, K, Ca, and Mg.

Uptake of nitrogen of marigold in vermicompost applied plots was significantly higher than that of FYM applied plots. This indicates the nitrogen mineralization in vermicompost-applied plots was greater as compared to FYM. The activity of 'N' fixers was higher with vermicompost applied plots the soil 'p' content and 'p' uptake in Rice was higher with vermicompost compared to FYM and chemical fertilizers alone (Bagyaraj and Powell, 1985). Application of vermicompost to paddy field has long range influence on soil, in improving chemical and biological properties (Kale *et al.*, 1992). Integrated application of worm cast with chemical fertilizer showed that increase in the nitrogen content of straw and seed and also increased the nitrogen uptake by wheat crop (Zhao and Haung, 1991). Stephens *et al.* (1994) reported that in sandy loam soils, presence of earthworms increased the nutrient uptake (N, P, K, Ca, Mg, Mn, Fe, S, Cu, Na & Zn) in wheat plants.

Gopal Reddy, (1997) observed higher dehydrogenase, urease and phosphatase activity was recorded with 100% substitution of RDN with vermicompost, poultry manure, biogas slurry and FYM in maize-soybean cropping system and it was at par with 50 and 75% substitution, while only inorganic fertilizer (RDF) recorded the lower urease activity. At Kasaragod (Kerala), Maheswarappa *et al.* (1997) revealed that FYM and vermicompost application to arrowroot crop decreased the bulk density, increased soil porosity and water holding capacity to a greater extent. In Malaprabha command area, on *Vertisols* significantly higher uptake of N, P_2O_5 and K_2O by sunflower crop was recorded with application of vermicompost @ 2 t ha^{-1} followed by FYM, cotton stalk and maize residues. Further, the available N, P_2O_5 and K_2O and S in soil at harvest of sunflower was higher with the application of vermicompost @ 2 t ha^{-1} followed by FYM (Kademani *et al.*, 2003). The vermicompost application significantly improved organic carbon, available P_2O_5 and K_2O and DTPA – extractable Zn, Fe, Cu and Mn content in the soil after harvest of chickpea (Singh and Yadav, 2004). Agrawal *et al.*, (2000) stated that an addition of organics either in the form of FYM or vermicompost @ 10 t/ha enhanced the organic carbon content of soil and make the soil porous by reducing the bulk density in forage crop field. The results were pronounced under vermicompost as compared to FYM on clay loam soil of Jabalpur. Jadhav *et al.* (1997) from a pot experiment on rice, reported that dry matter production and uptake of the major nutrients (N, P, K and Mg) were higher with the application of 75 kg N/ha as urea and 25 kg N/ha through vermicompost.

Effect Vermicompost on Quality of Agricultural Produce

Lopes *et al.* (1996) reported that an increase in level of vermicompost upto 10 t/ha significantly increased plant total nitrogen content in cowpea. Sreenivas *et al.* (2000a) working with ridge gourd found that increased rates vermicompost increased fruit quality like TSS. The vermicompost 10 t/ha + 50:25:25 kg NPK / ha increased the total soluble solid in ridge gourd cv. Pusa Nasdar.

Yadav and Vijyakumari (2004) carried out an experiment to assess the effect of vermicomposted vegetable waste on the biochemical characters of chilli and found that the protein was higher on 60 (113.37 mg/g) and 90 days (79.69 mg/g) after sowing. The carbohydrate content (15.34 mg/g) was higher in vermicompost treatment on 60 days after sowing. On 60 days after sowing, higher chlorophyll b (2.61 mg/g) and total chlorophyll (3.62 mg/g) contents were observed while on 90 days after sowing higher chlorophyll a (1.01 mg/g) and total chlorophyll (1.92 mg/g) content were observed with vermicompost alone. Chander *et al.* (2005) reported that the application of vermicompost @ 10 t /ha increased the N uptake over 100 % NPK alone by 71% in okra and application of vermicompost @ 25 t /ha by 149% in onion.

Advantages of Vermicompost

- Vermicompost is rich in all essential plant nutrients and contains valuable vitamins, enzymes and hormones like auxins, gibberellins etc.
- Provides excellent effect on overall plant growth, encourages the growth of new shoots / leaves and improves the quality and shelf life of the produce.
- Vermicompost is free flowing, easy to apply, handle and store and does not have bad odour.
- It improves soil structure, texture, aeration, and water holding capacity and prevents soil erosion.
- Vermicompost is rich in beneficial micro flora such as a fixers, P-solubilizers, cellulose decomposing micro-flora etc in addition to improve soil environment.
- Vermicompost contains earthworm cocoons and increases the population and activity of earthworm in the soil.
- It prevents nutrient losses and increases the use efficiency of chemical fertilizers and enhances the decomposition of organic matter in soil.
- Vermicompost is free from pathogens, toxic elements, weed seeds etc. and minimizes the incidence of pest and diseases.

Conclusion

Vermicomposting technology is known throughout the world and considered as a widely spread popular technology. As a process for handling organic residuals, it represents an alternative approach in waste management, in as much as the material is neither landfilled nor burned but is considered a resource that may be recycled. In this sense, vermicomposting is compatible with sound environmental principles that value, conservation of resources and sustainable practices. Vermicompost can improve physical, chemical and biological properties of soil and is an excellent organic fertilizer. Presence of microbiota and phenolic compounds in vermicompost help to effectively control a number of plant pathogens and pests. A number of growth, yield and quality parameters of various crops are positively affected by vermicompost. In most of the studies, vermicompost when applied in combination with chemical or other fertilizers has been proved as a substitute of using chemical fertilizers alone. However, it has been proved more effective than chemical fertilizers in few studies. At the same time, it is an effective tool for solid waste management also. As organic fertilizers are slow releasing and have to be applied in bulks because of their lower N, P, K values as compared to chemical fertilizers, application of vermicompost alone may be costlier than applying chemical fertilizers alone or applying vermicompost in combination with chemical fertilizers. Farmers must be educated and made aware for the use of organic amendments like vermicompost in combination with chemical or other fertilizers. Cost effectiveness of vermicompost should also be reflected in future studies. Net economics of applied vermicompost and inorganic fertilizers must be compared to know whether such organic amendments are cost-effective for farmers or not and how these amendments can be made more cost effective in future so that the farmers of both developed and developing world can take its advantage without hesitation.

REFERENCES

Abduli, M.A., L. Aimiri, E. Madadian, S. Gitipour and S. Sedighian (2012). Efficiency of Vermicompost on Quantitative and Qualitative Growth of Tomato Plants. *International Journal of Environmental Research*, 7(2): 467 - 472.

Agarwal, S. (1999). Study of Vermicomposting of Domestic Waste and the Effects of Vermicompost on Growth of Some Vegetable Crops. Ph.D. Thesis, University of Rajasthan, Jaipur.

Agrawal, S.B., K.M. Dubey, G.S. Thakur, R.K. Dubey and N.S. Raghuwanshi (2000). Soil Faunal Activities for Sustainable Forage Production. In: Natl. Sem. On "Bio-diversity Conservation Management and Utilization for Sustainable Development" held at JNKVV Jabalpur from 19-20 April, 2000. pp: 77.

Alam, M.N., M.S. Jahan, M.K. Ali, M.A. Ashraf, and M.A. Islam (2007a). Effect of Vermicompost and Chemical Fertilizers on Growth, Yield and Yield Components of Potato in Barind soils of Bangladesh. *Journal of Applied Sciences*, 3 (12):1879 - 1888.

Alam, M.N., M.S. Jahan, M.K. Ali, M.S Islam and S.M.A.T. Khandaker (2007b). Effect of Vermicompost and NPKS Fertilizers on Growth, Yield and Yield Components of Red Amaranth. *Australian Journal of Basic and Applied Sciences*, 1 (4): 706 -716.

Albiach, R., R. Canet, F. Pomares and F. Ingelmo (2000). Microbial Biomass Content and Enzymatic Activities After Application of Organic Amendments to a Horticultural Soil. *Bioresource Technology*, 75: 43 - 48.

Anonymous (1998). Annual Progress Report, All India Coordinated Research Project on Forage Crops, JNKVV, Jabalpur. pp. 46.

Ansari, A.A. (2008). Effect of Vermicompost on the Productivity of Potato (*Solanum tuberosum*), Spinach (*Spinacia oleracea*) and Turnip (*Brassica campestris*). *World Journal of Agricultural Sciences*, 4 (3): 333 - 336.

Ansari, A.A. and S.Jaikishun (2011). Vermicomposting of Sugarcane Bagasse and Rice Straw and Its Impact on the Cultivation of *Phaseolus vulgaris L.* in Guyana, South America. *Journal of Agricultural Technology*, 7 (2): 225 - 234.

Arancon, N. Q., C.A, Edwards and P.Bierman (2006). Influences of Vermicomposts on Field Strawberries: Effects on Soil Microbial and Chemical Properties. *Bioresource Technology*, 97: 831 - 840.

Arancon, N. Q., C.A. Edwards, P. Bierman, C Welch and J.D. Metzer (2004). Influence of Vermicomposts on Field Strawberries: Effect on Growth and Yields. *Bioresource Technology*, 93: 145 - 153.

Arancon, N. Q., C.A. Edwards, P. Bierman, J. D. Metzger, S. Lee and C.Welch (2003). Effects of Vermicomposts on Growth and Marketable Fruits of Field-grown Tomatoes, Peppers and Strawberries. *Pedobiologia*, 47: 731 - 735.

Arancon, N.Q,, C.A. Edwards, P. Bierman, J. Metzger, S. Lee and C. Welch (2002). Applications of Vermicomposts to Tomatoes and Peppers Grown in the Field and Strawberries Grown Unger High Plastic Tunnels. In: Proceedings of the International Earthworm Symposium, Cardiff Wales. September.P: 84.

Arancon, N.Q., C.A. Edwards, P. Bierman, J.D. Metzger and C.Lucht (2005). Effects of Vermicomposts Produced from Cattle Manure, Food Waste and Paper Waste on the Growth and Yield of Peppers in the Field. *Pedobiologia*, 49: 297 - 306.

Arguello, J.A., A. Ledesma, S.B. Nunez, C.H. Rodriguez and M.C.D. Galdfarb (2006). Vermicompost Effect on Bulbing Dynamics, Nonstructural Carbohydrates Content, Yield and Quality of '*Rosado Paraguayo*' Garlic Bulbs. *Horticulture Science*, 41 (3): 589 - 592.

Athani, S.I., N.C. Hulamanai, and A.M. Shirol,(1999). Effect of Vermicomposts on the Maturity and Yield of Banana. *South Indian Horticulture*, 47 (1-6): 4 - 7.

Athani, S.I., Revanappa and P.R. Dharmatti (2009). Influence of Organic Fertilizer Doses and Vermicompost on Growth and Yield of Banana. *Karnataka Journal of Agricultural Science*, 22 (1): 147 - 150.

Atiyeh, R. M., S.S. Lee, C.A. Edwards, N.Q. Arancon and J. Metzger (2002). The Influence of Humic Acid Derived from Earthworm Processed Organic Wastes on Plant Growth. *Bioresource Technology*, 84: 7 - 14.

Azarmi, R., Giglou, M. T and Taleshmikail, D. 2008. Influence of vermicompost on Soil Chemical and Physical Properties in Tomato (*Lycopersicum esculentum*) Field. *African Journal of Biotechnology*, 7(14):2397-2401.

Babalad, H.B. (1999). Integrated Nutrient Management for Sustainable Production in Soybean Based Cropping Systems. *Ph. D. Thesis*, Univ. Agric. Sci., Dharwad, Karnataka (India).

Badole, S.B. and S.D. More (2000). Yield and Nutrient Uptake as Influenced by Integrated Nutrient Supply System in Cotton. *J. Indian Soc. Improve.*, 25 (3): 161 - 165.

Bagyaraj, D.J. and C. L. Powell (1985). Effect of Vesicular Arbscular Mycorrhizal Inoculation and Fertilizer Application on the Growth of Marigold. New Zealand *J. Agri. Res.*, 28: 169 - 173.

Bairwa, H.L., Shukla, A.K., L.N. Mahawer, R.A. Kaushik, K.B. Shukla and K.D. Ameta (2009). Response of Integrated Nutrient Management on Yield, Quality and Physico-chemical Characteristics of Okra cv. Arka Anamika. *Indian Journal of Horticulture*, 66: 3 - 7.

Balaji, S.K. (1994). Effect of Vermicompost on Growth and Flower Yield of China Aster (*Callilstephus chinansis*). *M. Sc. (Agri.) Thesis*, Univ. Agric. Sci., Dharwad. Karnataka (India).

Balamurugan, R. and P. Sudhakar (2012). Influence of Planting Methods and Different Vermicomposts on the Growth Attributes, Yield and Nutrient Uptake in Rice. Journal of Current Agricultural Sciences, 2 (6): 20 - 23.

Barik, A.K., A. Das, A.K. Giri and G.N. Chattopadhyay (2006). Effect of Integrated Plant Nutrient Management on Growth, Yield and Production Economics of Wet Season Rice (Oryza sativa L). The Indian Journal of Agricultural Sciences, 76 (11): 657 - 660.

Brito, U., A. Yanez, A.C. Maldonado and L.S. Franco (2009). Effect of Pig Litter Composted on Growth of Maize (*Zea maiz*) and Havanam Pepper (*Capsicum chinense*) Plant. *Research Journal of Biological Sciences*, 4 (4): 514 - 518.

Chakraborty, B., A.K. Chandra and S.K.Chakraborty (2008). Effect of Integrated Nutrient Supply and Growth, Leaf Yield and Field Performance of Mulberry (*Morus alba*) Under Semi Irrigated Lateritic Soil Condition of West Midnapore District, West Bengal. *J. Environ. Sociobiol.*, 5 (2): 221 - 226.

Chamani, E., D.C. Joyce and A. Reihanytabar (2008). Vermicompost Effects on the Growth and Flowering of Petunia Hybrida 'Dream Neon Rose'. *American-Eurasian Journal of Agricultural and Environmental Science*, 3 (3): 506 - 512.

Chanda, G.K., G. Bhunia and S.K. Chakraborty (2011). The Effect of Vermicompost and Other Fertilizers on Cultivation of Tomato Plants. *Journal of Horticulture and Forestry*, 3 (2): 42 - 45.

Chander, G., D.Naveen and R.P. Sharma (2005). Effect of Vermicompost, Farm Yard Manure and Chemical Fertilizers on Yield, Nutrient Uptake and Soil Fertility in Okra (*Abelmoschus esculentus*) Onion (*Allium cepa*) Sequence in Wet Temperate Zone of Himachal Pradesh. *Journal of the Indian Society of Soil Science*, 57(3): 357 - 361.

Chaoui, H.I., L.M. Zibilske and T.Ohno (2003). Effects of Earthworms Casts and Compost on Soil Microbial Activity and Plant Nutrient Availability. *Soil Biology and Biochemistry*, 35(2):295-302.

Chavda, V.N. and R.B. Singh (2015). Performance Evaluation of Vermicompost on Yield of *Kharif* Groundnut and Cotton Crops. *Internat. J. Forestry & Crop Improv.*, 6 (2): 127-131.

Correa, J.D., M.L Barrios and R.P. Galdona (2004). Screening for Plant Growth Promoting Rhizobacteria in *Chamaecytisus proliferus* (tagasaste), a Forage Tree-shrub Legume Endemic to the Canary Islands. *Plant Soil*, 266: 75 - 84.

CRIDA (2003). Annual Report 2002-03. Central Research Institute for Dry Land Agriculture, *Annual report* Hyderabad, p: 122-127.

Devi-Dayal, S.K. Agrawal and D. Dayal (1998). Response of Sunflower (*Helianthus annus*) to Organic Manures and Fertilizers Indian J. Agron., 43(3): 469 - 473.

Edwards, C.A and I. Burrows (1988). The Potential of Earthworm Composts as Plant Growth Media. In: Edwards, C. A and Neuhauser, (Eds.), Earthworms in Environmental and Waste Management. SPB Academic Publishers, The Netherlands. P: 211 - 220.

Gholve, S.G., S.H. Shinde and C.B. Gaikwad (2005). Efficacy of Integrated Nutrient Management for Pigeonpea Pearl Millet Intercropping System Under Dryland Conditions. *J. Maharashtra Agric. Univ.*, 30 (1): 41- 43.

Gopal Reddy, B. (1997). Soil Health Under Integrated Nutrient Management in Maize-soybean Cropping System. *Ph.D. Thesis,* Acharya N.G.Ranga Agric. Uni., Rajendranagar, Hyderabad.

Guerrero, R.D. 2010. Vermicompost Production and Its Use for Crop Production in the Philippines. Int. J. of Global Environmental Issues 10(.3/4):378 – 383.

Guerrero, R.D. and L.A. Guerrero (2006). Response of Eggplant (*Solanum melongena*) Grown in Plastic Containers to Vermicompost and Chemical Fertilizer. *Asia Life Sciences,* 15 (2): 199 -204.

Gupta AK and Tripathi VK. 2012. Efficacy of *Azotobacter* and Vermicompost Alone and in Combination on Vegetative Growth, Flowering and Yield of Strawberry (*Fragaria* x *ananassa* Duch.) Cv. Chandler. Progressive Horticulture. 44(2):256-261.

Gupta, A.K., B. Ray, M.P. Singh and V. Upadhyaya (2011). Effect of Fertilizers and Vermicompsot and Growth, Yield and Biochemical Changes in *Abelmoschus esculentus. Plant Archives,* 11 (1): 285-287.

Han, J., L. Sun, X. Dong, Z. Cai, H. Yang, Y. Wang and W. Song (2005). Characterization of a Novel Plant Growth-Promoting Bacteria strain Delftia Tsuruhatensis HR 4 both as a Diazotroph and a Potential Biocontrol Agent Against Various Pathogens. *Systematic and Applied Microbiology,* 28: 66 - 76.

Hangarge, D.S., R.S. Raut, G.U. Malewar, S.D. More and S.S. Keshbhat (2002). Yield Attributes and Nutrients Uptake by Chilli Due to Organics and Inorganics on Vertisol. *J. Maharashtra Agric. Uni.,* 27 (1): 109 - 110.

Hasheminajol, K., M. Kalbari, A. Gulchin and H. Shariatma Dari (2004). Comparison of Vermicompost and Compost as Potting Media for Growth of Tomatoes . *Journal of Plant Nutrition,* 27: 1107 - 1123.

Hossaen, M.A., A.T.M. Shamsuddoha, A.K.Paul, M.S.I. Bhuiyan and A.S.M. Zobaer (2011). Efficacy of Different Organic Manures and Inorganic Fertilizer on the Yield and Yield Attributes of Boro Rice. The Agriculturists, 9(1&2): 117 - 125.

Jadhav, A.D., S.C. Talashilkar and A.G. Powar (1997). Influence of the Conjunctive Use of FYM, Vermicompost and Urea on Growth and Nutrients Uptake in Rice. J. Maharashtra Agric. Univ., 22 (2): 249 - 250.

Jadia, C.D. and M.H. Fulekar (2008). Vermicomposting of Vegetable Wastes: A Biophysiochemical Process Based on Hydro-operating Bioreactor. *African Journal of Bio-technology,* 7 (20): 3723 - 3730.

Jagvirsingh, H.B., B. Sreekrishna and M.R. Sundharaman (1997). Performance of Scotch Bannet Chilli in Karnataka and Its Response to Vermicompost. Indian Cocoa, *Arecanut Spice J.,* 21: 9 - 10.

Jambhekar, H.A. and M.R. Bhiday (1992). Effect of vermicompost on sugarcane planted in saline land. In: Proc. Natn. Sem. Natural Fmg., New Delhi. pp: 275 - 282.

Jat, R.S. and I.P.S. Ahlwat, (2004). Effect of Vermicompost, Bio-fertilizer and Phosphorus on Growth, Yield and Nutrient Uptake by Gram (Cicer arietinum) and their Residual Effect on Fodder Maize (Zea Mays). *Indian J. Agri Sci.,* 74 (7): 349 - 402.

Jayaprakash, T.C., V.P. Nagalikar, B.T. Pujari and R.A. Setty (2003). Effect of Organics and Inorganics on Yield and Yield Attributes of Maize under Irrigation. *Karnataka J. Agric. Sci.*, 16 (3): 451 - 453.

Kademani, M.B., B.M. Radder and N.S. Hebsur,(2003). Effect of Organic and Inorganic Fertilizers on Availability and Uptake of Nutrients by Sunflower in *vertisols* of Malaprabha Command. *Karnataka J. Agri. Sci.*, 16 (1): 48 - 53.

Kalantari, S., M. M. Ardalan, H.A Alikhani and M. Shorafa (2011). Comparison of Compost and Vermicompost of Yard Leaf Manure and Inorganic Fertilizer on Yield of Corn. *Communications in Soil Science and Plant Analysis*, 42: 123 - 131.

Kale, R.D., B.C. Mallesh, B.Kubra and D.J. Bagyaraj (1992). Influence of Vermicompost Application on the Available Micronutrients and Selected Microbial Populations in a Paddy Field. *Soil Biol. Biochem.*, 24 (12): 1317-1320.

Karmegam N, K. Alagermalai and T. Daniel (1999). Effect of Vermicompost on the Growth and Yield of Green Gram (Phaseolus aureus Rob.). Tropical Agriculture, 76: 143 – 146.

Karmegam, N. and T. Daniel (2000). Effect of biodigested Slurry and Vermicompost on the Growth and Yield of Cowpea [*Vigna unguiculata* (L.)]. Environment and Ecology, 18: 367 – 370.

Kondappa, D., B.M. Radder, P. L. Patil. N.S. Hebsur and S.C. Alagundagi (2009). Effect of Integrated Nutrient Management on Growth, Yield and Economics of Chilli (cv. Byadgi Dabbi) in a Vertisol. *Karnataka Journal of Agricultural Sciences*, 22: 438-440.

Krishnamoorthy, R.V. and S.N. Vajranabhiah (1986). Biological Activity of Earthworm Casts: An Assessment of Plant Growth Promoter Levels in Casts. *Proceedings of the Indian Academy of Sciences, Animal Science*, 95: 341 - 351.

Kumara, A., S. Sharma and S. Mishrab (2009). Application of Farmyard Manure and Vermin-compost on Vegetative and Generative Characteristics of *Jatropa curcas. Journal of Phytology*, 1 (4): 206 - 212.

Lal, R., B. Singh, B. Singh and M.R. Masih (2008). Efficient Recycling of Mustard Straw Through Vermicomposting for Sustainable Production of Barley in Semi Arid Easter Plain Zone of Rajashtan. *Asian J.of Hort. An Asian Journal of* soil Sci., 3 (2): 249 – 251.

Lazcano, C., G. Arnold, A. Tato, J.G. Zaller and J. Dominguez (2009). Compost and Vermicompost as Nursery Pot Components: Effects on Tomato Plant Growth and Morphology. *Spanish Journal of Agricultural Research*, 7 (4): 944 - 951.

Lopes, A.J., N.P. Stam Ford, M.V.B.N.A. Figueiredo and E.B. Ferraz (1996). Effect of Vermicompost Mineral Nitrogen and Mineralizing Agent on N Fixation and Yield in cowpea. *Revista-Brasileira-de-ciencia-do-solo*. 20 (1): 55-62.

Luishuxin, Liong, Zezhong and Wubebing (1991). Studies on the Effect of Earthworms on the Fertility of Red Arid Soil. In Advances in Management and Conservation of Soil Fauna. *Oxford and IBH Publishing Co. Pvt. Ltd*. New Delhi, pp. 543-546.

Maheswarappa, H.P., Nanjappa and M.R. Hegde (1997). Influence of Organic Manures on Yield of Arrowroot, Soil Physico-chemical and Biological Properties when Grown as a Intercrop in Coconut Garden. *Annals Agric. Res.*, 20 (3): 318-323.

Manivannan, S., Balamurugan, Parthasarathi, G. Gunasekharan and R.Ranganathan (2009). Effect of Vermicompost on Soil Fertility and Crop Productivity–beans (*Phaseolus vulgaris*). *Journal of Environmental Biology*, 30: 275 - 281.

Marjan Shishehbor, Hamid Madani1 and Mohammad Reza Ardakani. 2013. Effect of Vermicompost and Biofertilizers on Yield and Yield Components of Common Millet (Panicum miliaceum). Annals of Biological Research. 4(2):174-180.

Masciandaro, G., B. Ceccanti and C. Gracia (1997). Soil Agro-ecologica Management: Fertirrigation and Vermicompost Treatments. *Bioresource Technology*, 59: 199 - 206.

Mastiholi, A.B. and C.J. Itnal (1997). Response of Rabi Sorghum (Sorghum bicolor L. Moench) to Application of Biofertilizers under Dry Land Conditions. Karnataka J. Agric. Sci., 10(2): 302 - 306.

Mishra, T.D., S.K. Singh, S.N.S. Chaurasia, P. Kemaria and T.B. Singh (2009). Effect of Vermicompost and Biofertilizers on Okra (*Abelmoschus esculentus* (L.) Moench) Under Graded Dose of Nitrogen and Phosphorus. *New Agriculturist*, 20 (1 & 2): 9-13.

Mogle, U. P and D.R. Chamle (2011). Evaluation of Biofertilizers and Parthenium Vemicompost on Tomato Crop. *Journal of Ecobiotechnology*, 3 (2): 11 - 13.

Mrinal, S., D.J. Rajkhowa and M. Saikia (1998). Effect of Planting Density and Vermicompost on -Yield of Potato Raised from Seedling Tubers. J. Indian Potato Assoc., 25 (3-4): 141 - 142.

Munroe, G. (2007). Manual of On-farm Vermicomposting and Vermiculture. Publication of Organic Agriculture Centre of Canada, Nova Scotia, 39p.

Murali, M.K. and R.A. Setty (2000). Effect of levels of NPK, Vermicompost and Growth Regulator (Triacontanol) on Growth and Yield of Scented Rice (Oryza sativa L.). Mysore Journal of Agricultural Sciences. 34(4): 335 - 339.

Murarkar, S.R., A.S. Tayade, S.N. Bodhade and R.B. Ulemale (1998). Effect of Vermicompost on Mulberry Leaf Yield. J. Soil and Crops, 8(1): 85 - 87.

Murthy, D.K., S.P. Palaniappan, S.S. Narayan and S. Chelliah (2000). Effect of Organically Bound Micronutrients on Growth and Yield in Cotton. *J. Indian Soc. Cotton Improve.*, 25 (1): 44 - 45.

Muscolo, A., F. Bovalo, F. Gionfriddo and F.Nardi (1999). Earthworm Humic Matter Produces Auxin-like Effect on *Daucus carota* Cell Growth and Nitrate Metabolism. *Soil Biology and Biochemistry*, 31: 1303 - 1311.

Nethra, N., N, K.V. Jayaprasad and R.D. Kale (1999). China Aster [Callistephus chinensis (L)] Cultivation using Vermicompost as Organic Amendment. Crop Research (Hisar), 17: 209 –215.

Netwal, L.C. (2003). Effect of FYM and Vermicompost on Nutrient Uptake and Quality of Cowpea *[Vigna unguiculata* (L.) Walp] Grown under Saline Condition. M.Sc (Ag) Thesis, Rajasthan Agricultural University, Bikaner.

Orozco, F.H., J. Cegarra, L.M. Trujillo and A. Roig (1996). Vermicomposting of Coffee Pulp Using the Earthworm *Eisenia fetida*: Effects on C and N Contents and the Availability of nutrients. *Biology and Fertility of Soils*, 22: 162 - 166.

Parthasarathi K, Balamurugan M and Ranganathan LS. 2008. Influence of Vermicompost on the Physico-chemical and Biological Properties in Different Types of Soil along with Yield and Quality of the Pulse Crop Blackgram. Iranian Journal of Environmental Health Science & Engineering. 5(1): 51-58.

Patil, C.V., S.S. Prakash and N.A. Yeledhalli (1995). Crop Residue Management for Sustainable Agriculture. In: Proc. of *Seminar on Conservation of Natural Resources for Sustainable Production*. November 16-17, 1995, Univ. Agril. Sci., Dharwad (Indian), p. 18.

Patil, M.P., N.C. Hulamani, S.T. Athani, and M.G. Patil (1998). Response of New Tomato Genotype Mehga to Integrated Nutrient Management. Advance in Agri. Res. in India 9: 39-42.

Patil, S.L. and M.N. Sheelavantar (2000). Effect of Moisture Conservation Practices, Organic Sources and Nitrogen Levels on Yield, Water Use and Root Development of

Rabi Sorghum [Sorghum bicolor (L.)] in the Vertisols of Semiarid Tropics. Annals of Agricultural Research, 21(2): 32 – 36.

Pontillas L, Lugo E, Malate R, Lanioso A. 2009. Efficacy Evaluation of Vermicompost and Inorganic Fertilizer Applied in Low Land Rice. The Threshold Volume IV.. January – December, 2009. 66-75.

Premsekhar, M. and V. Rajashree (2009). Influence of Organic Manures on Growth, Yield and Quality of Okra. *American-Eurasian Journal of Sustainable Agriculture,* 3(1): 6 - 8.

Rajan, M.R. and R. Mahalakshmi (2007). Effect of Vermicompost Prepared from Hotel Wastes on Growth and Production of Radish and Cowpea. *Environment and Ecology,* 25 (Special 4) : 1194-1197.

Rakshit, A., N.C. Sarkar and D. Sen (2008). Influence of Organic Manures on Productivity of Two Varieties of Rice. *Journal of Central European Agriculture,* 9 (4): 629 - 634.

Rama Lakshmi, C.S., T. Sreelatha, T. Usha Rani, S.R.K. Rao and N.V. Naidu (2011). Effect of Organic Manures on Soil Fertility and Productivity of Sugarcane in North Coastal Zone of Andhra Pradesh. Indian J. Agric. Res., 45 (4): 307 – 313.

Ramdhan, K. (2004). Effect of NPK and Vermicompost on Growth, Yield and Quality of Cauliflower cv. Pusa Katki. M.Sc. (Ag.) Thesis, Submitted to Rajasthan Agricultural University, Jobner, Rajasthan.

Ranganathan, L.S and K.Parthasarathi (2000). Enhanced Phosphatase Activity in Earthworm Casts is more of Microbial Origin. Current Science, 79: 1158–1159.

Rasool, A,, Parviz SZ and Mohammad RS. 2008. Effect of Vermicompost on Growth, Yield and Nutrition Status of Tomato (Lycopersicum esculentum). Pakistan Journal of Biological Sciences. 11:1797-1802.

Rather SA and Sharma NL. 2009. The Effect of Integrated Use of Vermicompost, Biofertilizer (Azotobacter chroococcum) and Inorganic Fertilizers (N, P, K and Zn) on Yield and Nutrient Content and their Uptake by Wheat. International Journal of Agricultural Sciences. 5(2):371-373.

Raut, R.S. and S.S. Mehetre (2008). Integrated Nutrient Management in Hirsutum Cotton cv. NHH- 44 under Summer Irrigated Conditions. *J. Cotton Res. Dev.,* 22(1): 48 - 49.

Reddy, G.B. and M.S. Reddy (1999). Effect of Integrated Nutrient Management on Soil Available Micronutrients in Maize – Soybean Cropping Systems. Journal of Research (ANGRAU), 27(3): 24 - 28.

Reddy, R., M.A.N. Reddy Y.T.N. Reddy N.S. Reddy N.Anjanappa and R. Reddy (1998). Effect of Organic and Inorganic Sources of NPK on Growth and Yield of Pea [Pisum sativum(L)]. Legume Research, 21(1): 57 – 60.

Roberts, P., G.E. Jones and D.L. Jones (2007). Yield Responses of Wheat (*Triticum aestivum*) to Vermicompost. *Journal of Compost Science and Utilization,* 15(1): 6- 15.

Rodriguez, H. and R. Fraga (1999). Phosphate Solubilizing Bacteria and their Role in Plant Growth Promotion. *Biotechnology Advances,* 17:319-339.

Sailaja Kumari, M.S. and K. Ushakumari (2002). Effect of Vermicompost Enriched with Rock Phosphate on the Yield and Uptake of Nutrients in Cowpea (Vigna unguiculata). J. of Tropical Agriculture, 40: 27 - 30.

Samawat, S., A. Lakzian and A. Zamirpour (2001). The Effect of Vermicompost on Growth Characteristics of Tomato. *Journal of Agricultural Science and Technology,* 15 (2): 83-89.

Shailaja, K. (2005). Effect of Different Sources on Quality of Vermicompost and their Influence on Performance of Maize (*Zea mays* L.). M.Sc (Ag) Thesis, Department of Soil Science and Agricultural Chemistry, Acharya N.G. Ranga Agricultural University, Rajendranagar, Hyderabad.

Sharma, R.P., N. Datt and G. Chander (2009). Effect of Vermicompost, FYM and Chemical Fertilizers on Yield, Nutrient Uptake and Soil Fertility in okra [*Abelmoschus esculentus* (L.) Moench] – Onion (*Allium cepa*) Sequence in Wet Temperate Zone of Himachal Pradesh. *Journal of Indian Society of Soil Science*, 57 (3): 357-361.

Sharma, T.R., A.K. Pandey, S.D. Updhyaya and S.B. Agrawal (2010). Effect of Vermicompost on Yield and Quality of *Kharif* Season Okra [*Abelmoschus esculentus* (L.) Moench]. *Vegetable Science*, 37 (1-2): 181-183.

Shirisha, D. (2002). Nature and Properties of Soil Humic Substances and the Available Nutrient Status as Influenced by the Incorporation of Organic Residues. M Sc (Ag.) Thesis Submitted to Acharya N G Ranga Agricultural University, Hyderabad.

Shivalingayya, G. (2010), Effect of Nutrient Management and Plant Protection Practices in Organic Cotton Production. *M. Sc. (Agri) Thesis*, Univ. Agric. Sci., Dharwad, Karnataka (India).

Shiwei, Z. and H. Fu-zhen (1991). The Nitrogen Uptake Efficiency from 15N Labeled Chemical Fertilizer in the Presence of Earthworm Manure (cast). In: Veeresh, G.K., Rajagopal, D., Viraktamath, C.A. (Eds.), Advances in Management and Conservation of Soil Fauna. Oxford and IBH Publishing Co, New Delhi. P: 539 - 542.

Singh LN, Singh RKK, Singh AH and Chhangte Z. 2005. Efficacy of Urea in Integration with Azolla and Vermicompost in Rainfed Rice (Oryza sativa) Production and their Residual Effect on Soil Properties. Indian Journal of Agricultural Science. 75(I):44-45.

Singh, K., C.R. Hazra and G.P. Shukla (1998). Effect of Organic and Inorganic Fertilizers on Fodder Yield of Oats under multi Environment Testing. Forage Res., 24(3): 127 - 129.

Singh, R., R.R. Sharma, S. Kumar, R.K. Gupta and R.T. Patil (2008). Vermicompost Substitution Influences Growth, Physiological Disorders, Fruit Yield and Quality of Strawberry (*Fragaria xananassa* Duch). *Bioresource Technology*, 99 (17): 8507 - 8511.

Singh, R.K. and B.S. Yadav (2004). Effect of Vermicompost and Fertilizers on Productivity of Gram (*Cicer arietinum*) and Soil Fertility. *Indian J. Agric. Sci.*, 77 (11): 613 - 615.

Sinha, R.K., D. Valani, K. Chauhan, and S. Agarwal (2010b). Embarking on a Second Green Revolution for Sustainable Agriculture by Vermiculture Biotechnology using Earthworms: Reviving the Dreams of Sir Charles Darwin. *Agricultural Sciences*, 2 (7): 113 - 128.

Sinha, R.K., S. Agarwal, K. Chauhan and D. Valani (2010a). The Wonders of Earthworms & Its Vermicompost in Farm Production: Charles Darwin's 'Friends of Farmers', with Potential to Replace Destructive Chemical Fertilizers from Agriculture. *Agricultural Sciences*, 1 (2): 76 - 94.

Sreenivas, C., S. Muralidhar and M.S. Rao (2000a). Vermicompost, a Viable Component of IPNSS in Nitrogen Nutrition of Ridge Gourd. Annals of Agricultural Research, 21(1): 108 –113.

Sreenivas, C.H., S.Muralidhar and M.S. Rao, (2000b). Yield and Quality of Ridge Gourd Fruits as Influenced by Different Levels of Inorganic Fertilizers and Vermicompost. *Annals of Agricultural Research*, 21 (1): 262 - 266.

Stephens, P.M., C.W. Davoren, M.H. Ryder and B.M. Double (1994). Influence of Earthworm. Aporrectoda Trapezoides on the Colonization of Survival of Rhizobium Meliloti in Soil. *Biol. Fert. Soils*, 18: 63-70.

Surindra, Suthar (2009). Impact of vermicompost and Composted Farmyard Manure on Growth and Yield of Garlic (*Allium sativum* L.) Field Crop. *International Journal of Plant Production*, 3 (1): 44 - 46.

Szczeck, M.M. (1999). Suppressiveness of Vermicompost against Fusarium Wilt of Tomato. *Journal of Phytopathology*, 47: 155 - 161.

Tapan Kumar Garai (2013). An Alternative Approach in Rice Production Towards Reducing Chemical Fertilizer Using Bio-fertilizer and Compsot for Sustainable Yield, Soil Health and Biodiversity in Old Alluvial Zone of Burdwan, West Bengal. Ph.D Thesis, Department of Environmental Science, University of Burdwan, Burdwan-713104, West Bengal.

Tharmaraj, K., P. Ganesh, K. Kolanjinathan, R.S. Kumar and A. Anandan (2011). Influence of Vermicompost and Vermiwash on Physic Chemical Properties of Rice Cultivated Soil. *Current Botany*, 2 (3): 18 - 21.

Theunissen, P.A., Ndakidemi and C.P. Laubscher (2010). Potential of Vermicompost Produced from Plant Waste on the Growth and Nutrient Status in Vegetable Production. *International Journal of Physical Sciences*, 5 (13): 1964 - 1973.

Tomati, U., E. Galli, A. Grapppelli and G. Dihena (1990). Effect of Earthworm Casts on Protein Synthesis in Radish (*Raphanus sativum*) and Lettuce (*Lactuca sativa*) Seedlings. *Biology and Fertility of Soils*, 9: 288 - 289.

Uma, B and Malathi MV. 2009. Vermicompost as a Soil Supplement to Improve Growth and Yield of Amaranthus Species. Research Journal of Agriculture & Biological Sciences. 5(6):1054.

Usha Kumari, K., P. Prabha Kumari and P. Padamaja (1999). Efficiency of Vermicompost on Growth and Yield of Summer Crop of Okra (*Abelmoschus esculentus*). *Journal of Tropical Agriculture*, 37(1/2): 87 - 88.

Vadiraj, B.A., Siddagangaiah and S.N. Potty (1998). Response of Coriander (*Coriandrum sativum* L.) Cultivars to Graded Levels of Vermicomposts. *Journal of Spices and Aromatic Crops*, 7:141-143.

Vanmathi, J.S. and M.N. Selvakumari (2012). The Influence of Vermicompost on the Growth and Yield of *Hibiscus esculentus*. *Elixir Applied Botany*, 44 (2012): 7416-7419.

Vasanthi, D. and K. Kumarswamy (1996). Efficacy of Vermicompost on the Yield of Rice and on Soil Fertility. In: *Organic Farming for Sustainable Agriculture*, Abstracts of National Seminar, at Trivandrum October 9-11, 1996, p. 40.

Vitakar, M. N., R. R. Manolikar, S.D. Vasmate, B.M. Kalalbandi and M.F. Patil (2007). Effect of Organic and Inorganic Fertilizers on Growth and Green Fruit Yield of Chilli (*Capsicum annum* L.). *Asian Journal of Horticulture*, 2 (2): 273-276.

Warman, P. R and M. J. AngLopez (2010). Vermicompost Derived from Different Feed Stocks as a Plant Growth Medium. *Bioresource Technology*, 101: 4479 - 4483.

Yadav, G.L. (2014). Effect of Nitrogen and Bio-organics on Growth, Yield and Quality of Okra [*Abelmoschus esculentus* (L.) Moench]. M.Sc (Horticulture) Thesis, Department of Horticulture, S.K.N. College of Agriculture, Jobner, Rajasthan.

Yadav, R.H. and B.Vijayakumari (2004). Impact of Vermicompost on Biochemical Characters of Chilli (*Capsicum annum*). *Journal of Ecotoxicology and Environmental Monitoring*, 14: 51 - 56.

Yadav, S.S. and N.Yadav (2010). Effect of Integrated Nutrient Management on Yield of Okra in *Zaid* Crop. Bhartiya Krishi Anusandhan Patrika, 25: 2 - 4.

Yasir, M., Z. Aslam, S. Won Kim, S.W. Lee, C.O. Jeon and Y.R. Chung (2009). Bacterial Community Composition and Chitinase Gene Diversity of Vermicompost with Antifungal Activity. Bioresource Technology, 100: 4396 - 4403.

Zhao, S.W. and F.Z. Haung (1991). The Nitrogen Uptake Efficiency from N Labeled Chemical Fertilizer in the Presence of Earthworm Manure (cast) In: Advances in Management and Conservation of Soil Fauna (Eds. G.K. Veeresh D. Rajgopal and C.A. Virakthmath) Oxford and IBH Publishing Pvt. Ltd, New Delhi, pp. 539 - 542.

INDEX